IMAGES of America

UNION COUNTY RIVER TOWNS

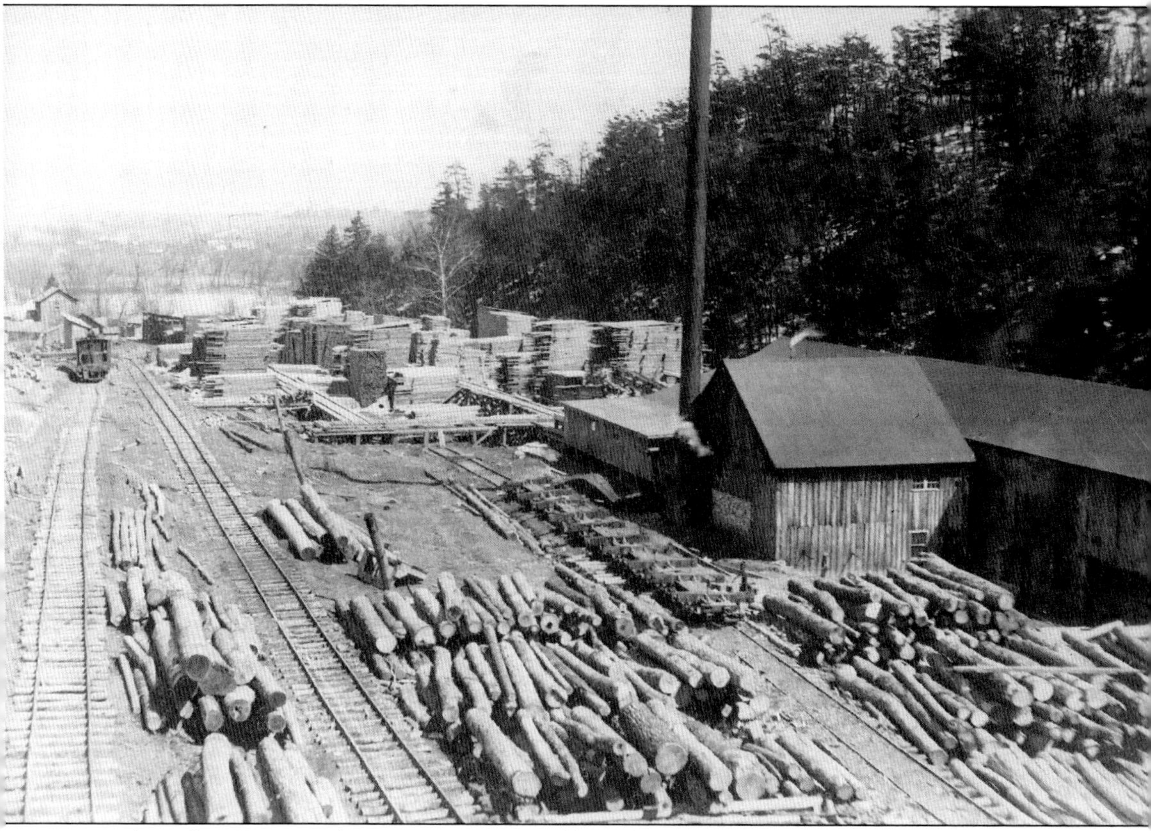

The White Deer Lumber Company's sawmill, on the right, was located just north of White Deer on the west side of the road to Williamsport. Looking east, the Susquehanna River is in the background while the log pond is out of sight on the left. The locomotive, called the *Pot*, rests on the tracks. The Reading Railroad line is in the middle, curving into piles of finished lumber. (Union County Historical Society [UCHS] 2010.21.108e.)

ON THE COVER: The White Deer Flouring Mill's milldam on White Deer Creek was a destination for families. Several real-photo postcards of it were made between 1907 and 1911. On the back of one, the writer tells his friend in Lancaster, "We are enjoying ourselves up here in these mountains." The field adjacent was used as a local baseball diamond in the early 1900s. (Ardith Wilkins.)

IMAGES
of America

UNION COUNTY RIVER TOWNS

Jeannette Lasansky

ARCADIA
PUBLISHING

ISBN 978-0-7385-7458-5

Published by Arcadia Publishing
Charleston, South Carolina

Printed in the United States of America

Library of Congress Control Number: 2010937086

For all general information, please contact Arcadia Publishing:
Telephone 843-853-2070
Fax 843-853-0044
E-mail sales@arcadiapublishing.com
For customer service and orders:
Toll-Free 1-888-313-2665

Visit us on the Internet at www.arcadiapublishing.com

Contents

ACKNOWLEDGMENTS

Teamwork made *Union County River Towns* possible. Those who scoured their respective communities for photographs, postcards, and more were Ardith Wilkins and Jack Fisher on Allenwood, Spring Garden, and White Deer; Terri Stump and Bill Clemens on New Columbia; and Susan Ohl Wirth on West Milton. Jack Fisher was the group's fact-finder supreme.

While the Union County Historical Society (UCHS) was the single largest resource, many individuals came forward with hundreds of special items: Joan Bastian, Gilbert Bennett, Susan Berkheimer, Joan Blank, Doris M. LaForm Caris, Bill Clemens, Allen Dershem, Rita Eisley, Hattie L. Fisher, Jack Fisher, Kay Golfieri, Nelson Hauck, Helen Fair, Elisabeth J., Sara, and Susan E. Helsman, Sharon and Bill Herald, Jean LaVan Hormel, Bill Houtz, Stephen Huddy, Drew Hyman, Phyllis Keiser, Minnie Troxel Koch, Patricia Longley, Lycoming County Historical Society, Harry Mann, Helen Frontz Myers, Ronald Nornhold, Amos and John Persing, Paul Prowant, Dorothy Ranck, Katherine V. Reitz, David and Pam Keifer Russell, Ruthann and David Schooley, Clara Shearer, Jean Showers, William Showers, Susan Snoddy, Terri Stump, Jack Wertz, Ardith Wilkins, Donald Wilver Sr., Susan Wirth, Sherry Wolf, Elizabeth Yost, and Ethel Yost. Images that appear in this volume courtesy of the Union County Historical Society (UCHS) are followed by a collection number.

Bill Clemens and Alan Richard expertly scanned nearly 1,000 images from which the final selections were made. All contributed to the research and writing of captions while Pat Longley reviewed the text, as did our final copy editor, Betsy Robertson, a volunteer for numerous society projects. Lois Huffines, coauthor for the UCHS's first Arcadia book on Lewisburg, another Union County river town, helped me navigate the publisher's guidelines while Shawn McLaughlin contemplated these towns' futures.

Joining me on "country rides" for this volume was William Lasansky. Country rides have been a family tradition since we came to live, work, and celebrate in Union County in 1968. This is a pastime learned firsthand from Merrill W. Linn, the granddaddy of exploring less-traveled paths and making new acquaintances along the way.

Come join in that exploration and feel the pulse of the past history as we all look forward to Union County's bicentennial in 2013.

Introduction

The West Branch of the Susquehanna River runs nearly 21 miles along the eastern edge of Union County, and its river towns, from north to south, are Allenwood, White Deer, New Columbia, West Milton, Winfield, and Lewisburg. Some of these communities had different names at earlier times. The northernmost town was laid out in 1815 by John McCurdy as Uniontown, and by the 1860s, it had its post office named Slifer and train station named Cairo. All were renamed Allenwood after the entrepreneurial Allen family, which laid out lots, kept a general store, and then built a large brick store and warehouse in 1880. White Deer, previously called White Deer Mills, began as Hightown, named for Henry High, owner of the town's gristmill in the late 1840s. West Milton was first called Datesman's Station in 1834 after land and store owner John Datesman.

Well before settlers like Hawkins Boone arrived in the 1770s, Native Americans traversed the area by foot, including the waterways. A major Indian path went northwesterly from the mouth of White Deer Creek through the White Deer Mountains to the area now known as Spring Garden. The path continued across the White Deer Valley to a gap near present-day Elimsport, then into Nippenose Valley and beyond. White Deer Valley is bounded by the imposing White Deer and Nittany Appalachian Mountains.

The Treaty of Fort Stanwix, which was made with the Iroquois in 1768, and the New Purchase gave proprietors Thomas and Richard Penn six special proprietary manors and awarded land to the officers of the Pontiac War, while the majority of tracts was allotted to settlers via a lottery held on April 3, 1769. Applications with one's name and a description of the land desired were placed in a trunk and drawn, then numbered in the order of the drawing. Settlers got a warrant, had land surveyed, and then patents were issued. There were 2,782 applications for land on the first day. This era of extensive land surveying is encapsulated in a large hand-drawn map showing these patents that is located in the Union County Courthouse on the wall across from the deed office. The 1769 patents from Black Run south to Shikellamy's Bluff started with Bernard Bonner, then Edward Miner, James Bell, Daniel Ryan, Robert Iredell, Samuel Iredell, Margaret Blythe, Elizabeth Blythe, John Potter, John Zimmerman/Robert McCorley, Deetrick Rees, William Armstrong/Samuel Dale, Michael Diets/John Hoffman, John Fisher, Joseph Hutchens, and Michael Wheyland; from Turtle Creek south to Blue Hill were Thomas Lowery, George Palmer/John Lee, Alexander Craig, Andrew Culbertson, William Huffman, Henry Masser, and John Calloway. Some names resonate historically, while others seem not to have left their marks except as early landholders. In 1772, this area of Northumberland County became Buffalo Township. White Deer Township split from Buffalo in 1776.

During the American Revolution, committees of safety were formed, but many people fled the area by 1779 because of marauding Indians and few places of refuge. When stability returned, a stream of settlers arrived. Landholders and tenants, farmers and craftsmen, those of substance and those with less came by foot or horse and wagon across Tulpehocken Road from Berks, Chester, and Lancaster Counties. Transportation of goods and people proved to be vital to the establishment and growth of these river towns, their outlying farms, and later industries.

Present Gregg Township, bounded by Black Run on the north and the White Deer Mountains on the south, is where Allenwood, Spring Garden, and Alvira were situated. It has an interesting and complex political history. Among its earliest settlers, starting in the 1760s, were the Browns, Follmers, Hunters, and Oakeses. When Union County was formed from Northumberland County in 1813, this area was the northeasternmost section of the new county. It was not long before residents successfully petitioned to join Lycoming County since its county seat of Williamsport was closer to them than New Berlin, the seat of Union County. Thus was formed Washington, later renamed Brady Township. However, after 1855, when Union was split in two and Union's new county seat moved north to Lewisburg, some residents of Brady Township petitioned Pennsylvania's state government to rejoin Union County in 1861. After much contention, a vote was taken in 1865. The "yeas" achieved a narrow majority and this land area, renamed Gregg Township for a supportive legislator, was reconnected to Union County.

In the 1830s, the Pennsylvania Canal reached the east side of the Susquehanna and small ferries transported goods and people from Northumberland, Montandon, Milton, and Watsontown on the east side to river towns on the west banks. Railroads changed the equation starting in the 1860s by providing greater carrying capacity and faster links to people and cities farther away. Towns throughout Union County were made or became obsolete with the emergence or absence of this new mode of transportation. For instance, Datesman's Station had its post office named West Milton when the Catawissa Railroad crossed the river from Milton in 1871. In 1882, the Shamokin, Sunbury & Lewisburg Railroad also came into West Milton, and the construction of an engine house transformed West Milton into a transportation hub in 1901.

The narrow gauge White Deer and Loganton Railroad factored greatly in the industrial growth and social life of the northern river towns as it connected communities and the tramways of successive lumber barons Ario Pardee, John Duncan, and Monroe Kulp. Remnants of rail beds still lace the woods. These trains carried workers to lumber camps in the northern interior of Union County and brought felled timber back to the Susquehanna at White Deer. At times, these steam locomotives pulled a couple of passenger cars with their finely dressed customers for an idyllic day at Tea Springs. Near the train tracks were the large dam and reservoir built in 1898 that provided the water supply for New Columbia, West Milton, Milton, and Lewisburg.

Along the White Deer Pike was an array of small industries dependent on the area's natural resources and White Deer Creek, or Opaghtanoten. A half-mile west of White Deer Creek was a large, six-storied wooden structure that housed a manufacturer of woolen goods and then hats. Active from 1850 to 1879, the mill employed as many as 100 at its peak of operation and supplied thousands of blankets to the Union army. The mill had various owners over time, including Stratton, Maar, Griffey, Brumbaugh, and Pardee. Farther up the White Deer Creek and Pike was Forest Iron Works, which made cast iron fleetingly—from 1845 to around 1855. A larger and longer-lasting iron furnace operation using ore from the Shamokin Mountain and limestone from a local quarry was situated in Winfield and was called the Union Furnace. Geddes, Marsh & Company was managed by Dr. Levi Rooke of Winfield and, with financial backing from brothers Thomas Beaver of Danville and Peter Beaver of Lewisburg, operated in Union Township from 1854 to 1891. The Union Furnace was among the first employers of free African Americans in the county, as was the Berlin Iron Works at Glen Iron.

The cool woods and high points above Spring Garden, where Dr. William Devitt built his successful institution for tubercular patients in 1912, had many real-photo postcards attest to its scenic and open-air environment. In the 1960s, Devitt's Camp became the Home of the Aged of the United Church of Christ and now is the White Deer Treatment Center. In 1909, a river bluff just below West Milton became Central Oak Heights (COH), an Evangelical Church summer retreat that celebrated family living and is still thriving. Real-photo postcards and vivid Kodachromes illuminate the good times that families and young people had there over many decades, both in tents and, later, wooden cottages. It was the very site where Oneida chief Shikellamy camped periodically in the late 1720s, and it is still referred to as Shikellamy's Bluffs.

Low roads beside the river allowed for permanent houses and camps and, later on, motor homes and RVs, particularly in the Winfield area. River islands, like Cat Bird near Winfield, and nearby groves, as in Allenwood, became seasonal retreats. Duck and deer hunting counted among many recreational sports that still attract visitors as well as area residents. Sawmills dotted the landscape, especially close to creeks like White Deer, where logs were floated through a series of splash dams to get to sawmills at the Susquehanna River's edge or for easy transport downriver. Allenwood Lumber Company operated mills near the mouth of White Deer Hole Creek and had the capacity to cut 40,000 feet per day from trees as large as three feet in diameter. On the ridges and deep in the woods were numerous hunting cabins.

With the coming of the automobile, Union County river towns again embraced a new mode of transportation. Many major dirt roads were paved under Pennsylvania governor Gifford Pinchot (1923–1927 and 1931–1935). The primary highway that ran parallel to the Susquehanna was aptly called River Road and ran north from Turtleville in Union Township. It was supplanted by a two-lane highway that was later widened to four lanes. What ultimately was called Route 15 went south to Harrisburg and continued to Virginia. It ran north to Williamsport and then to Rochester, New York. When Route 15 was first built, it accommodated buildings that were near its path like the enormously long, stone-ended Eyer barn in Winfield, the site of the founding of the Evangelical Church. But, over time, wider versions of Route 15 that had skirted the river towns would take whole sections of them. West Milton, for example, had access ramps constructed where family homes and farms had stood for generations. Between New Columbia and White Deer, trucking businesses would emerge to take advantage of the junction of the major east-west and north-south arteries: Routes 80 and 15. New endeavors thrived and some, like Reptiland in Allenwood, became nationally known institutions. But road building often altered the village streetscapes irrevocably as in White Deer, West Milton, and Winfield, where local landmarks like Yankee Spring were demolished and paved over.

The federal government similarly took whole towns in the name of progress. Just as 12 farms were purchased to form the Northeast Federal Penitentiary site outside of Lewisburg in the early 1930s, so were 8,500 acres taken by eminent domain west and north of Allenwood to create the Pennsylvania Ordnance Works for making TNT in World War II. The explosives facility was short-lived (1942–1950), and the acreage later became the Allenwood Federal Correctional Complex, which currently houses 3,636 inmates, and State Game Lands No. 252. The entire town of Alvira, including three old churches and the Alvira one-room school, was razed, but it was not forgotten as presentations and publications kept memories of the community alive.

Lutheran, Baptist, Methodist, Reformed, Evangelical, and Presbyterian churches built from the 1830s onward are still evident and active in this region, though not all are in every town. Usually, there are one or two, maybe three denominations, while other congregants have to travel greater distances to attend services. The churches reflect the Germanic and English/Scots-Irish mix of the area, with the Germanic being less dominant than in other parts of the county.

White Deer Township residents immediately accepted Pennsylvania's Public School Law of 1834 with a favoring vote of 52-26, contrasting with Union Township residents, who voted negatively, 0-205. The *Miltonian* proclaimed, "The little township of White Deer has contracted with a mechanic [John Fisher] for the building of five schoolhouses—all to be built of brick [on good stone foundations] and to be 25' x 30' [at a fixed cost of $1,450 or $490 a school]." Other townships eventually followed suit, and by 1854 Union County's first superintendent of schools, J.S. Whitman, supervised 172 male and 12 female teachers.

As late as 1910, Allenwood built a new school, and West Milton built its Washington Primary School in 1926. Atypical construction included Allenwood's two-story frame building and the "temporary" prefabricated West Milton Primary School. The latter was used for 29 years.

Consolidation of schools in 1955 brought profound change to these river towns since, with the exception of the Winfield area, only the primary grades of White Deer Township were educated in Union County, in the White Deer Elementary School that was newly built in New Columbia in 1955. West Milton area students were bused to Milton if they lived in White Deer Township or to the Lewisburg School District if they lived in Kelly Township. Gregg Township families were initially given a choice: Warrior Run, Milton, or Montgomery School Districts; later, all Gregg students were sent to Warrior Run. The local one-room schools—symbols of community pride—were either converted to private homes or were razed, as were the schools named Allenwood, Alvira, and Russell, which was known as "Fairview."

Many times, the photographic images of these places when contrasted with present-day observation tell of metamorphic change and stark contrasts. When oral accounts and manuscripts such as maps, newspaper clippings, and letters home are combined, the transitions from isolated rural to connected modern become very personal. Yet, these river towns are still small communities with many family names going back two centuries.

The story of *Union County River Towns* is told through pictures. Before most families owned a camera, many relied on professionals to take their photographs in the studio or at their home or farm. Cabinet photographs—mounted on a large stiff board—were the work of Williamsport or Milton studios. The Wilson Studio, established in 1885 in Milton, produced images of Central Oak Heights (COH) and Allenwood. Until 1917, Milton studio photographer John Swanger made large series of real-photo postcards of COH and Devitt's Camp and panoramas of towns. Arthur R. Ishiguro (1887–1956), a Japanese immigrant, bought Swanger Studio, which he operated from around 1923 to 1950.

Amateurs, who limited themselves to photographing friends and family or their residences, included Malinda Drumm, a shopkeeper and resident in Winfield in the early 1900s, and Mary Barber Hagey (1891–1967) of White Deer. Hagey stands out for providing a vivid picture of the lives of children.

Other amateurs became semiprofessional from 1905 to 1920 when the real-photo postcard came of age and flourished. Lewis D. Thomas (1883–1949) grew up on a farm outside Spring Garden. In 1903, he received a Century Grand camera from his mother, and it opened an area of interest that occupied his life when not farming with his wife, Mary Ellen Reaser, of the Alvira area. Their ninth child, Marlin Thomas, writes in *Lewey and Mary Ellen, Moving On* (2005), "So that she would not feel so far from home, Lewis took pictures of the valley [White Deer] which he printed as picture postcards and mailed them up there to his sister [Susan] in New York [prior to January 1909 when she died suddenly]." Many of Thomas's real-photo postcards of White Deer Valley date from 1903 to 1911. From 1912 to 1917, he worked for the Swanger Studio in Milton before returning to a family farm.

Steven B. Horton (born 1882), a boarder at the West Milton Hotel operated by George and Clara Fenstermacher, sold Uneeda Biscuits throughout Union County as well as in Snyder, Northumberland, and Montour, and he photographed these places from 1907 to 1911. Probably, Horton's postcards were sold upon his return to the same stores, as his work focused on businesses or street scenes with people assuming a minor role. Ralph Fuller (born 1840 and raised in Muncy Hills) opened a photography business in Turbotville in 1907 and produced postcards of area towns including Allenwood. In the 1920s, when the real-photo postcard era started to decline, Fuller transformed his shop into a hardware store. Nelson Adelbert Caulkins (1874–1965) was the only one of this group who was a semiprofessional photographer all of his life. From Unidella, New York, Caulkins set up a studio in Slate Run in central Pennsylvania's Pine Creek Valley. He traveled from Slate Run to other central Pennsylvania sites and lived in Watsontown from 1914 to 1917 before returning to the Pine Creek area.

These photographers, along with countless unknown others, have left a body of work that allows us to better understand our past and present.

One

Allenwood, Spring Garden, and Alvira

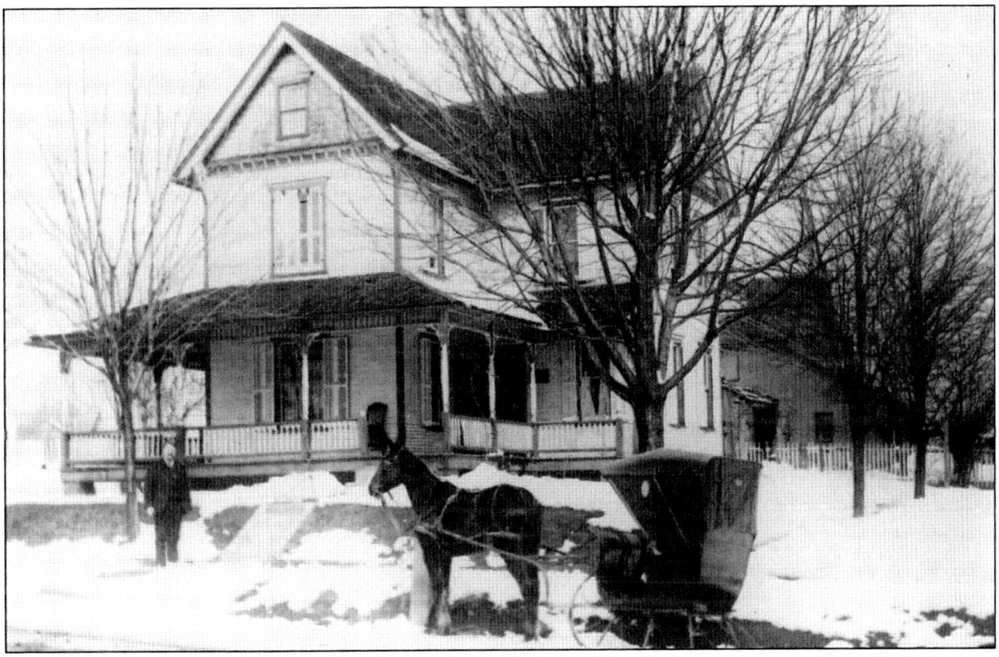

Dr. Amos Persing, who practiced medicine from 1892 until he died in 1938, stands ready for house calls by his Allenwood home and office on Bridge Street in 1904. He often made house calls throughout the White Deer Valley. Persing married Estel Pensyl of Elysberg, and among their children were two doctors: William and Amos Jr. They also had two daughters; Katherine was a schoolteacher and Martha married William Schooley. (Amos and John Persing.)

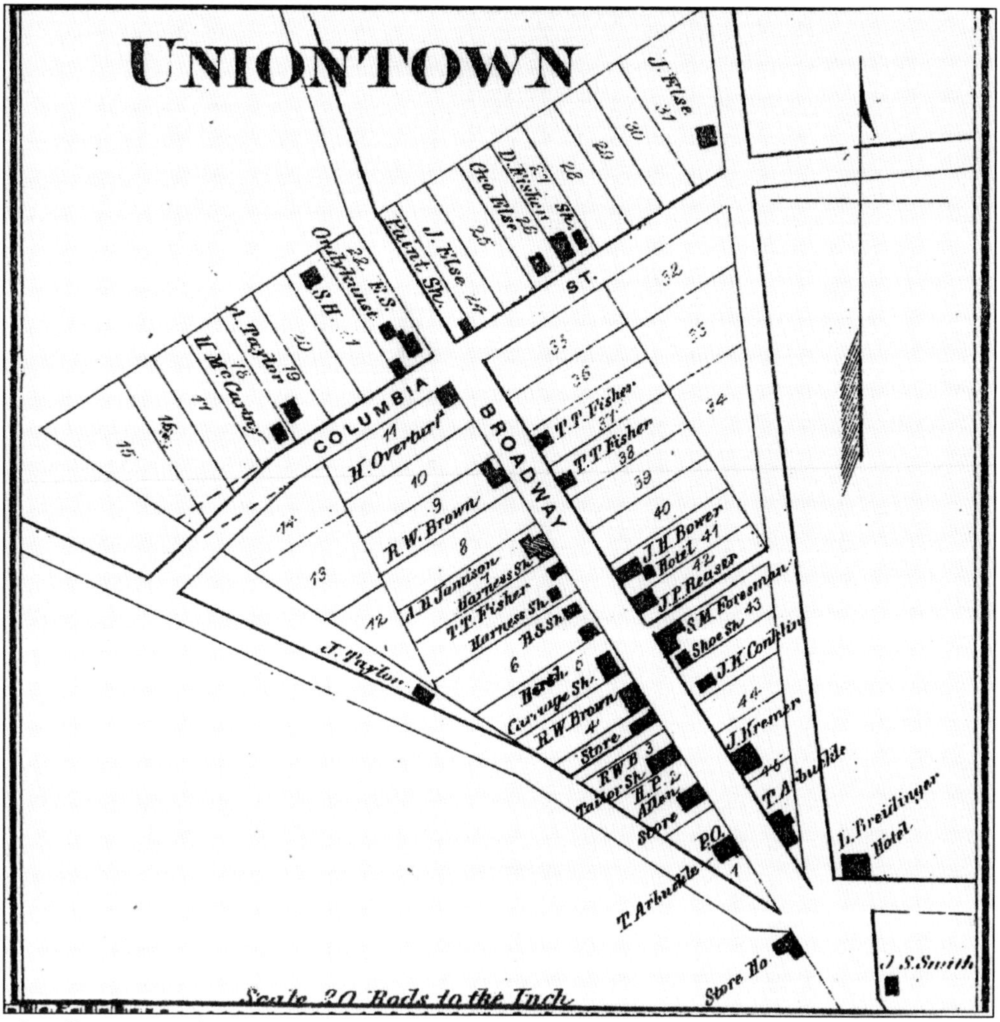

This illustration of Uniontown (later named Allenwood) in the 1868 *Pomeroy's Atlas of Union and Snyder Counties* shows the post office in Thomas Arbuckle's store. H.P. Allen's store (next to the post office) was followed by a cluster of related businesses: the carriage, blacksmith, and harness shops of T.T. Fisher and A.H. Jamison, all north on Broadway (now Route 15). Arbuckle's store later became Anthony Armstrong's store. The Breidinger Hotel became the Allenwood Hotel. It was located on the northeast corner of Bridge Street, aptly named for the bridge that, in 1852, crossed the Susquehanna to Dewart and to the Erie Railroad. A second hotel is farther north on Broadway. The store and dwelling on the southwest corner of Routes 15 and 44 was later operated by the Ungards. Allenwood's post office moved between several locations, this store being one of them. (UCHS.)

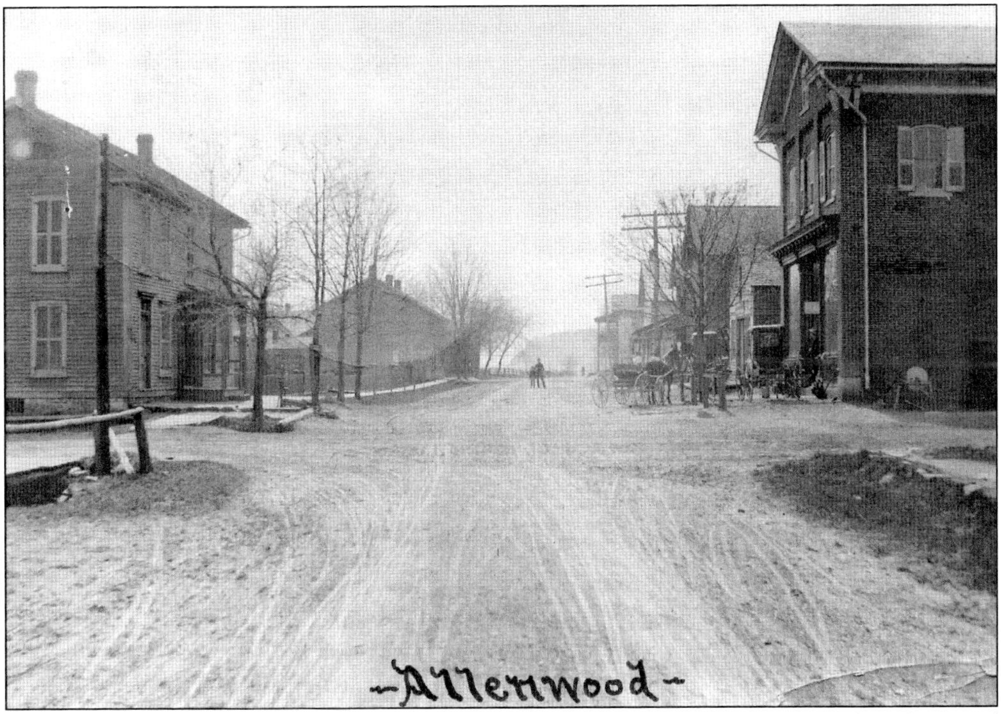

The photographer of the above image stood in Allenwood's main street and looked south toward the eastern tip of White Deer Mountain. Allen's Store (still standing) is on the near right, pictured around 1908. The Philadelphia and Reading Railroad curve south of Allenwood was at the base of the White Deer Mountains, as seen up-close in another real-photo postcard of the same period (below). The sender of that card wrote, "We got done making hay this week and we killed 3 big snakes inside of a week." Copperheads, water moccasins, and rattlesnakes are known in the area, but harmless black snakes are more common. (Both, Jean L. Hormel.)

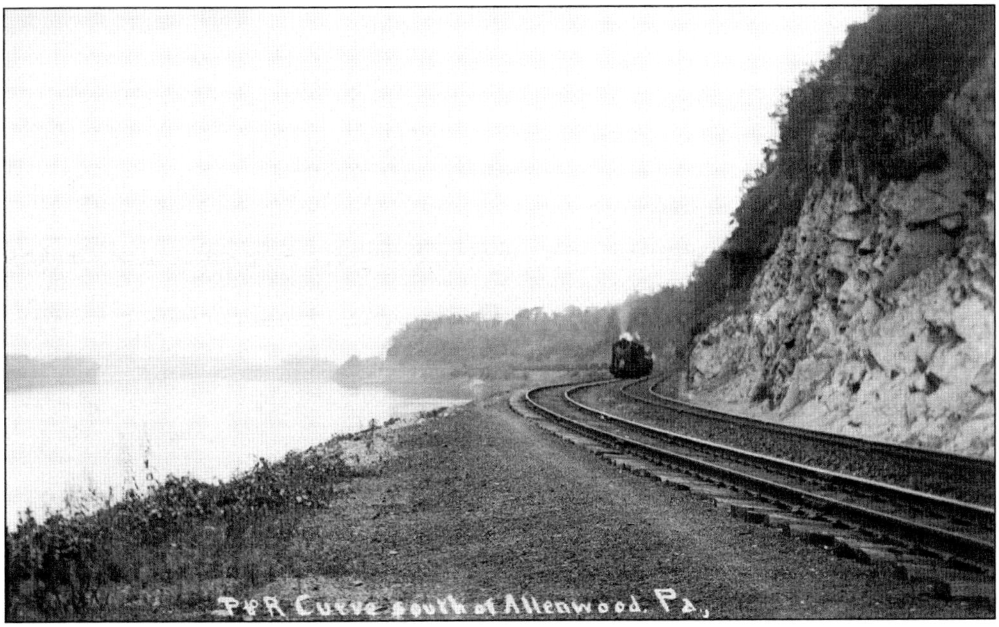

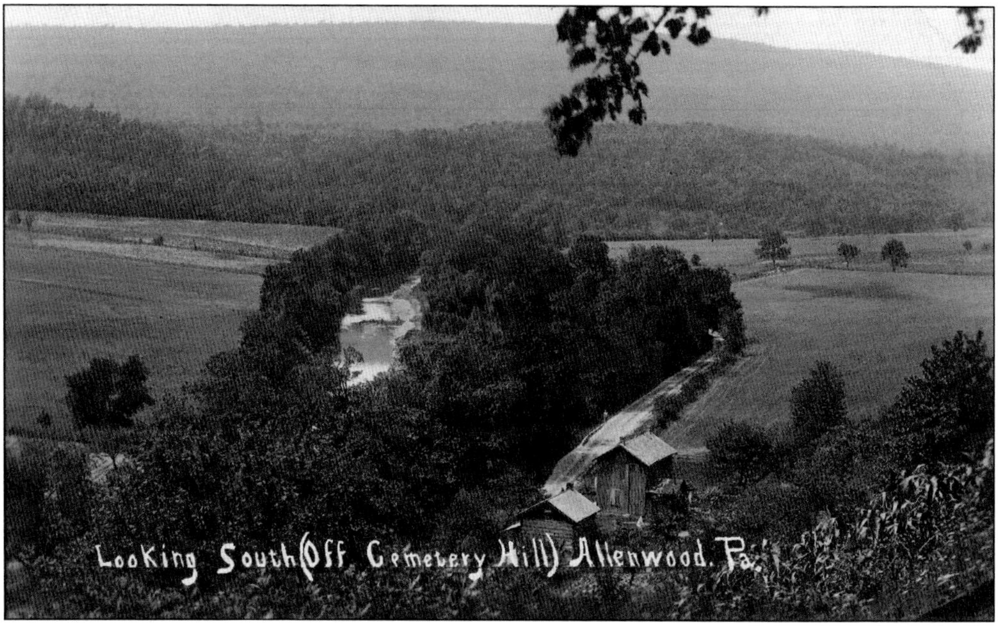

The above real-photo postcard, which reads "Looking South (Off Cemetery Hill) in Allenwood," aims the viewer more westerly than south and toward the White Deer Mountains. The cemetery, now called Allenwood, was earlier called Uniontown. In a second view (below), the scene is in a northeasterly direction, taking in much of the town. The Susquehanna River can be seen in the mid-background. (Both, UCHS 2004.17.3 and 94.5.21.)

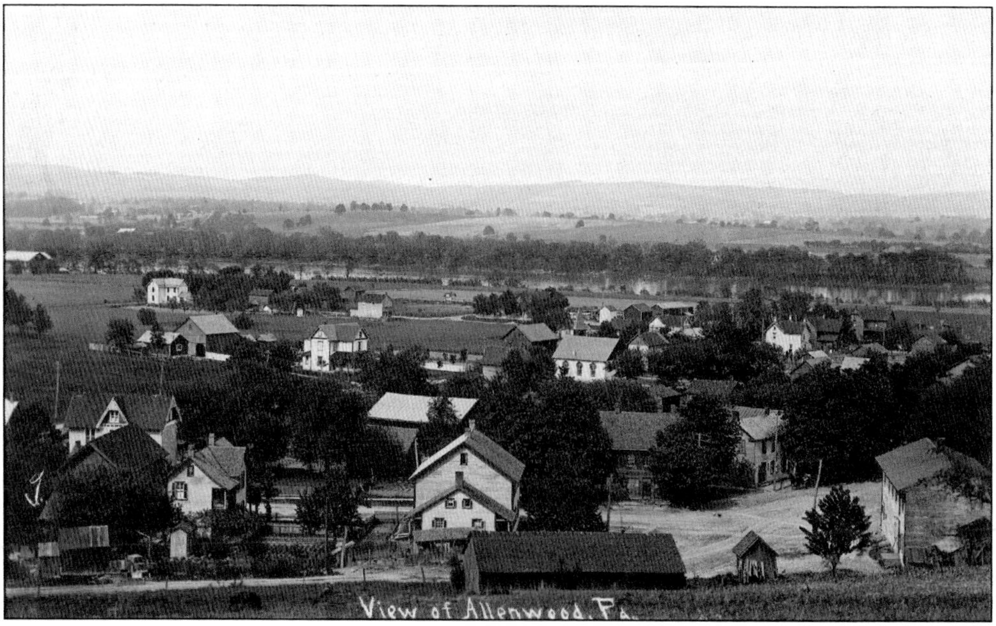

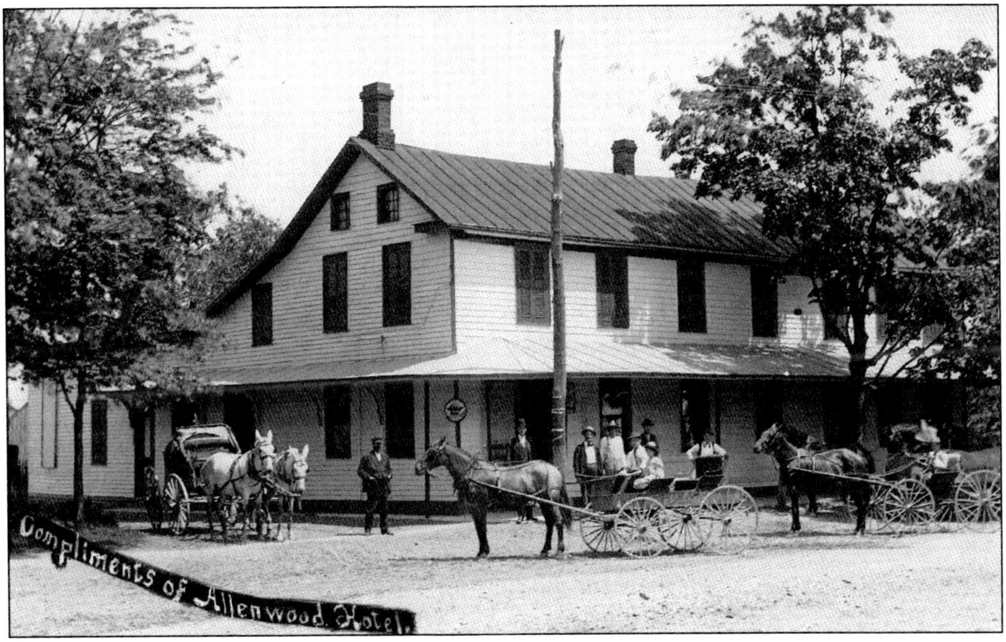

William F. Ungard (1853–1923), a Watsontown coal merchant, and his wife, Elizabeth A. (1853–1934), moved to Allenwood between 1901 and 1906. Initially, Ungard was the proprietor of the Allenwood Hotel (above). His son Donald C. Ungard (1893–1919) sent this complimentary real-photo postcard of the hotel. The lodging was razed between 1910 and 1920 when a new home was built at the site for William, who was then a store owner. The real-photo postcard below features Ungard's new home on Bridge Street (center), which still stands. In the 1910s, the town's post office was located in the two-story frame building (left) that housed Walter Meek's grocery store. From 1945 to 1952, the first beauty shop in Allenwood, run by Hattie Fisher, was on the second floor. Her rent was $25 a month. (Above, UCHS 95.2.1; below, Jack Fisher.)

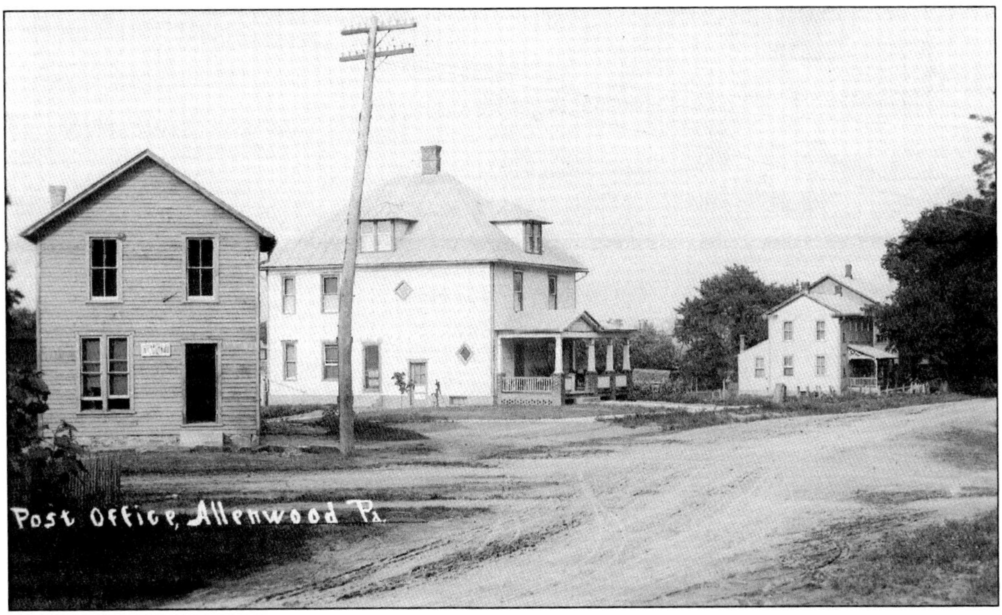

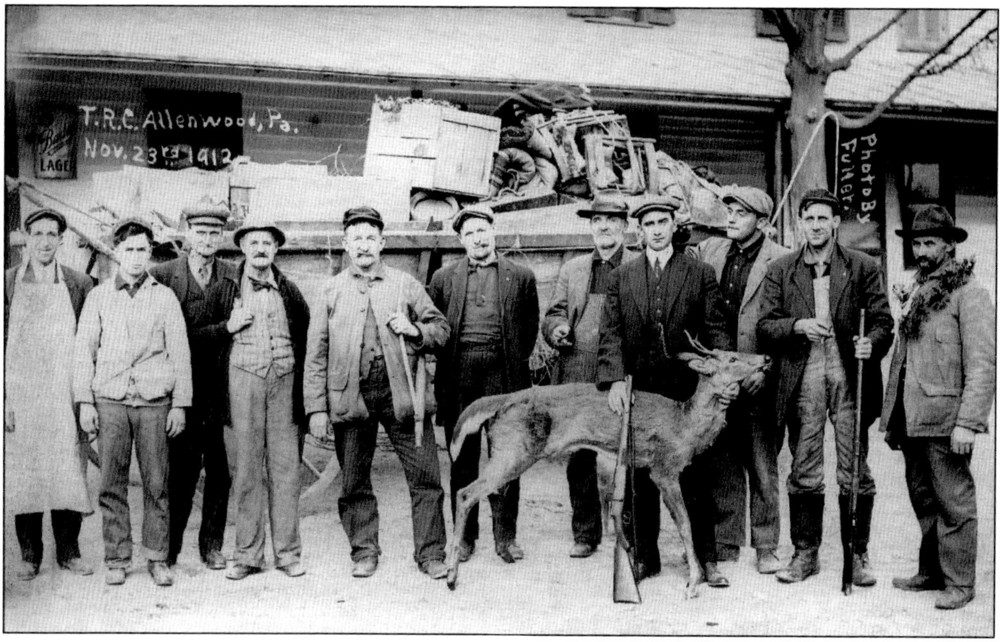

Ralph Fuller of Turbotville photographed the Turbotville Recreation Club (TRC) in front of the Allenwood Hotel on November 23, 1912. The men pose with a rather scrawny deer in front of a large wagon holding their gear. Their stone camp was located west of Elimsport, Lycoming County, at Fourth Gap. (UCHS 2005.52.4.)

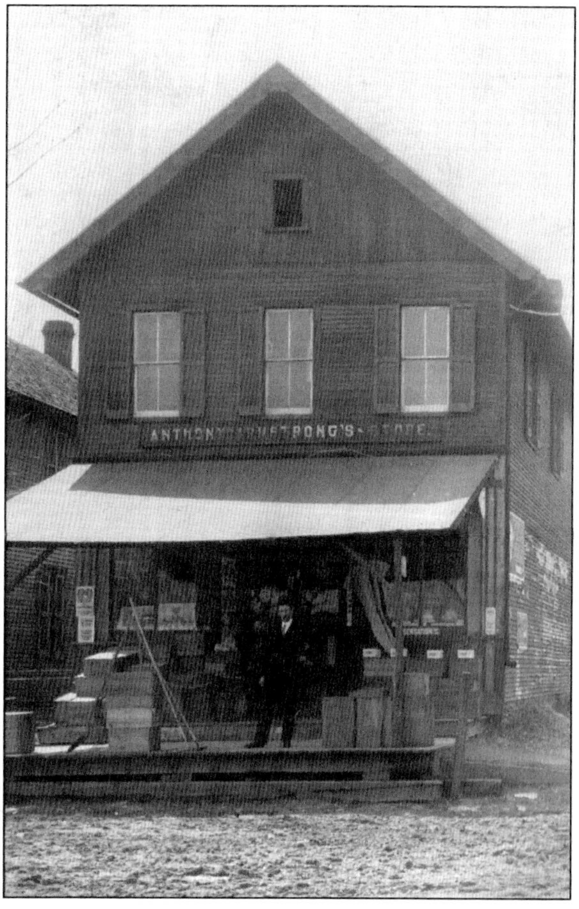

Anthony Armstrong (1852–1924) and Kate Griffey Armstrong (1860–1909) owned and operated a general store on Broadway, Allenwood, seen here in the early 1900s. Their son Richard "Dick" (1898–1942) later ran the store. (Jean L. Hormel.)

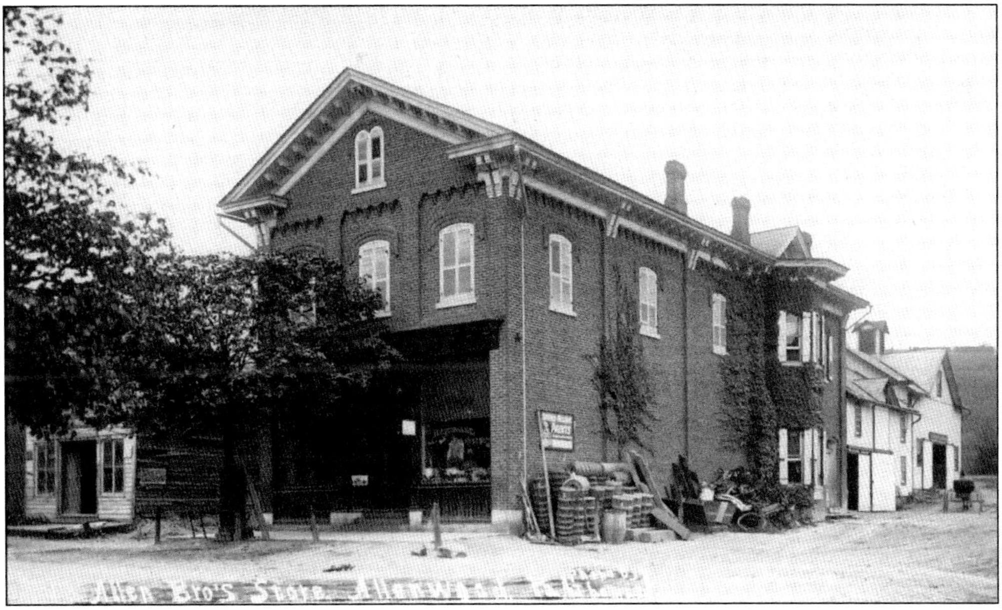

The Allen family, after whom the town is named, operated a large brick hardware store and warehouse north of Armstrong's store. The Allens also had an automotive and heavy equipment dealership. The real-photo postcard above by Lewis Thomas from about 1907 is of the front of their business. The c. 1910s–1920s photograph below shows several tractors at the side and rear. (Both, Jean L. Hormell.)

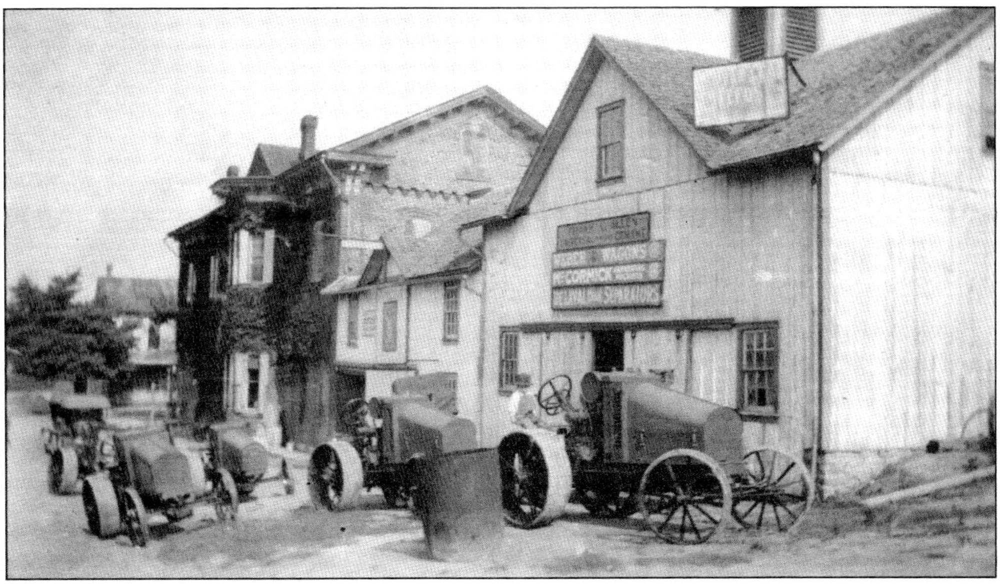

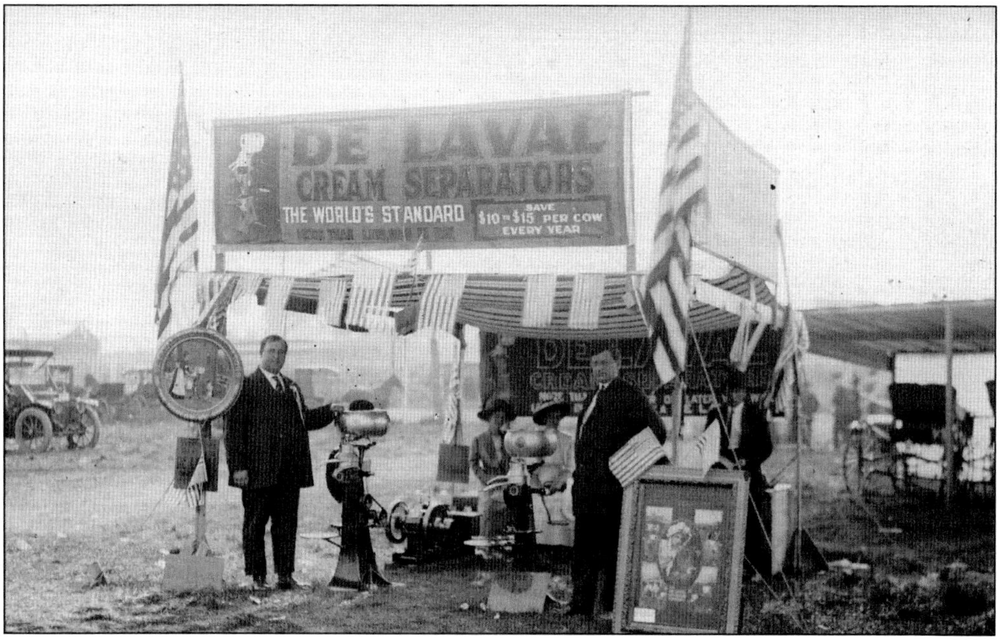

Herman and Elizabeth Jane (Armstrong) Allen's sons (above) pose as agents for DeLaval cream separators at a local fair around 1910. Frank Levan Allen (left) was born in 1882, and Drew Armstrong Allen (right) was born in 1871. Below, Carl Klapp (far left) and Carl Kesty (far right) pose with a Dort car being sold at Frank L. Allen's dealership in Allenwood. Dorts were made in Flint, Michigan, and used a Lycoming engine (now part of Textron) that was made in Williamsport and was popular in various automobiles and airplanes. (Both, Jean L. Hormell.)

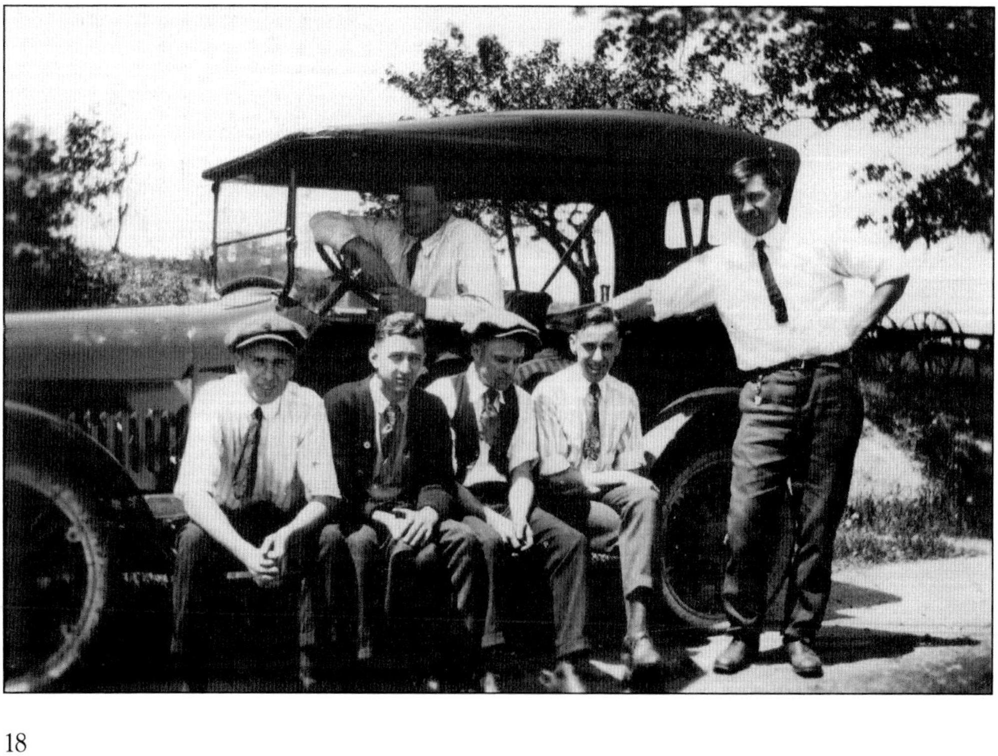

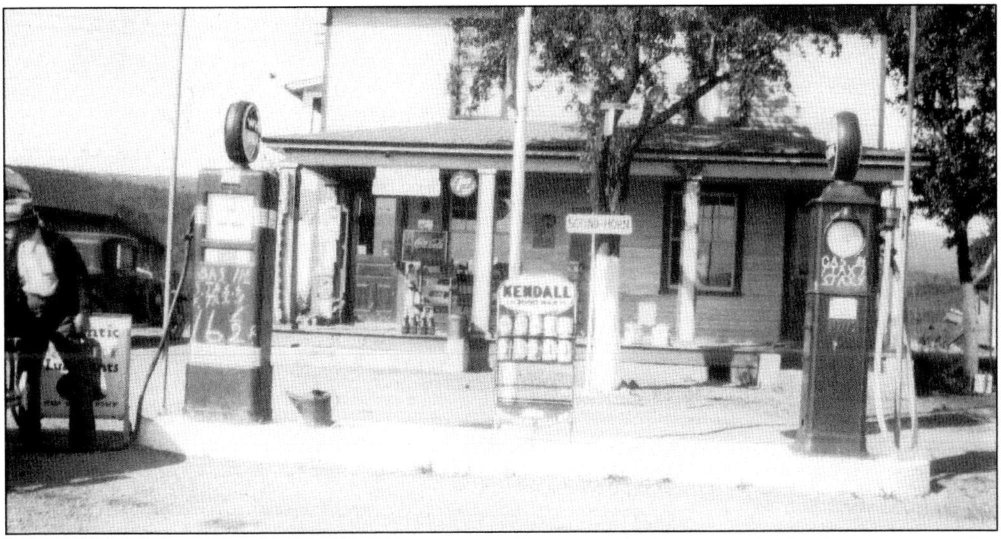

Edward J. Schooley's Atlantic Gas Station in Allenwood (1936–around 1960) was among the earliest filling stations between Lewisburg and Williamsport on Route 15. Edward and Blanche (Allen) Schooley's home served as a convenience store that sold Stroehman's bakery items, penny candy, Coca-Cola, Nehi soft drinks, Sheffer's ice cream, snacks, and tobacco products. In the summer, honey and raspberries were added to the inventory. Gas then was 16.5¢ per gallon. (Ruthann and David Schooley.)

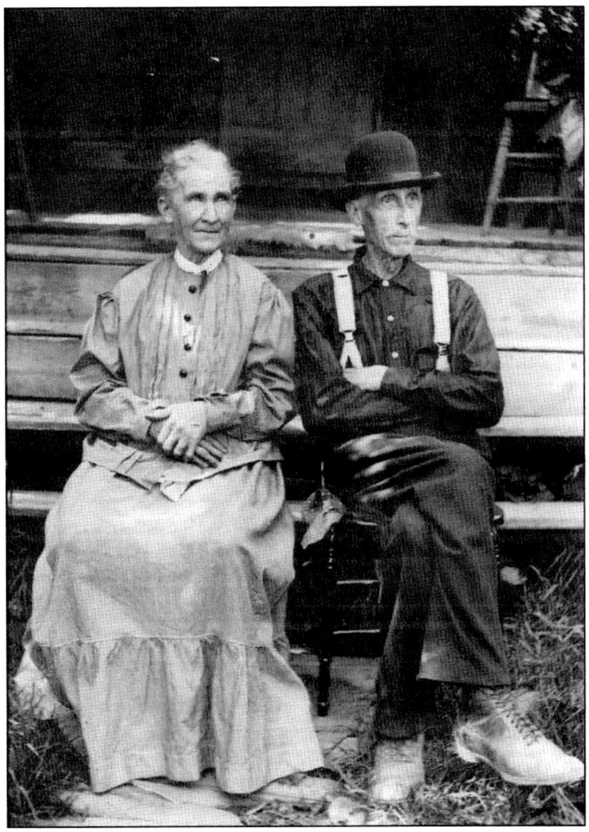

Fred and Kate Goldy were the toll keepers of the Allenwood/Dewart Bridge around 1900. In the 1870s, Fred Goldy had been a shoemaker and bridge toll keeper. (Donald Wilver Sr.)

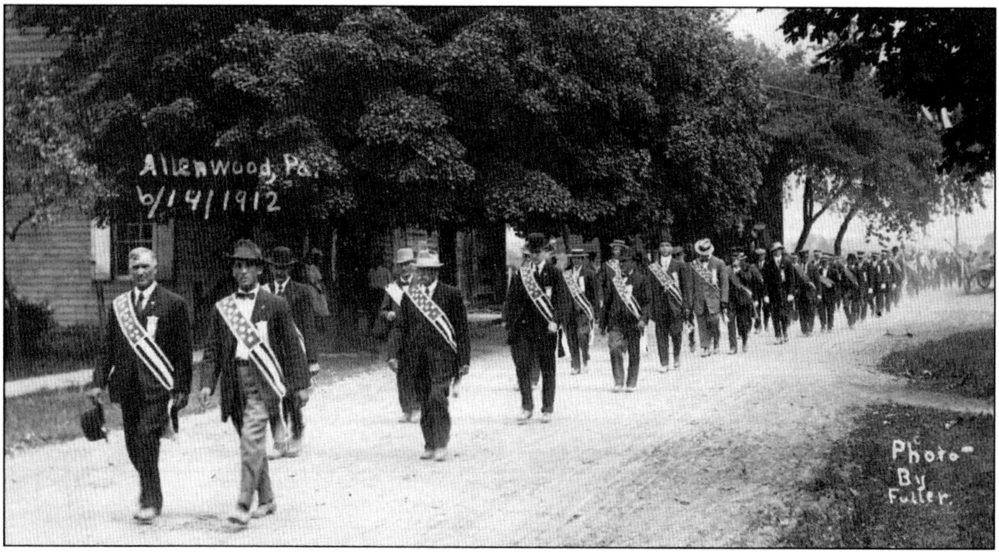

On June 14, 1912, a Flag Day parade in Allenwood proceeded on Bridge Street going west and was captured in real-photo postcards produced by Ralph Fuller of Turbotville. Above, the Allenwood Hotel is on the left. Four decades later, the Fireman's Parade and Carnival in Allenwood, always well attended, included a pet event usually held on Thursday night. Susan and Sara Helsman, below, are dressed for the parade in 1951. Susan is in her tutu, and Sara is in her stroller. The following year, the Helsman sisters portrayed the old lady and the shoe. The girls, about six and two here, won first place on two occasions, which meant tickets for rides and some spending money. (Above, UCHS 2003.7.2; below, Susan Helsman.)

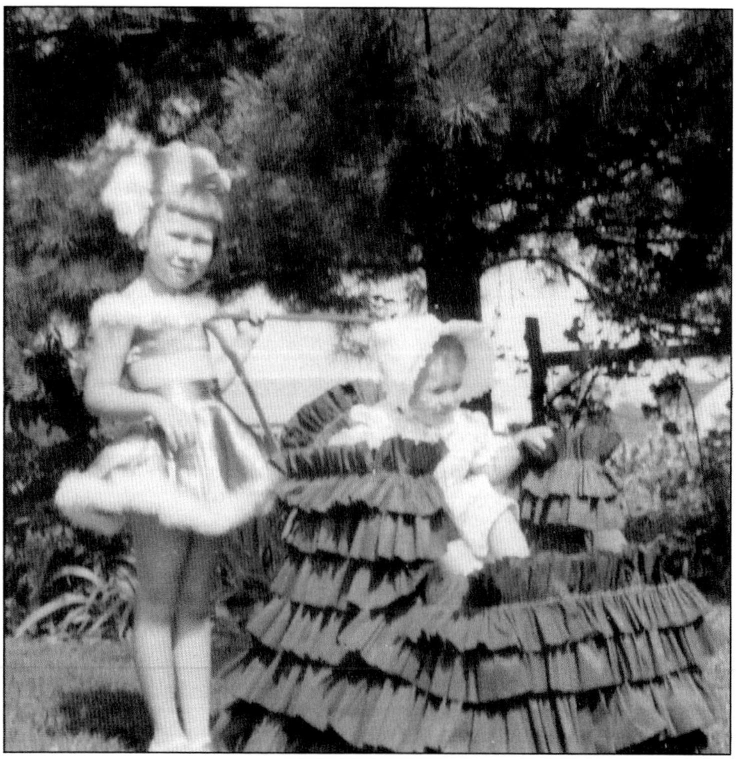

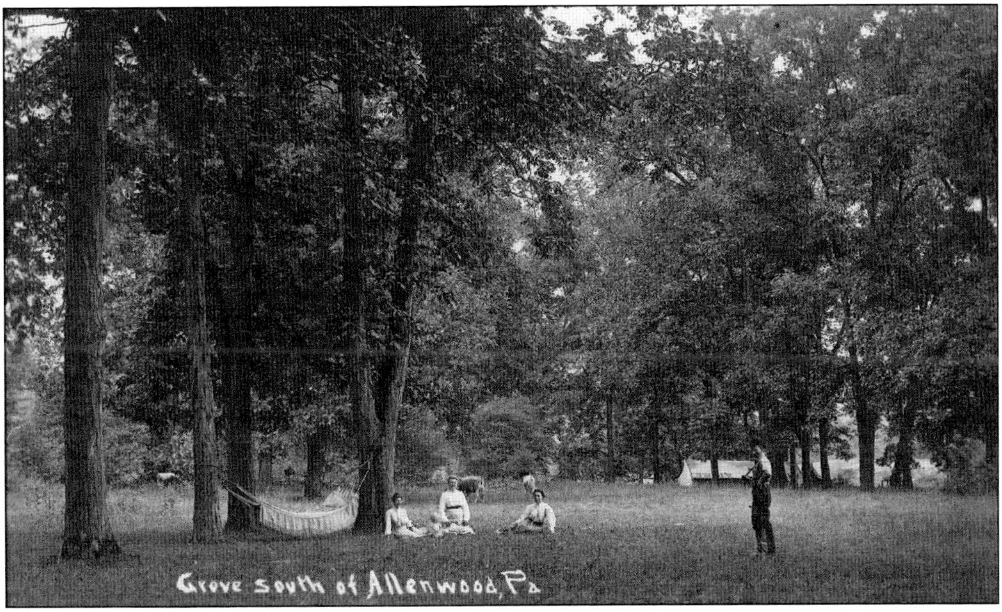

The real-photo postcard above labeled "Grove south of Allenwood" appears to be the same setting for local campers and the Dead-Gamers (below), who came in numbers from Lancaster to camp, hunt, and relax. It is believed the grove was located on the Gudykunst Mill tract, the description of which noted an orchard field or grove. The tract, presently off Old Mill Road, has the White Deer Hole Creek on three sides and includes a large level field. The cabinet photograph below is one in a series taken in 1908 by Wolf of 6 Prince Street, Lancaster, of the Dead-Gamers. Their ballooning was also captured by Turbotville photographer Ralph Fuller, who issued a series of real-photo postcards of the group. (Above, Patricia Longley; below UCHS 2006.21.20.)

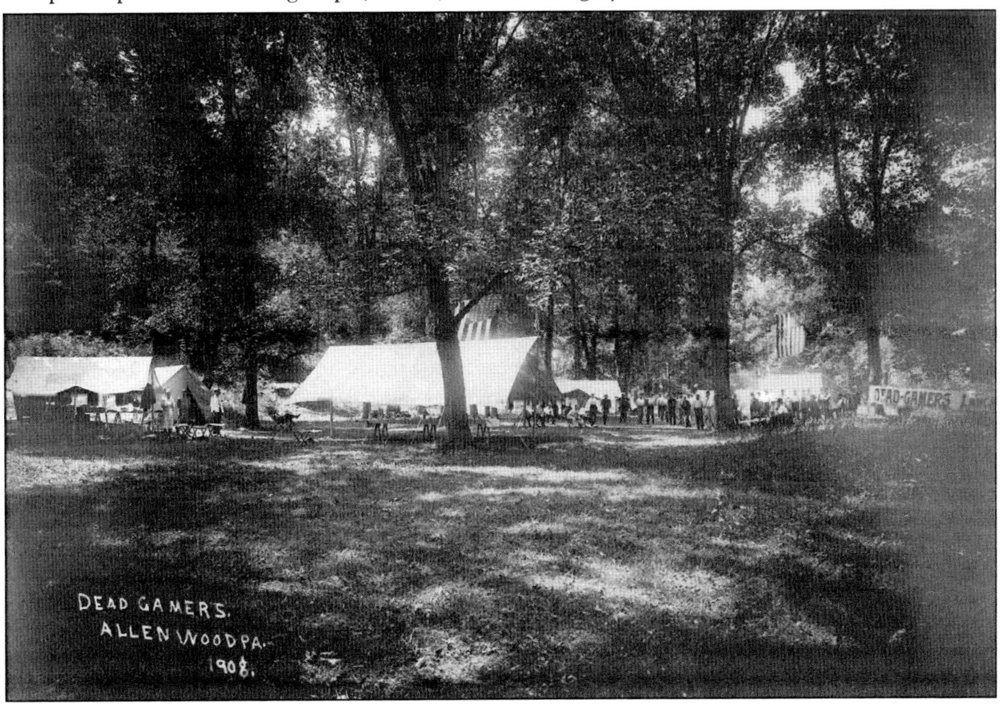

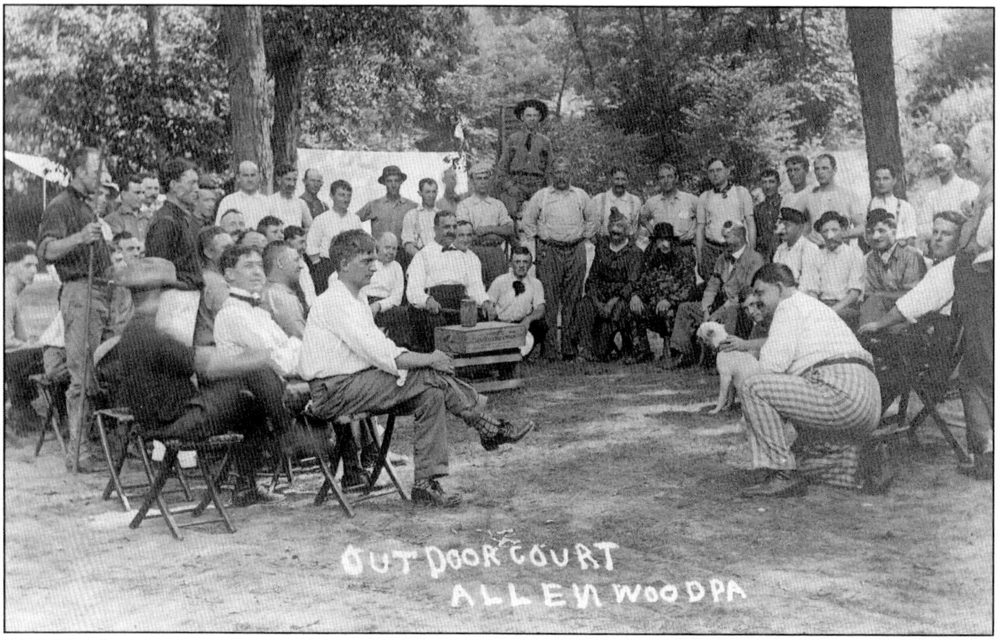

The Outdoor Court was a tongue-in-cheek event most likely held on the Gudykunst tract. On the reverse side of this postcard is written, "Sunday Court at Allenwood. All criminals were found guilty of course? Pop Gates Sr., the jury of six men, see man with small hat on head and white collar, Doebler Judge." (Ronald Nornhold.)

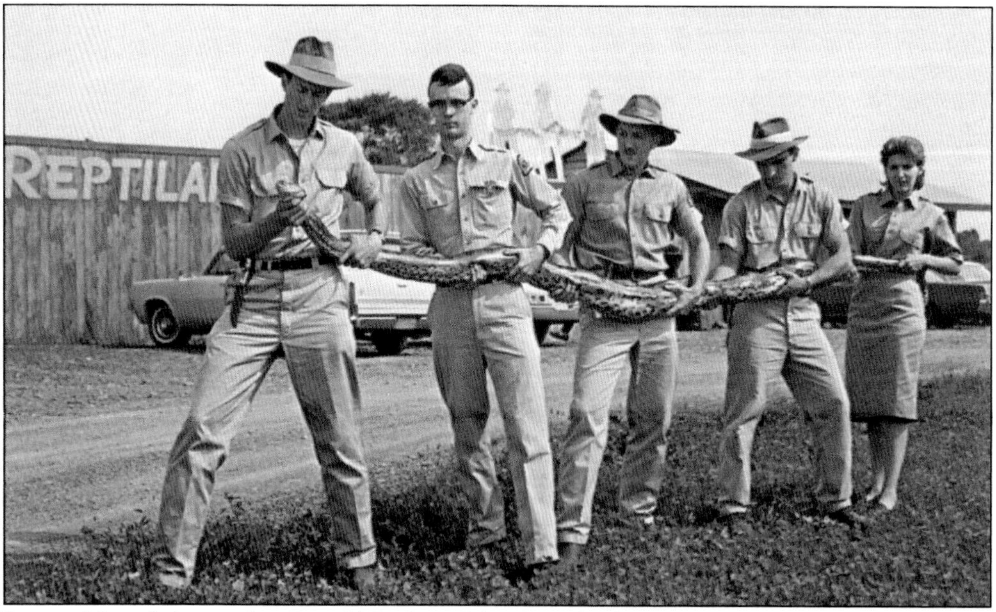
Pictured from left to right, Donald Peeling, John Strawbridge, Clyde Peeling, William Ely, and Virginia (Arthur) Peeling hold a 15-foot anaconda on this 1960s Kodachrome postcard. Clyde Peeling's Reptiland, a specialized zoo for reptiles and amphibians, was founded in 1964 and is accredited by the Association of Zoos and Aquariums (North America). In addition to the Allenwood site on Route 15, Reptiland has seven exhibits that travel nationwide, a program that was started in 1999. (UCHS 2003.7.13.)

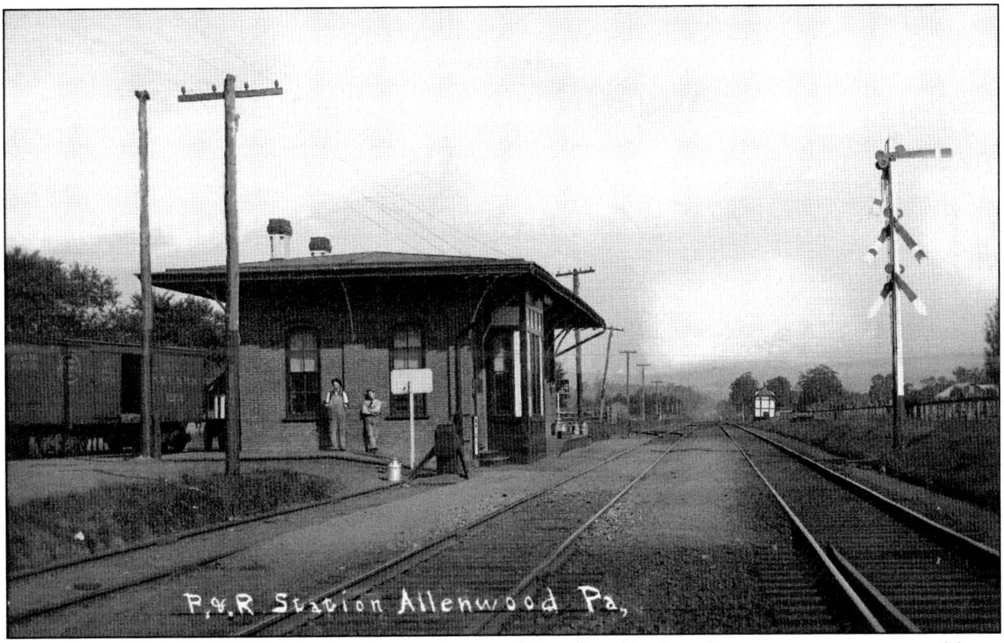

North of town was Allenwood's Philadelphia and Reading Railroad train station, pictured here around 1907. (Sharon and Bill Herald.)

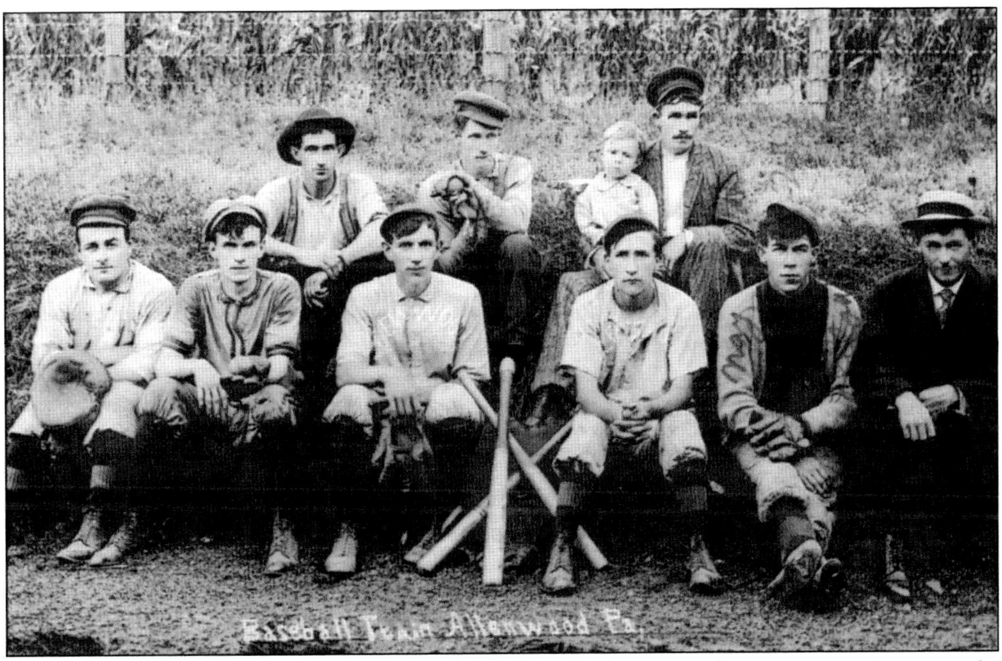

An Allenwood baseball team from the early 1900s poses for a group photograph. (Elizabeth Helsman.)

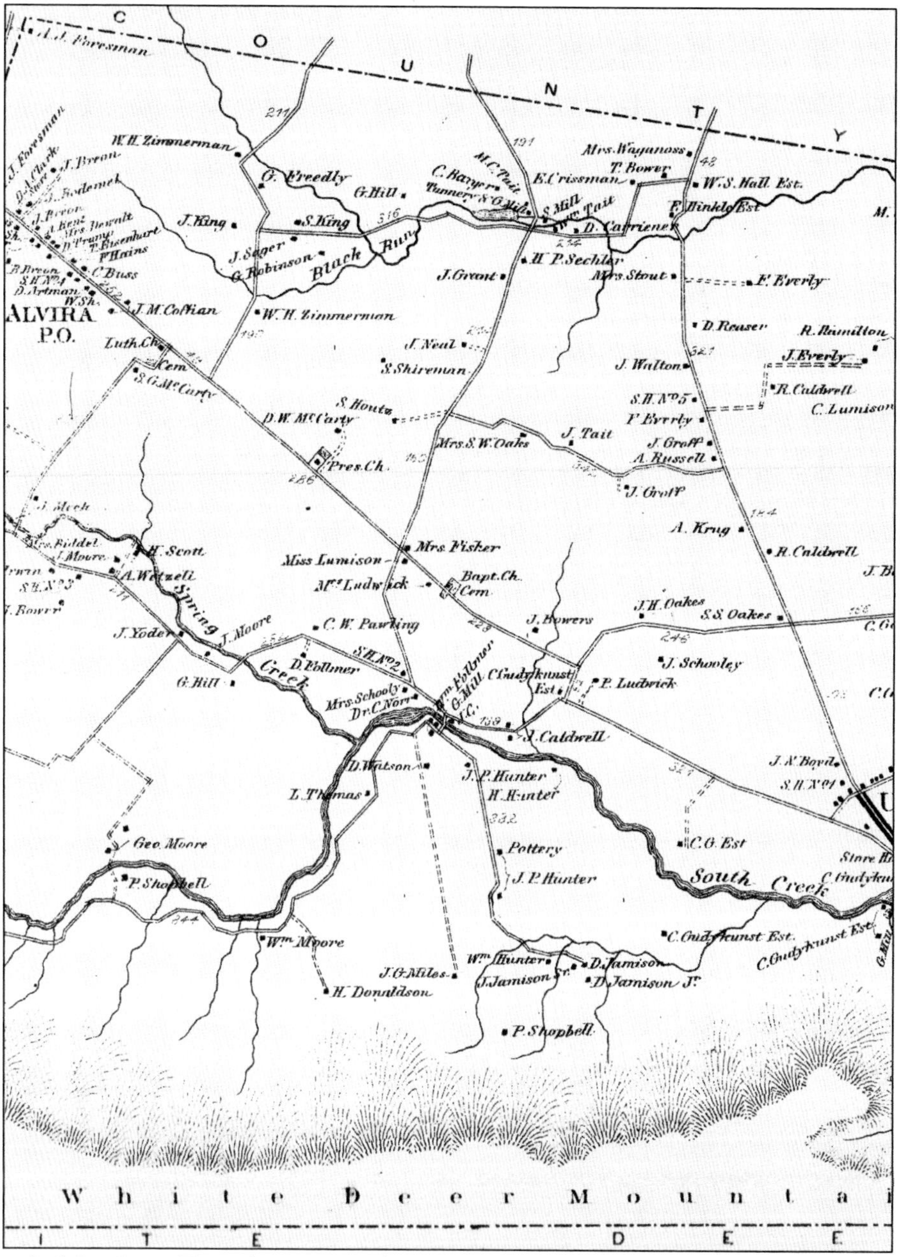

A detail of the Gregg Township map in the 1868 *Pomeroy's Atlas of Union and Snyder Counties* shows locations of the township's five schools. Schoolhouse 4 (upper left) is on Alvira's main street and was constructed in 1865 on land of Benjamin Breon. It was rebuilt in 1885 and closed in 1934. Schoolhouse 3 (middle left), known as "Wetzel's" and located near Spring Creek on the road to Elimsport, was built in 1856 on the land of Jacob Slenker and closed around 1951 (it still stands). Schoolhouse 2 (middle), known as "Spring Garden," was erected on the land of Daniel Follmer and was closed by 1958. It still stands. Schoolhouse 1, slightly north of Uniontown on the road to Williamsport, was built in 1885 on the land of Michael Fisher and closed in 1958. Schoolhouse 5, known as "Russell" or "Fairview," was located north on the Williamsport Road and was constructed in 1864 on the land of James Russell. It closed in 1921 and was recently razed. (UCHS.)

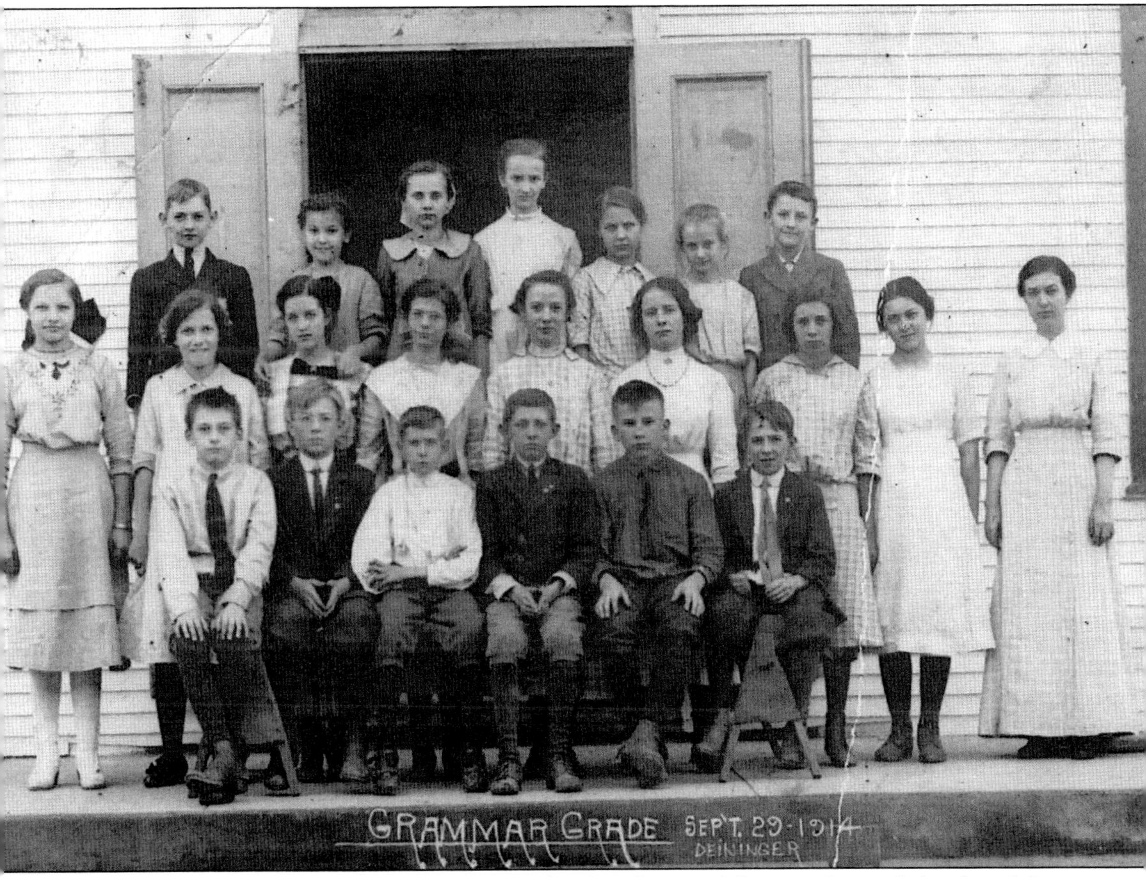

This 1914 photograph of Allenwood Grammar School students and their teacher includes, from left to right, (first row) Roland Campbell, William Cunningham, Raymond Fisher, Mark Gudykunst, Chester Cunningham, and unidentified; (second row) Christine Fairchild, Virdella Russell, Daisy Miller, Clarice Fisher, Idella Jamison, Pearl Shutt, Josephine Overdorf, Mary Beck, and teacher Mary Brown; (third row) ? Fairchild, Grace Zimmerman, Marguriete Johnson, Grace Else, Helen Morehart, Margaret Johnson, and Amos Persing. The school was located at the north edge of Allenwood and closed in 1959. (Donald Wilver Sr.)

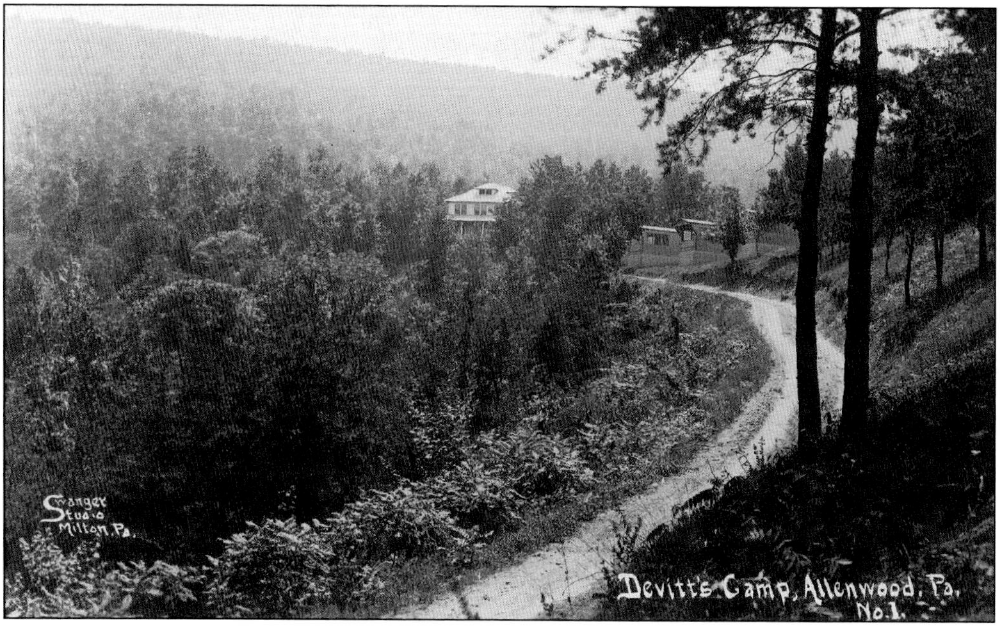

In 1912, Devitt's Camp, started inauspiciously in a barn, treated tubercular patients. Through the generosity of Philadelphia physician William Devitt and local physicians and members of the community, the sanatoriums at Devitt's Camp treated, cared for, and housed patients and their families. The approach to Devitt's Camp, as it appeared between 1912 and 1923 (above), was the first in a series of at least 18 real-photo postcards produced by the Swanger Studio of Milton. A second postcard (below) shows a nurse with patients, including Spry Arthur Sparks (third from left), of the Philadelphia area. At the close of World War I, the US Public Health Service and the Veterans Bureau sent men who had been gassed in the war to Devitt's Camp for rehabilitation. Veterans comprised more than half of the patients at that time. (Both, UCHS 96.1.2 and .1.)

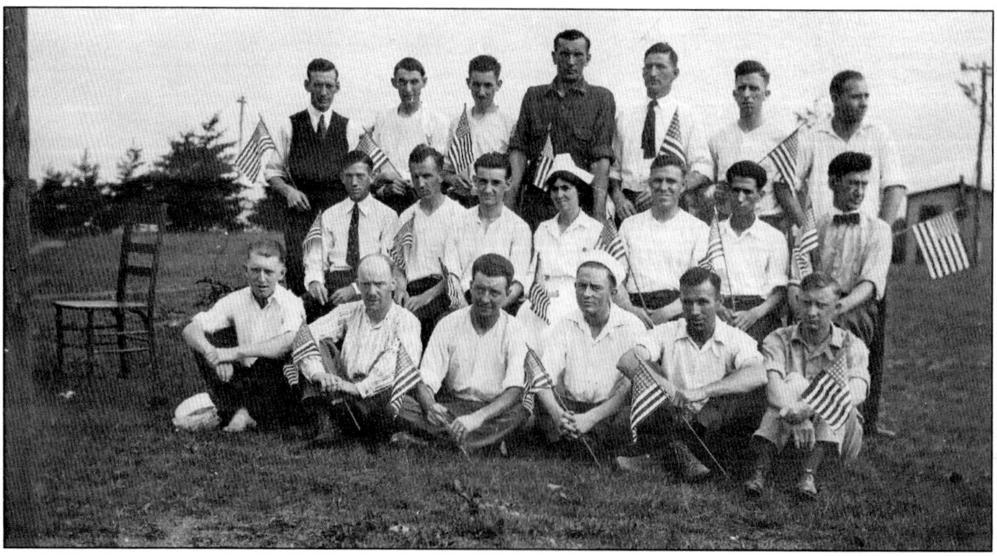

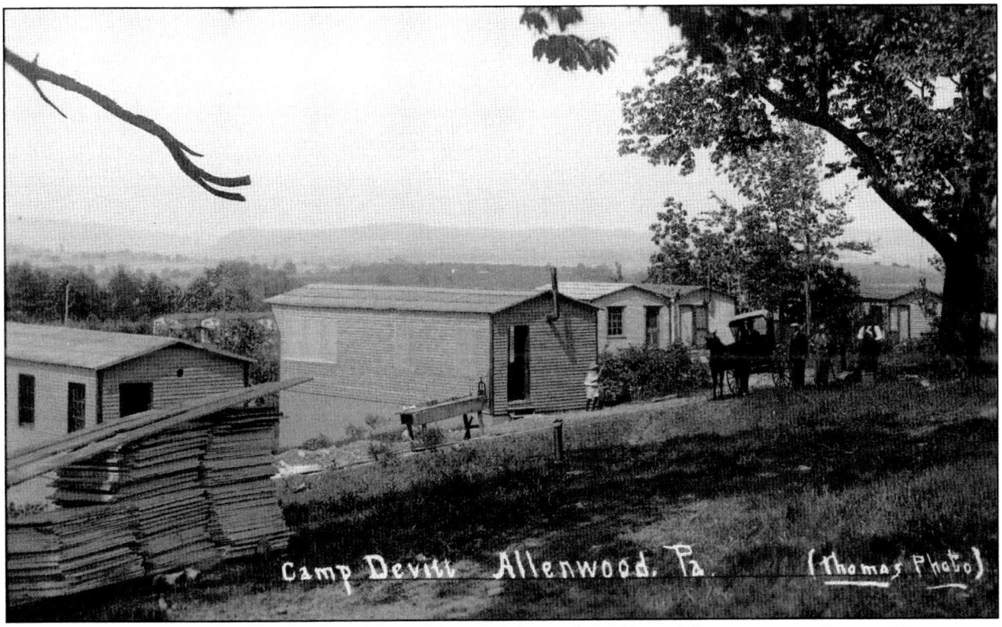

Cottages (above) were built on the north slope of the White Deer Mountains to house 30 patients in 1918, increased to 100 patients a year later. Below, a photographer captured the beauty and enormous space of rich farmlands below the facility for tuberculars. That land is occupied now by the Federal Correctional Complex at Allenwood on half of the 8,500 acres taken by the federal government in 1942 for an ammunitions facility. In 1950, the Federal Bureau of Prisons housed 110 minimum-security inmates from the Northeast Federal Penitentiary at what was then called the Allenwood Camp. Eventually, 500 acres on the east side of Route 15 were sold back to original landowners; 3,018 acres formed State Game Lands No. 252; 220 acres were sold to Lycoming County for the White Deer Golf Course, and 445 acres were given to the Williamsport Area Community College. (Above, Susan Snoddy; below, UCHS 2000.10.13.)

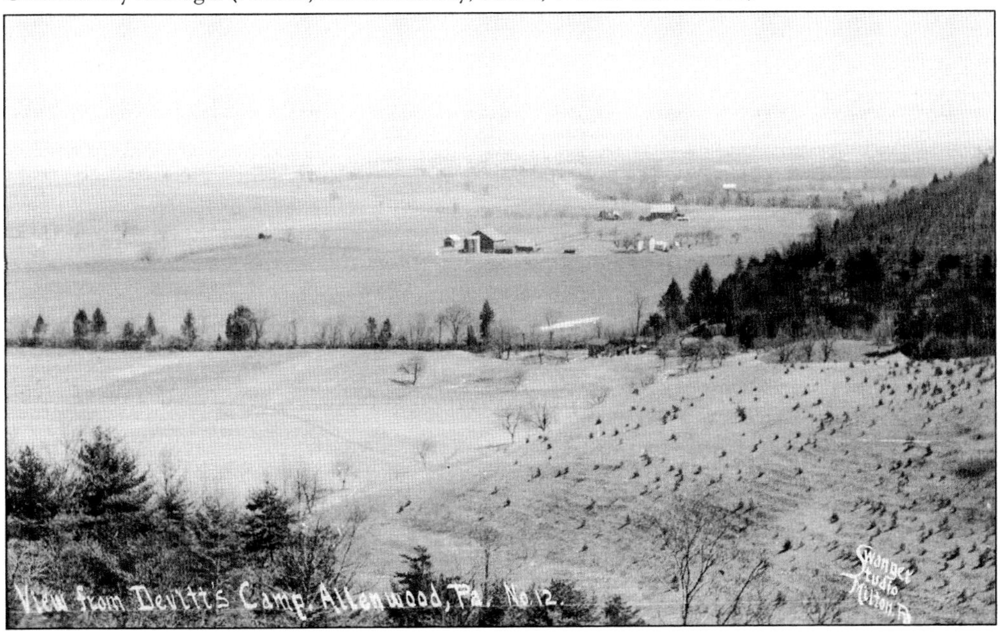

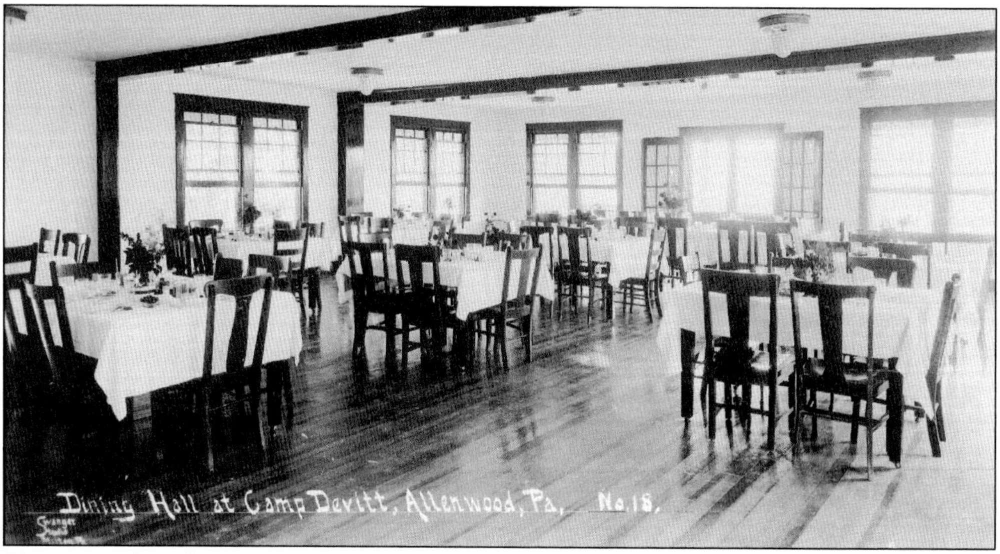

The airy quality of Devitt's Camp's dining room was captured in the photograph above by Swanger Studio. A 1949 menu detailed a dinner of prime rib or roulade of beef, mashed potatoes, creamed celery, beans, and ginger cake with whipped cream. Supper included orange or grapefruit juice, barley soup, Canadian bacon and scrambled eggs, baked potatoes, vegetable salad, and peaches or junket. Below, an aerial photograph—one of at least three different aerials produced in the 1950s—includes dining, administrative, treatment, and housing facilities that had evolved since the institution's founding. With tuberculosis in decline, St. Peter's United Church of Christ in Kelly Township used the facilities as a nursing home for upwards of 100 patients from 1956 to 1963. In 1970, the site became, and still is, the White Deer Run Treatment Center, a drug and alcohol rehabilitation facility. (Both, UCHS 2000.10.15 and 87.21.7.)

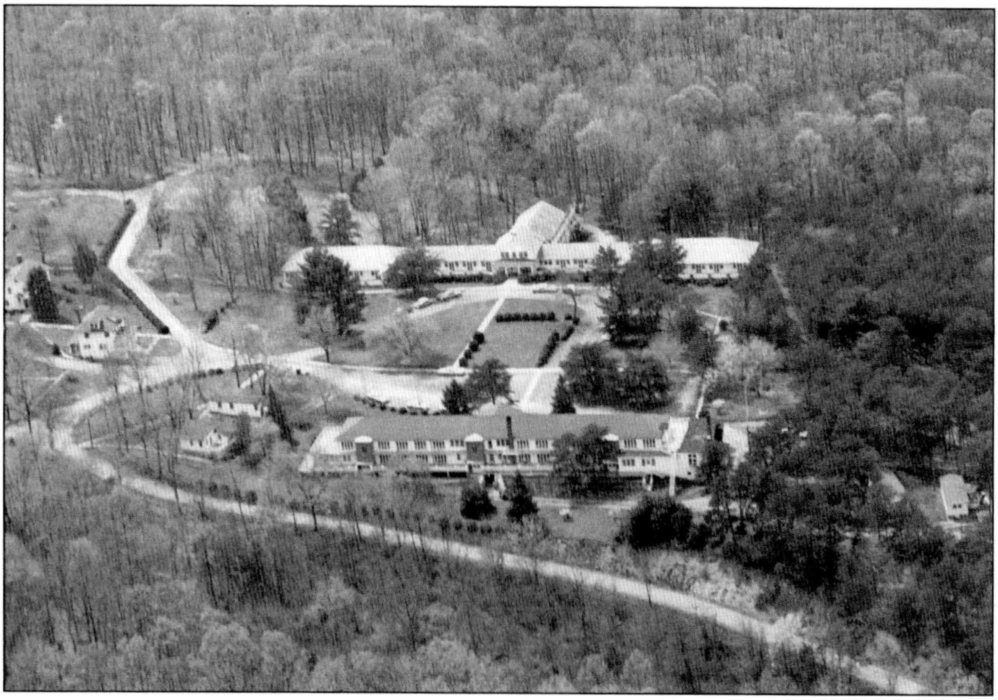

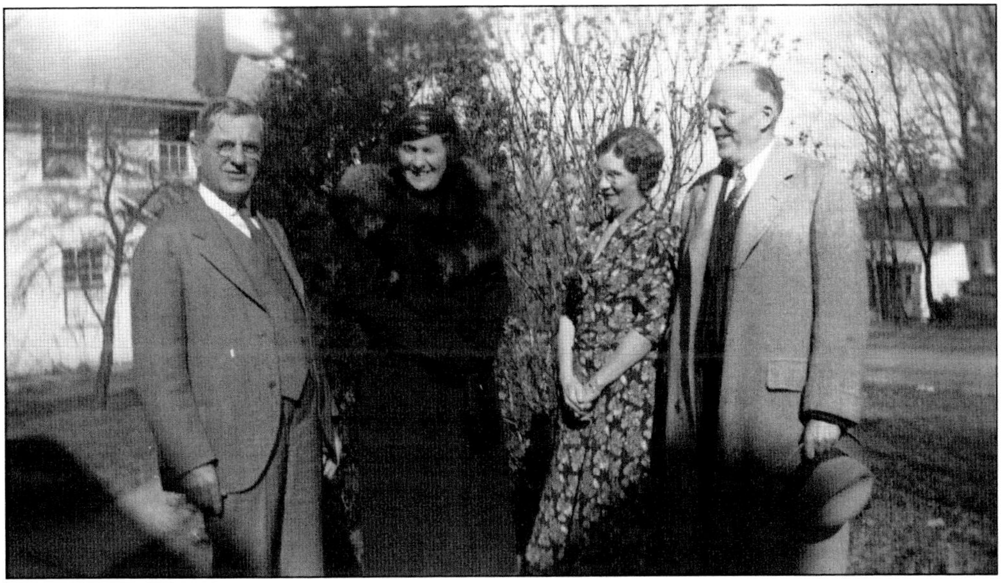

Candid photographs from 1934 to 1940 document hospital staff and others. At right are nurses Helen Frontz (left) and Martha Foresman. Above are the head of Geisinger Medical Center, Dr. Harold Foss (far right), and Mrs. Foss (in dark coat) at Devitt's Camp. The Fosses, from Danville, were visiting Dr. William Devitt (far left) and his wife (wearing flowered dress) at the tubercular facility. Both institutions were begun in the early 1900s and were unusual in their organization and treatment of patients. Geisinger, patterned on the Mayo Clinic of Rochester, Minnesota, was one of the pioneering large group practices in the nation. (Both, UCHS 87.21.4-.5.)

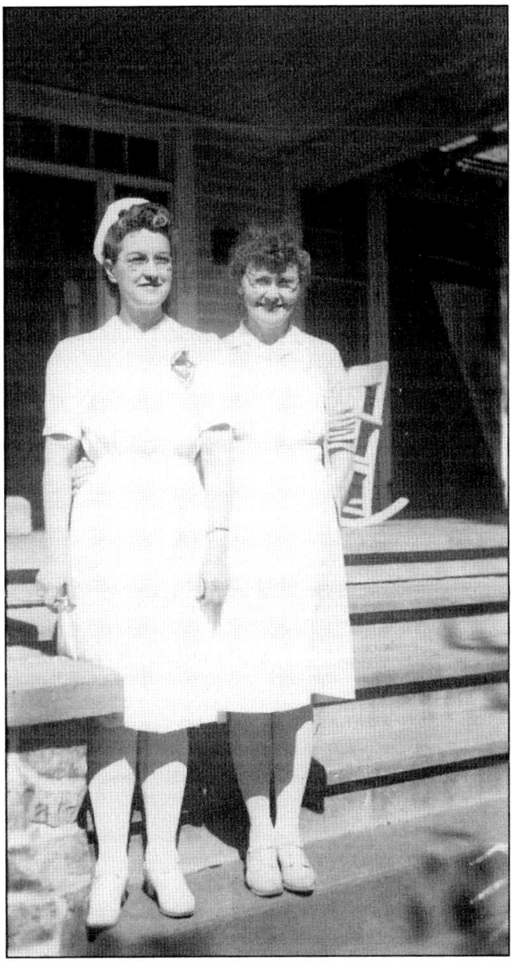

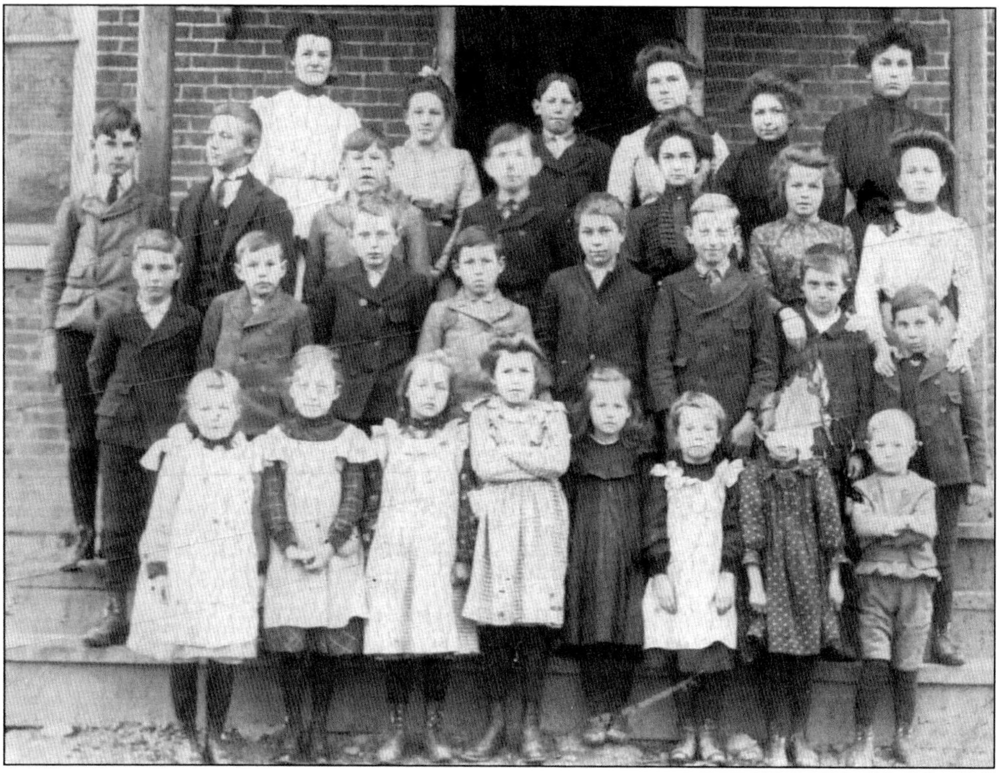

The Spring Garden School, pictured above around 1898, shows teacher Annie (Schooley) Ashcroft in the fourth row at the far left. In the class are John, Luther, and Madeline Snoddy and the Jamison twins, Olive and Brown. The more recent picture from 1954–1955 (below) shows, from left to right, (first row) Delmar Achenbach, Sandy Joe, David Ferguson, David Jamison, and David Masser; (second row) unidentified, Glenda Fisher, Florence Strassner, Beth ?, Sharon Phone, Mary Ann Clinger, Susan Helsman, Audrey Jamison, and Earl Wertman; (third row) unidentified, Jane Ulrich, Helen Williams, Margaret Reid, Marie Staggert, Janice Jamison, Mary Staggert, Betty Clinger, Bonnie Jamison, and two unidentified. Teacher Grace Saylor took the photograph. Susan Helsman was the fourth generation of Jamisons to attend this one-room school, which is perhaps a record in Union County. (Both, Elizabeth Helsman.)

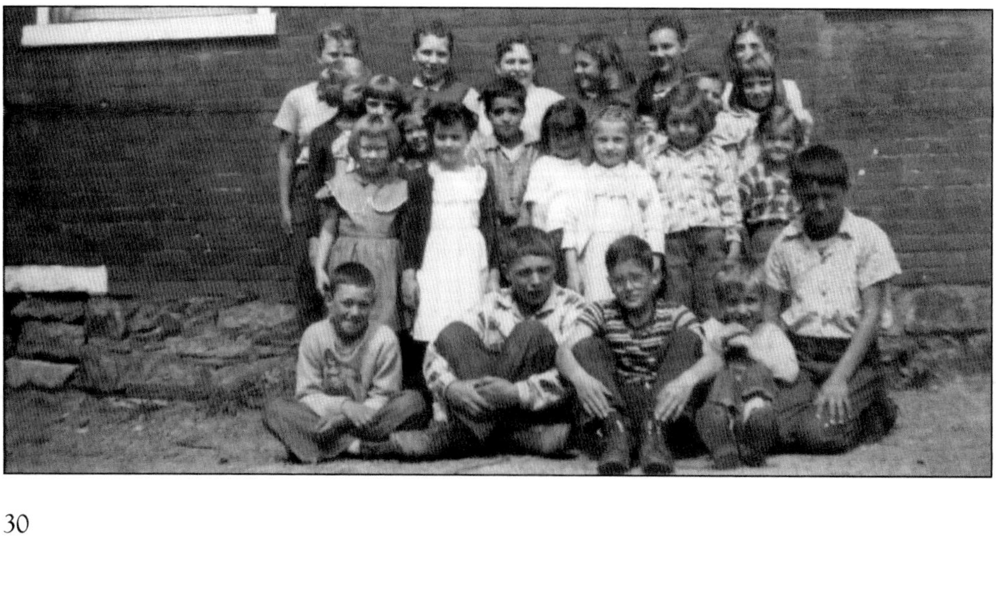

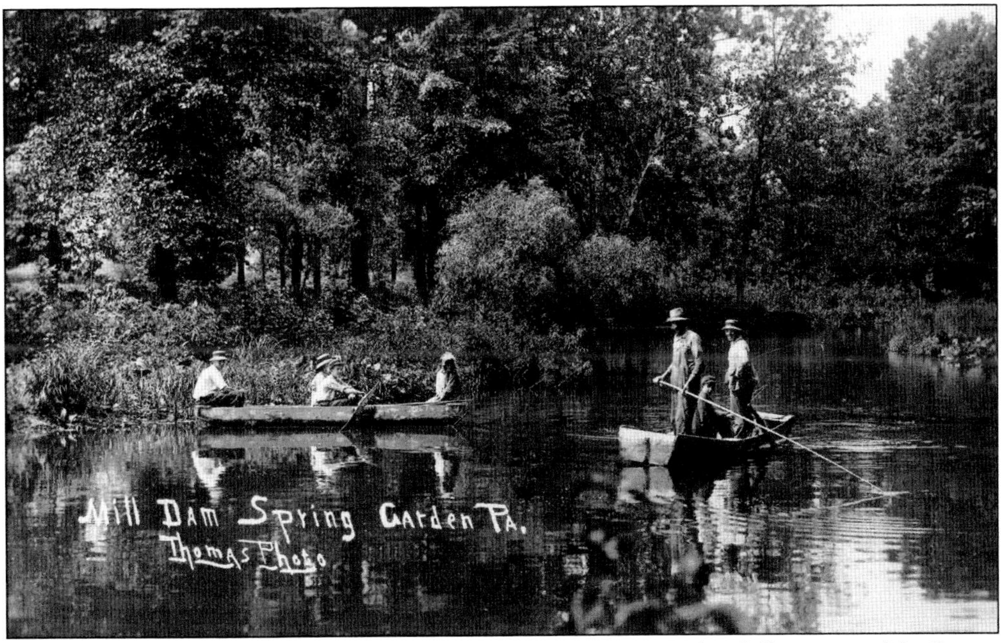

These real-photo postcards, taken between 1906 and 1911, capture the idyllic waters of the Spring Garden's gristmill dam and the physical relationship of the milldam, the north facade of the mill, the white miller's house (razed in 2008) across from the mill, the barely seen covered bridge (far left), and North White Deer Mountain. A gristmill was established at this site by Frederick Follmer around 1796. Ludwig Stitzel built the second gristmill location in the Allenwood area around 1820. It became known as "Gudykunst's" for Stitzel's son-in-law, an astute businessman who ran an oil mill and forge at the gristmill site just south of Allenwood (on the present Old Mill Road). The Stitzel-Gudykundst stone house still stands, but the mill, razed between 1906 and 1917, has no photographic record. (Above, Susan Snoddy; below, UCHS 2009.2.2.)

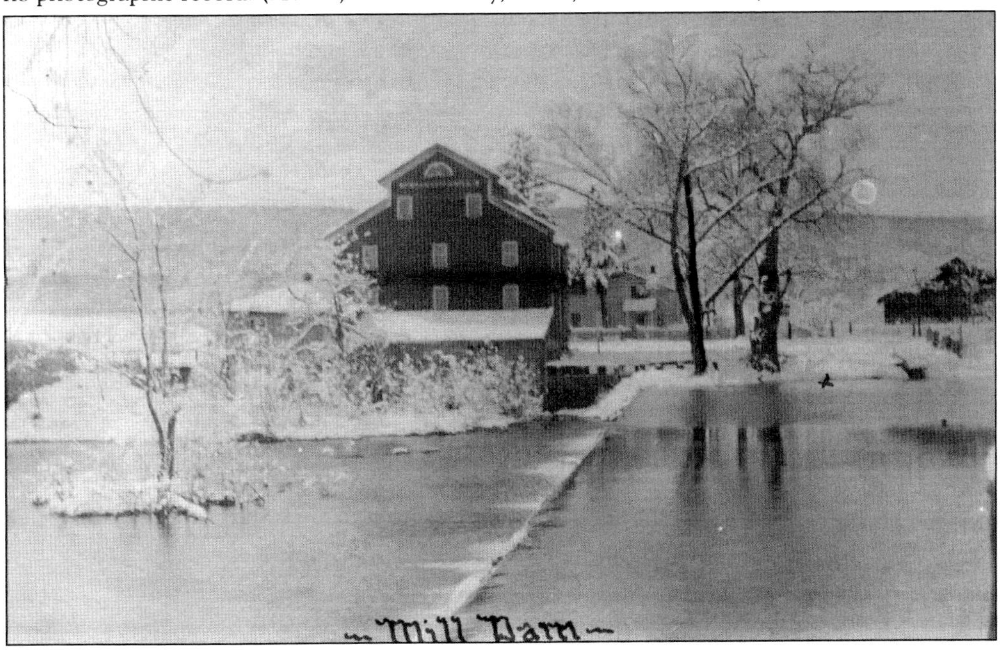

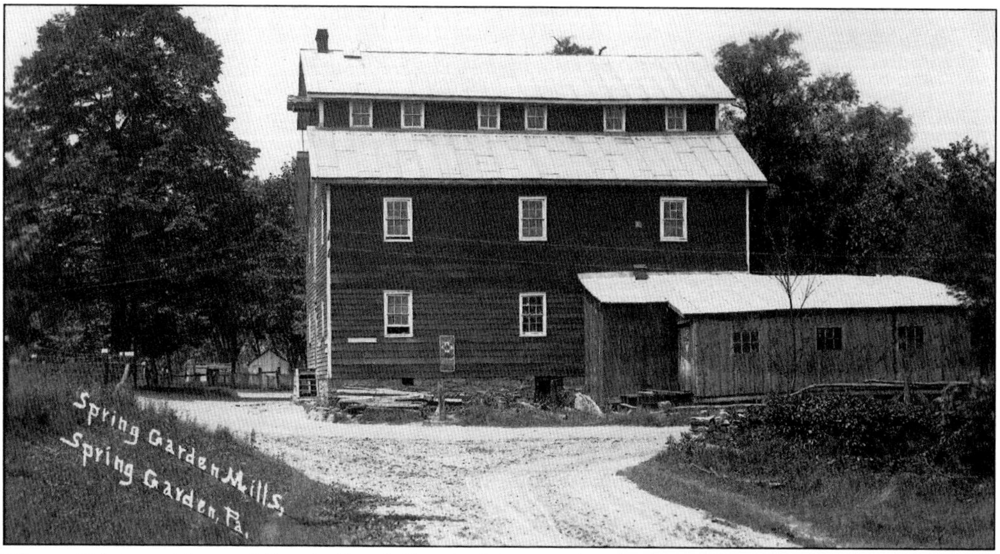

The mill (above) fronted South Creek Road while another highway going to the covered bridge on the right is barely visible. South and Spring Creeks joined just above the mill to form White Deer Hole Creek. In the postcard below are the home of Henry Jacob Sypher, who was then the current mill owner (far left), the millrace (center left), and the aging covered bridge. The postcard was sent in 1912 by Mary Sypher to her Aunt Jennie in Milton. The mill closed in the early 1930s and was razed by then-owner Calvin Webster Rider (1933–1936) after the 1936 flood destroyed it. Having been replaced by an iron bridge in 1951, the covered bridge was torn down by Bob Joe in 1956. An opaque paper mask made a distinctive, decorative frame when developing this real-photo postcard. (Both, Ronald Nornhold.)

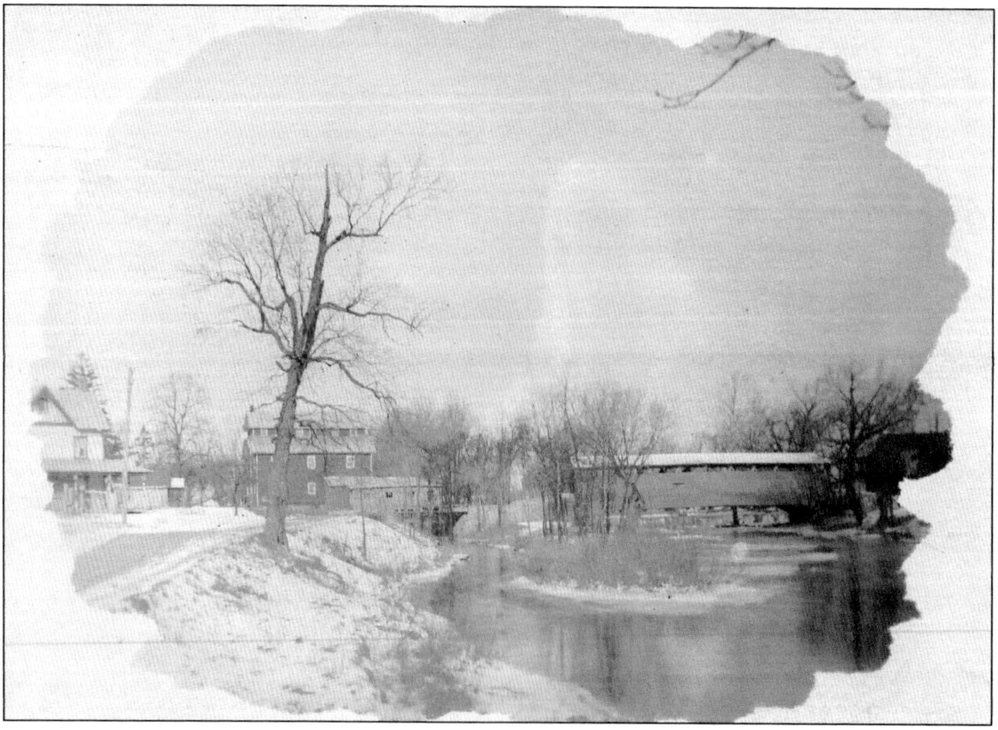

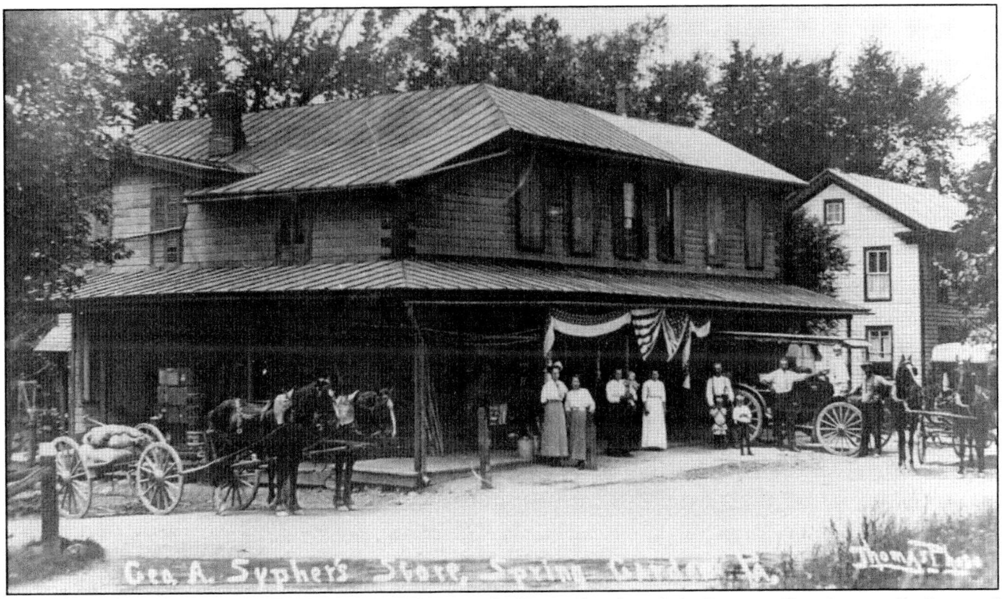

George Sypher's store, located across the creek from the family's Spring Garden mill, fronted Route 44, about 1.5 miles from Allenwood. Dr. James Headache Powder, Uneeda Biscuits, Buckles Roasted Coffees, and Breinigs' Linseed Oil Paints were sold here. The store burned around 1932. A house now occupies the site. Nearby was Quality Nursery, which was operated for 60 years, until 1987, by Ira Harvey Frontz Sr. (1908–1987). Originally located on Old Nursery Road, the business—including a log cabin—had to relocate in the 1940s to Route 44, Spring Garden, because of the federal government's Pennsylvania Ordnance Works, a facility for the manufacture of trinitrotoluene (TNT). In 1935, the Works Progress Administration had a program at the nursery. Workers included Ira Frontz (standing in left foreground), Clarence "Mac" Smith (kneeling, second from right), and Millard "Penny" Koch (kneeling, far right) of White Deer. (Above, Ronald Nornhold; below, Ardith Wilkins.)

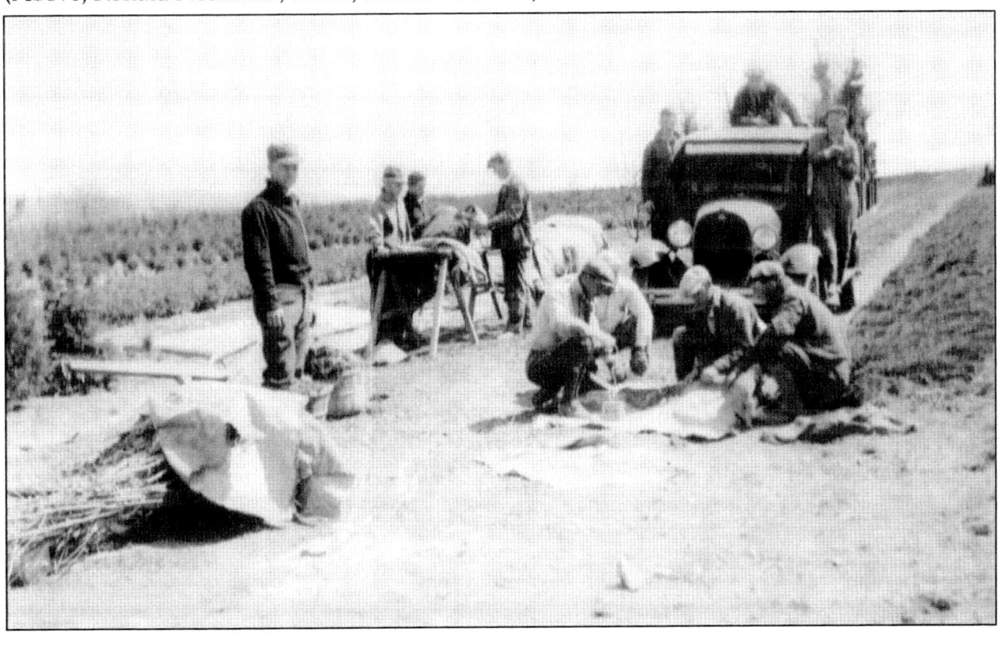

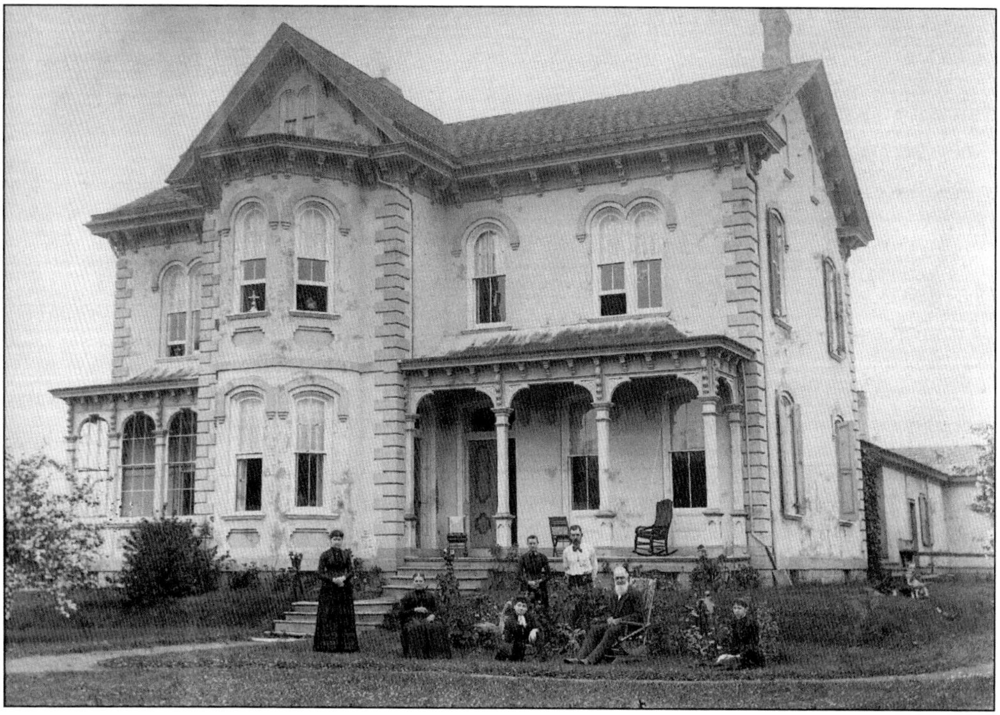

Pictured around 1910, unidentified members of the Derr family, who were tenant farmers, pose in their Sunday best for James S. Brown, a Lewisburg studio photographer. The family occupied entrepreneur Benjamin Griffey's 1880s home, near the Lycoming County line on Route 44. The house was badly damaged by fire in 1980 and has been vastly altered. It is known as the Fairchild Home, named after World War I nurse Helen Fairchild (1884–1918) who grew up there, and it is on the National Register of Historic Places. Nearby, a barn raising takes place at the Oscar McCormick farm, located close to the Baptist church. The McCormick farm was razed when the Ordnance took the property. (Above, UCHS 1984.16.2; below, Helen Frontz Myers.)

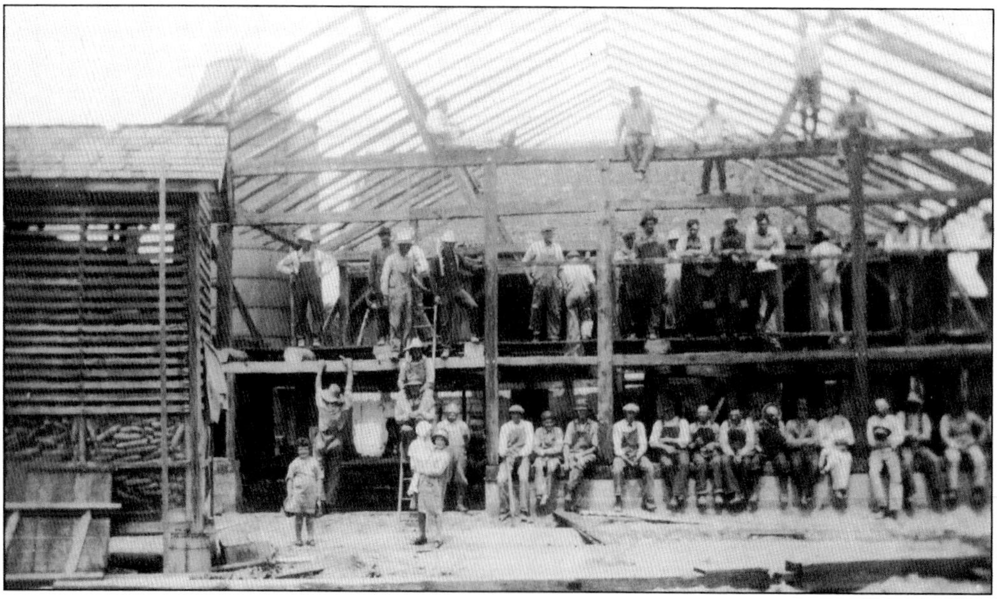

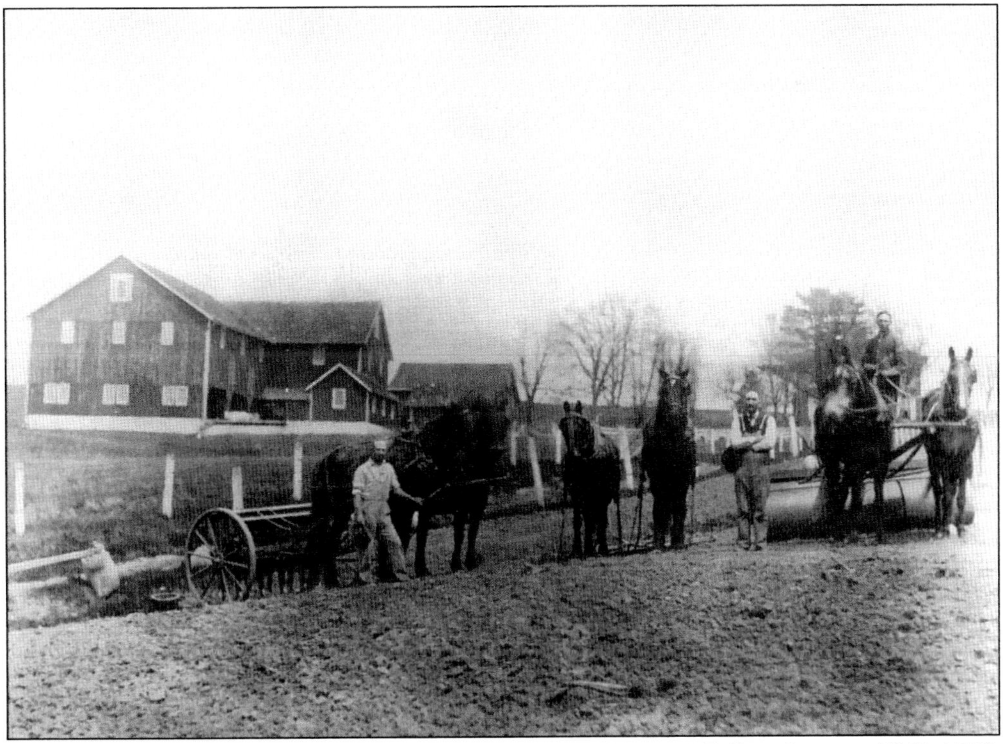

Above, Harry Jamison (1884–1962), left, his father, Brown "Brownie" Follmer Jamison (1860–1932), center, and hired hand George McCormick (1893–1980) were photographed in 1915 on the McCarty farm, located near the Washington Presbyterian Church (no longer standing), north of Alvira Road. Pictured below in 1917, Harry, left, and Brownie are shown flanking two unidentified hired hands as they work with their grain binder. (Both, Elizabeth Helsman.)

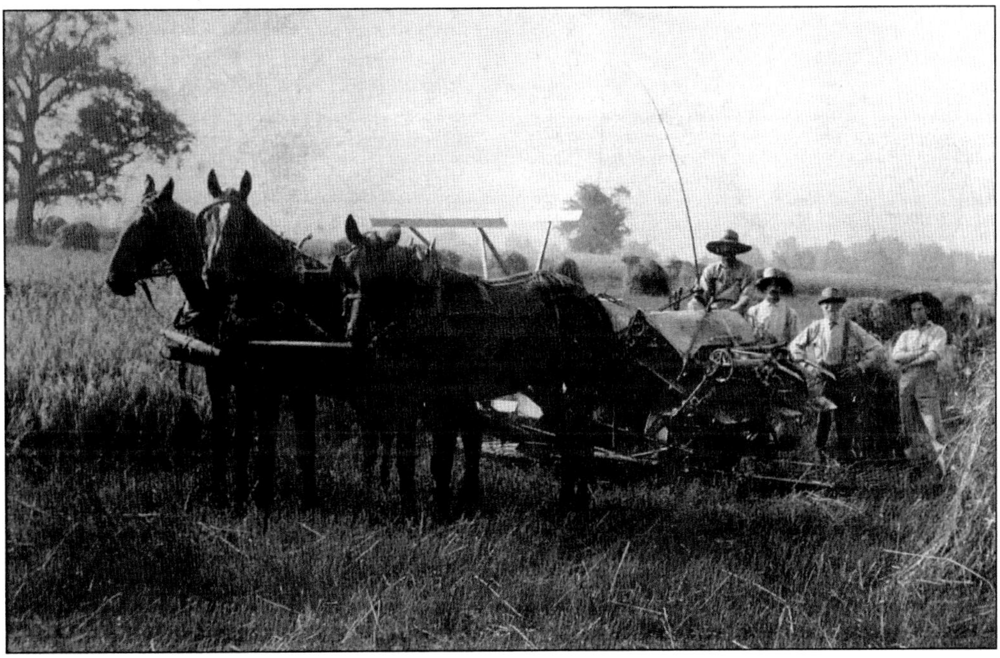

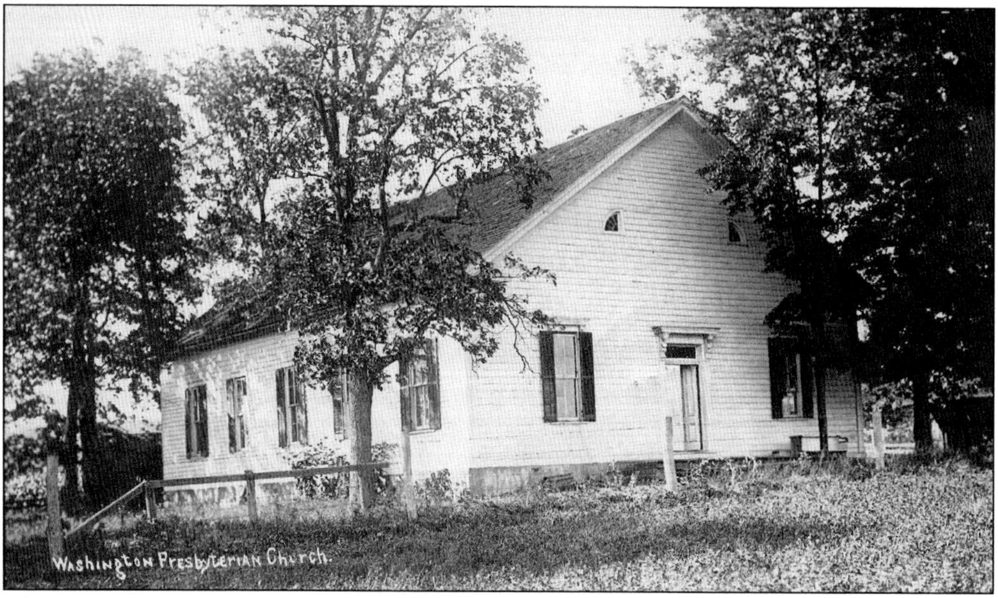

Along the Culbertson Trail Old State Route 44, now known as Alvira Road, stood four early churches with active congregations in 1940. From east to west were the 1837 White Deer Baptist Church, the 1849 "Pine Knot" Messiah Lutheran Reformed Church, the 1832 Washington Presbyterian Church, and the 1877 St. John's United Evangelical Church. The Lutheran Reformed, Presbyterian, and Evangelical churches were boarded up in the Ordnance purchase of 1942, fell into physical decline, and finally were razed in the 1960s. The Washington Presbyterian Church, seen in these c. 1907–1920 real-photo postcards, was very similar in overall appearance to the still standing and still active White Deer Baptist Church, which has a modern parsonage and a cemetery. White Deer Baptist Church stands just outside the grounds of the Federal Correctional Complex at Allenwood. (Above, UCHS 2000.10.8; below, Susan Snoddy.)

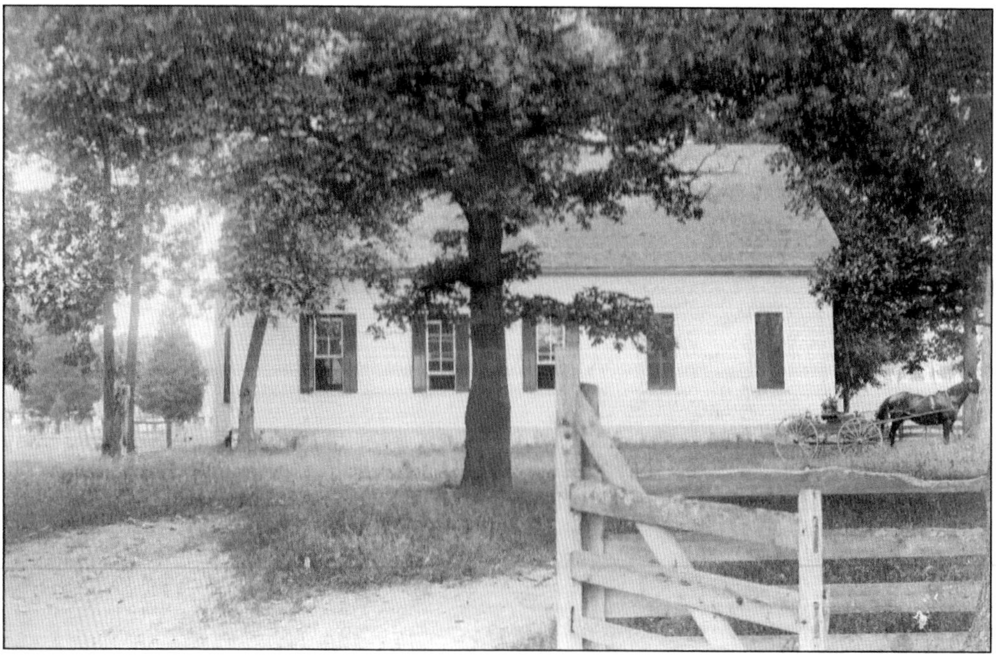

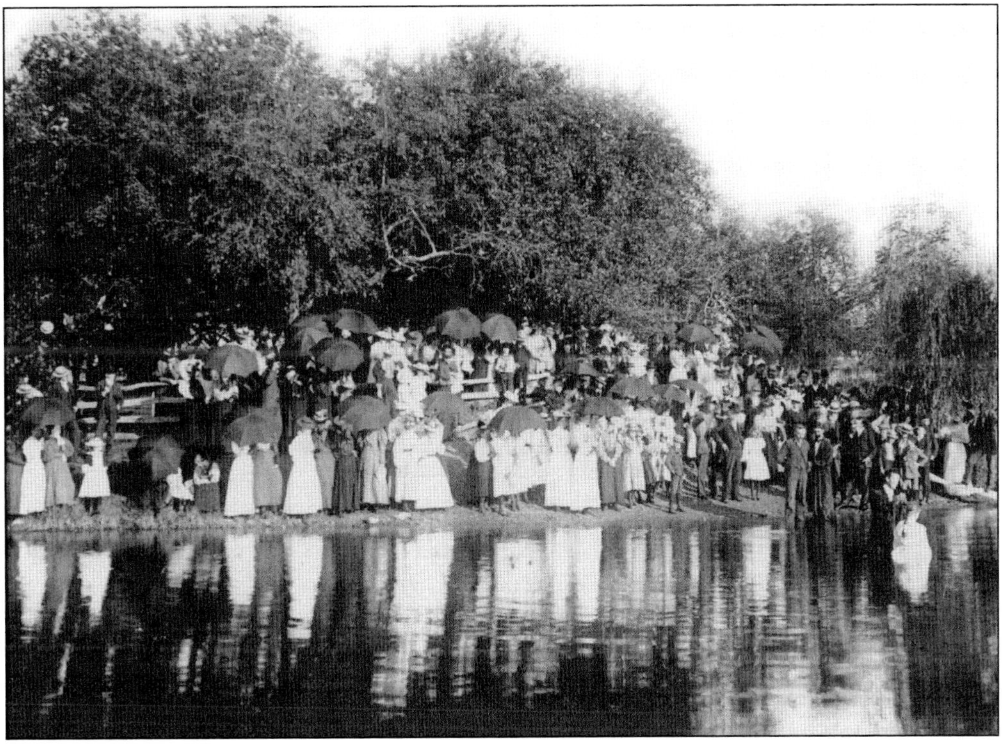

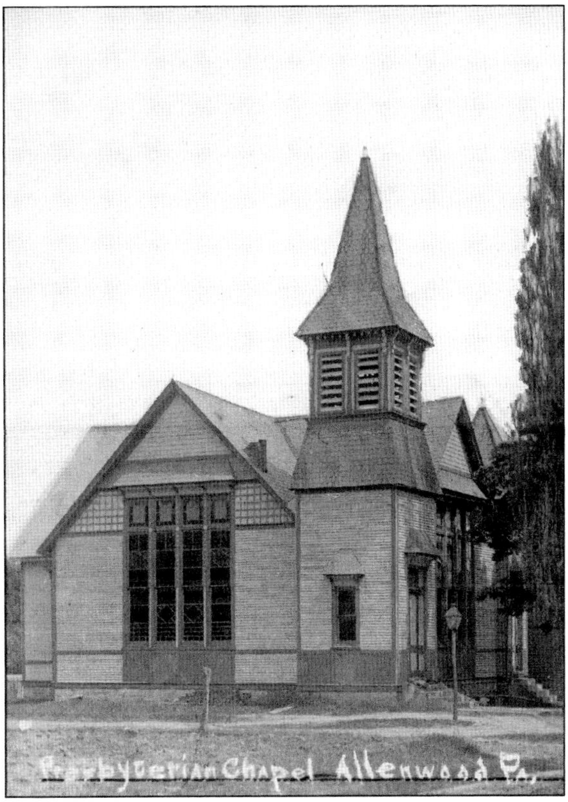

Spring Garden's millpond was the site for group baptisms, as photographed above around 1905. Local Baptists, organized by Elder Thomas Smiley, first built a log church and then a frame one in 1837. The neighboring Washington Presbyterian Church, under the leadership of Rev. Hugh Morrison of the Buffalo Cross Roads congregation, first met in a log structure around 1790 and then constructed a frame church in 1832. Around 1907, the Presbyterian chapel in neighboring Allenwood was newly built (right). At the time, two buildings were served by the same minister. Two of the six elders of Alvira's Presbyterian church also served as elders of the Allenwood chapel. When the Ordnance closed Alvira's Presbyterian church in 1942, its members then attended services at the Allenwood chapel. (Both, UCHS 89.5.2.20 and 96.1.3.)

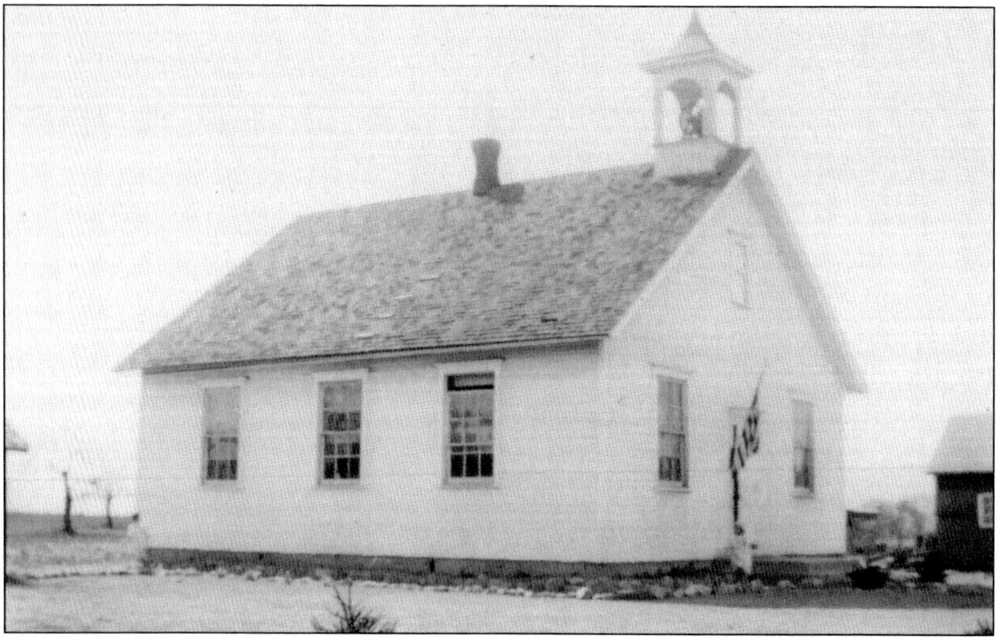

Wisetown was named after Henry Wise, a shoemaker, who settled on one of the town's original lots after 1825. Around 1864, the community became known as Alvira, and by 1900, it had 75 residents, a one-room frame school built in 1885 (above), and several churches. Below is a rare photograph of teacher W.Y. Baker inside the school. Alvira's main road was gravel. In 1932, electricity came to town—10 years before Alvira would disappear through an act of eminent domain by the federal government. Within weeks of the imposed purchases, Stone and Webster, the Ordnance's general contractor, had boarded up or razed Alvira. School was no longer held in the town after April 1942, and 150 area families were displaced. (Above, private collection; below, Lycoming County Historical Society 2006.103.)

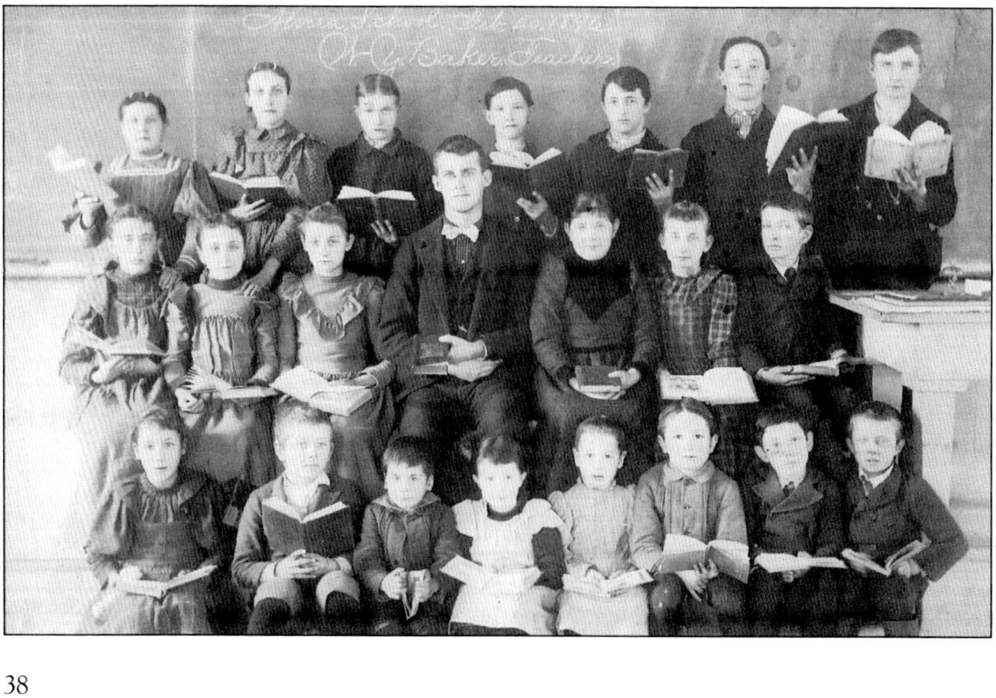

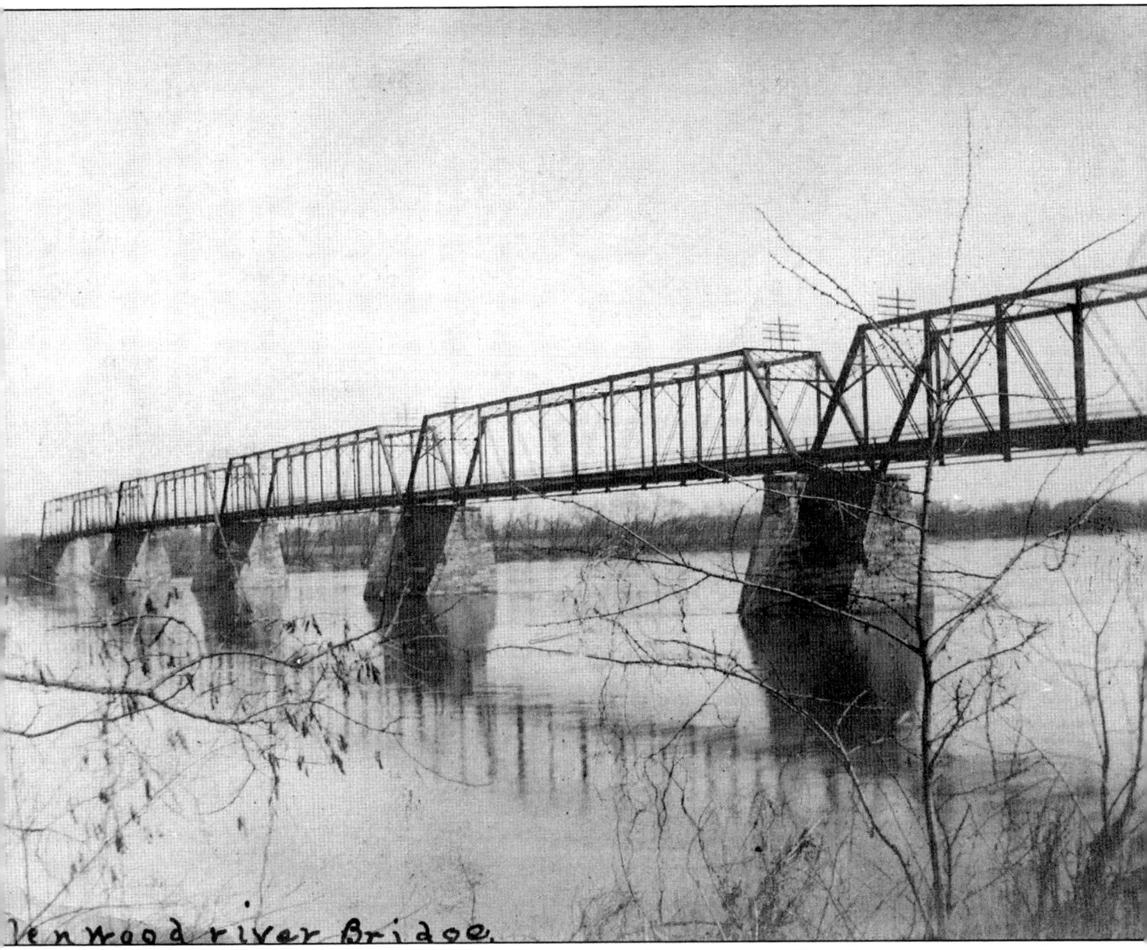

Nearly 10,000 workers were included in the demolition of Alvira, as well as the construction of the Ordnance. Many workers were housed in trailer homes at White Deer Trailer Park or the Ranck farm. Actual production of explosives involved one-third of the workers from February 1943 to April 1944. Some 150 concrete storage igloos, each 64 feet in diameter, comprised the Ordnance in Gregg and Brady Townships, along with 300 buildings, nearly 66 miles of roads, and 17 miles of rail bed. In April 1944, the Pennsylvania Ordnance Works was decommissioned for the manufacture of TNT and redesignated the Susquehanna Ordnance Depot (SOD) with the mission of storing munitions being transported from the Allies' victorious Pacific theater to the continuing European theater. The SOD used all the igloos and hundreds of additional earthen revetments to store munitions that were in transit. The railroad bridge at Allenwood, seen here in a real-photo postcard, would have been especially busy during these years. (UCHS #2003.7.9.)

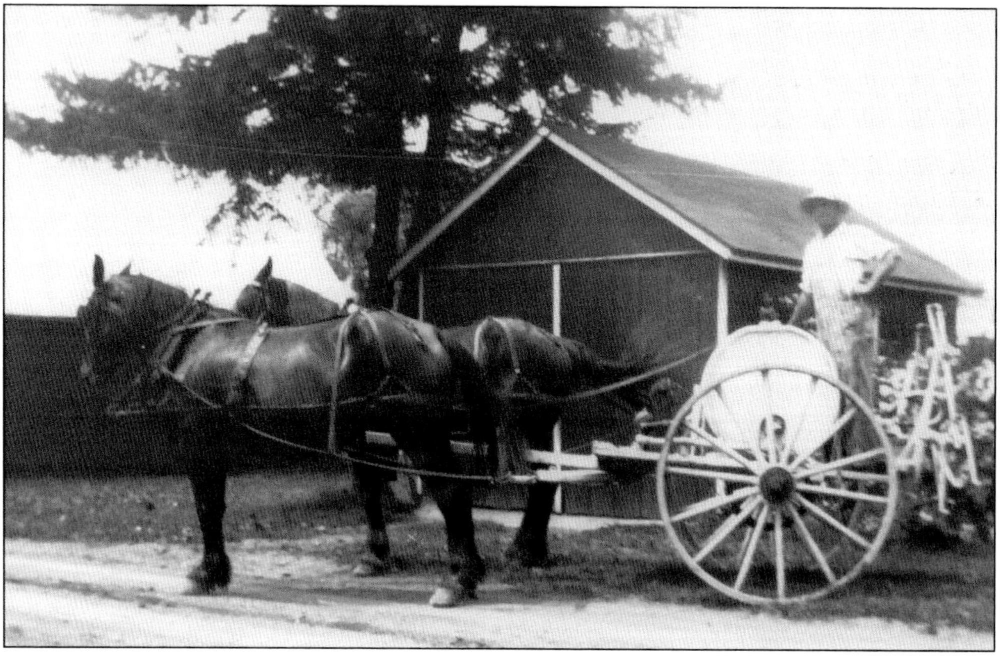

The White Deer Valley never completely returned to the rural paradise it had been before the Ordnance. This c. 1910 real-photo postcard depicts an earlier time when Harry Jamison (1884–1962) had the first potato sprayer in the White Deer Valley. Jamison raised potatoes and harvested as much as 422 bushels per acre. (Elizabeth Helsman.)

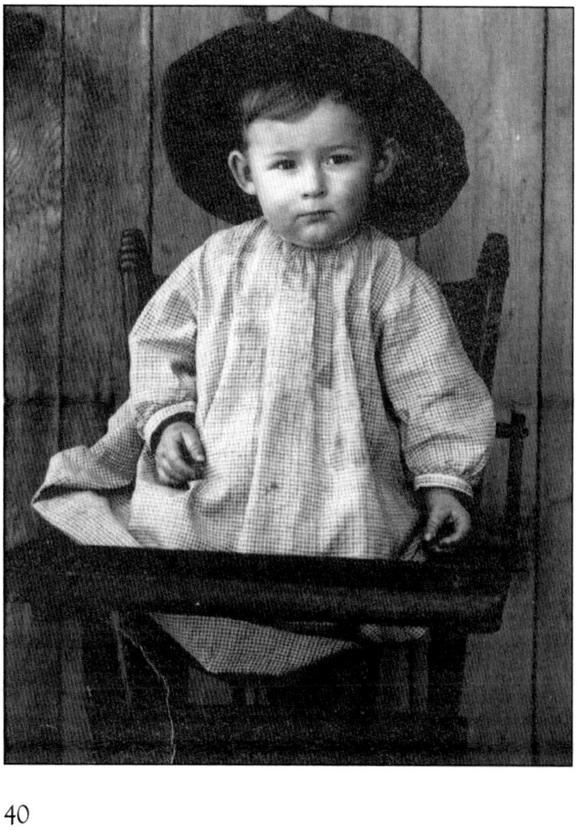

Many from the eastern end of White Deer Valley would consider Allenwood their town. In 1907, a real-photo postcard was sent as a valentine to a young Allenwood resident, Master Richard "Dick" Armstrong (1898–1942). His parents, Anthony Armstrong (1852–1924) and Kate Griffey (1860–1909), for many years owned and operated a general store in Allenwood. Dick later operated it. (UCHS 2007.23.7.)

Two

WHITE DEER

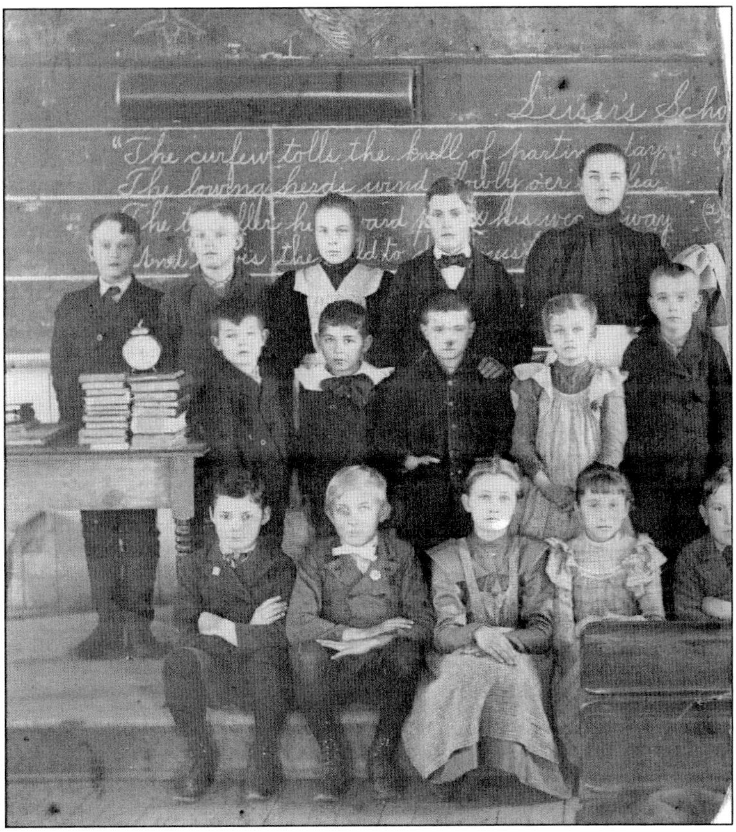

White Deer took the lead in Union County's public school education. Sullivan's School was built there in 1836. In the winter of 1852, teacher Luther Ranck reported 115 students enrolled with as many as 99 present daily. Due to crowded conditions, land was purchased for the construction of a new school, called Leiser. A rare interior photograph from the late 1880s shows the pupils and teacher at Leiser; all are unidentified. (Paul Prowant.)

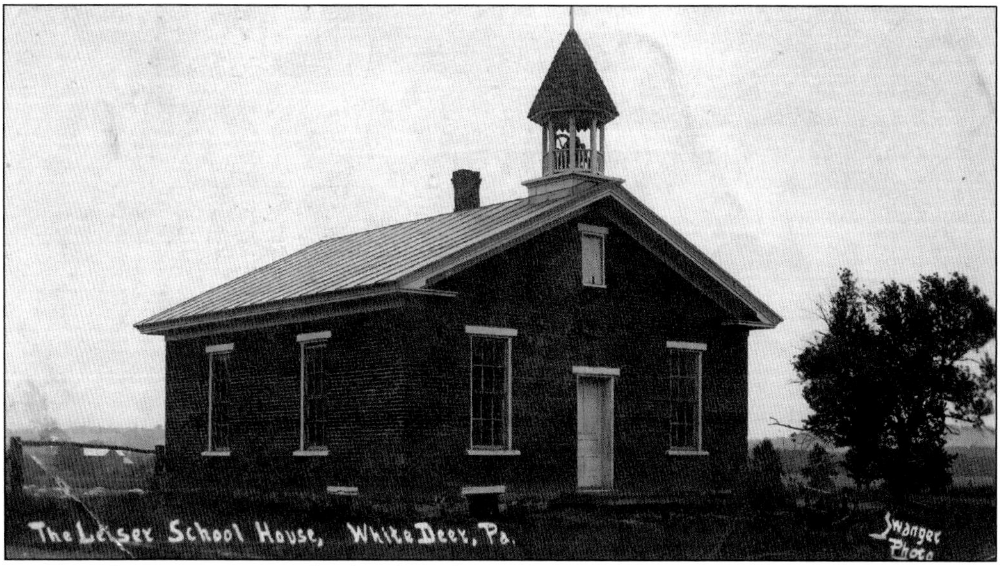

A postcard captures Leiser School's relatively small size, with two side windows rather than the customary three. The photograph below from 1929–1930 shows, from left to right, (first row) Floyd Koch, Fred Dingle, Donald Koch, Dan Walter, and Jim Fisher; (second row) Donald Brungard, Lois Strausser, Bessie Dingle, Dorothy Ketler, Ida and Jane Dingle; (third row) Frank Walter, Helen Condern, Bernie Strausser, Marie Prowant, Margaret Condern and Grace Prowant, Charles Walters, teacher Evelyn Koch, Isabel Ketler, and Erma Walters. This was one of nearly 50 one-room schools in Union County at the turn of the century. They were usually placed two miles apart so that children did not have to walk too far, and they typically had from 25 to 40 pupils in grades one through eight. A school year normally ran from September 1 to March 31. (Both, Paul Prowant.)

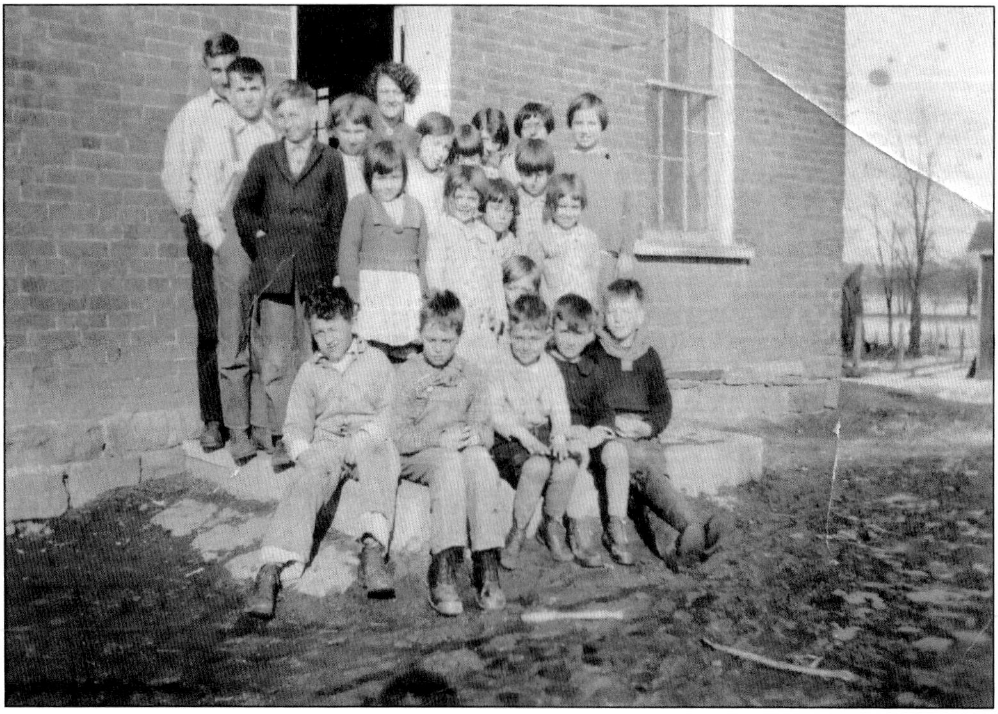

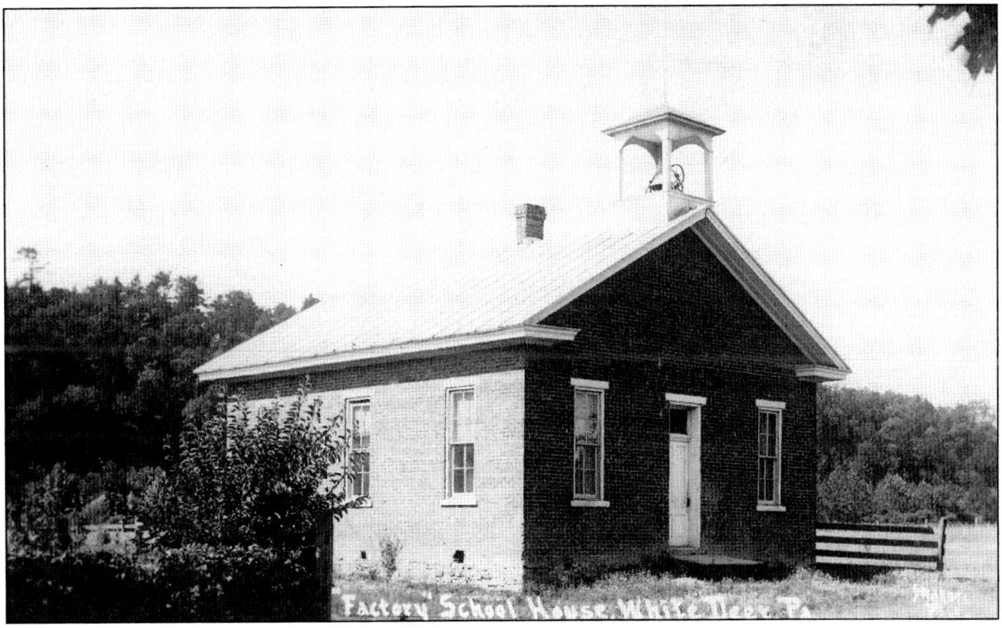

The Leiser School became so overcrowded that White Deer citizens petitioned the school board for a new school. In 1883, Factory School was constructed. Below, students in 1921–1922 were, from left to right, (first row) Woodrow Harrison, Bob Huff, Thelma Huffman, Claire Koch, Freda Bryan, Bill Huff, Hazel Fisher, Gladys Ranck, Julia Wagner, and Bill Wertz; (second row) Cyrus Wagner, Paul Brungard, Leon Huff, John Harrison, Jennie Huff, Alma Smith, Lois Koch, Martha Bryan, Helen Smith, Faye Koch, Dorothy Hagey, Alice Seaman, Violet Fisher, Willard Simpler, Fred Koch, and Alfred Smith; (third row) Paul Fisher, Mary Snyder, Harry Brungard, Esther Brungard, Gladys Huff, Ruth Snyder, Mildred Harrison, Susan Huff, George Wagner, Helen Badger, Hazel Reeser, Mary Romig, Mason Wagner, Harry Koch, Darrell Reeser, Millard Koch, Bob Smith. Teacher Lester Hartman is at the far right of the third row. (Above, UCHS 84.59.5; below, William Showers.)

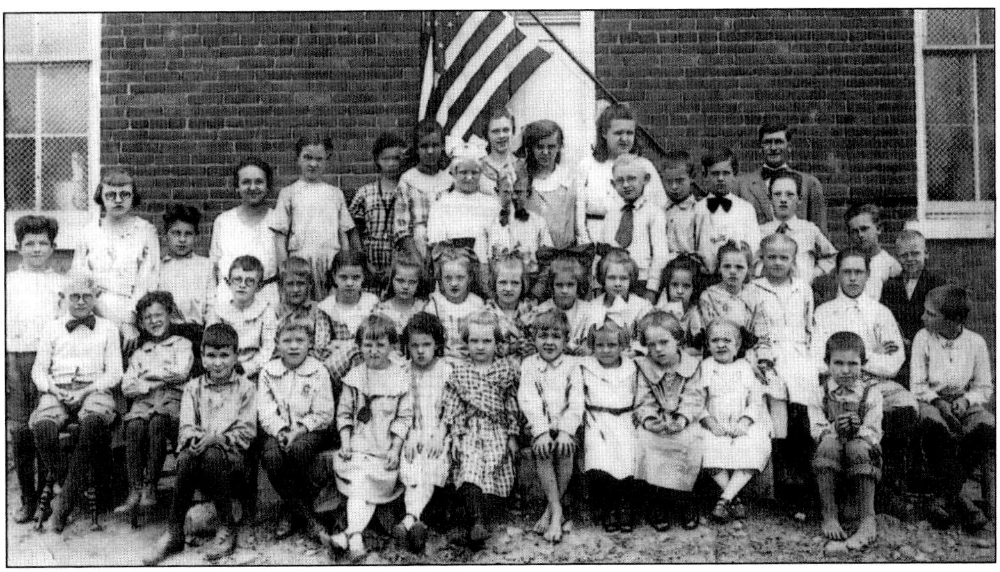

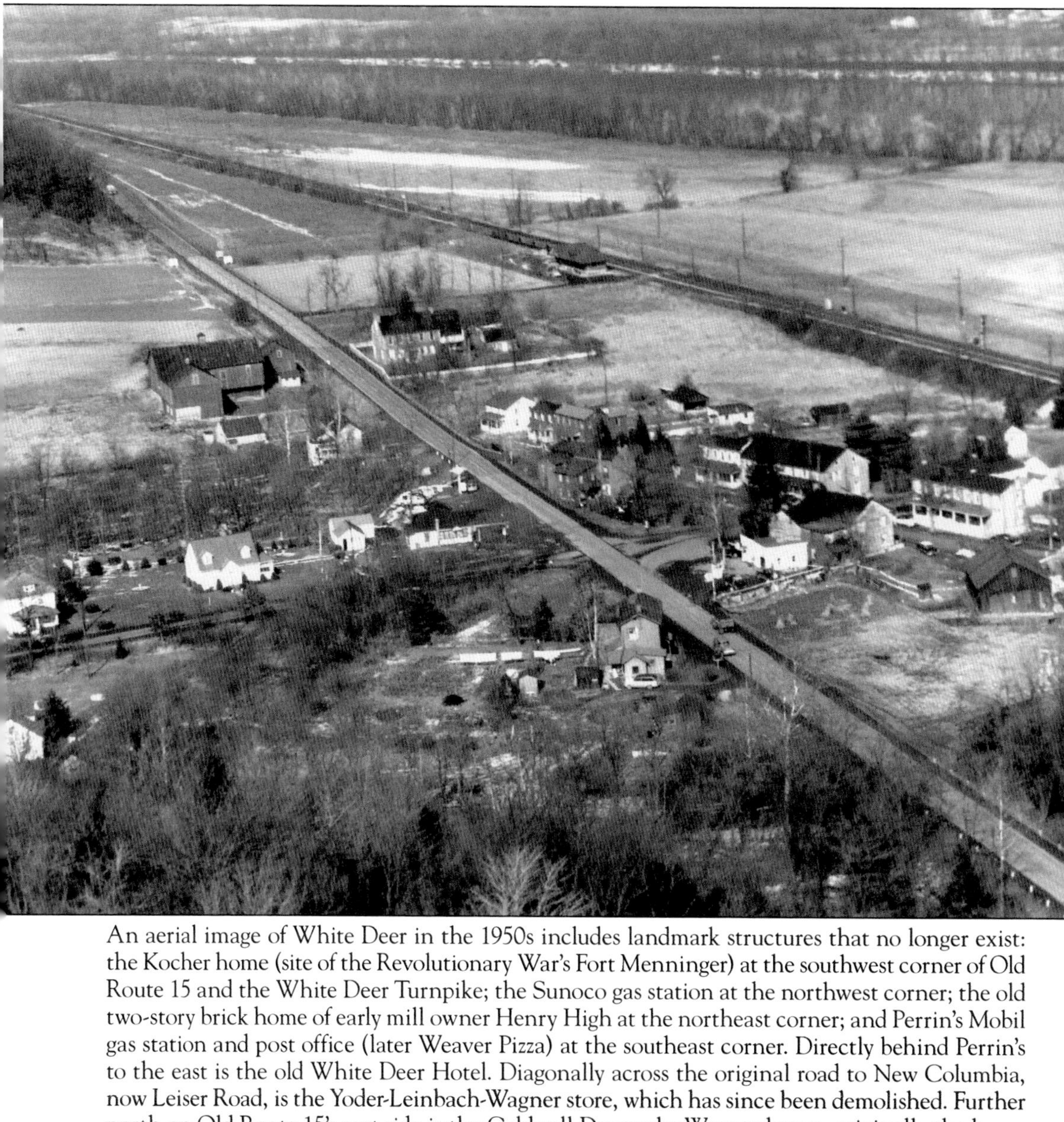

An aerial image of White Deer in the 1950s includes landmark structures that no longer exist: the Kocher home (site of the Revolutionary War's Fort Menninger) at the southwest corner of Old Route 15 and the White Deer Turnpike; the Sunoco gas station at the northwest corner; the old two-story brick home of early mill owner Henry High at the northeast corner; and Perrin's Mobil gas station and post office (later Weaver Pizza) at the southeast corner. Directly behind Perrin's to the east is the old White Deer Hotel. Diagonally across the original road to New Columbia, now Leiser Road, is the Yoder-Leinbach-Wagner store, which has since been demolished. Further north on Old Route 15's east side is the Caldwell-Danowsky-Wagner house, originally the home of Catherine Smith, who was buried across Route 15 in the old settlers' graveyard near the barn, which was razed in the construction of the new Route 15 in the mid-1960s, as were all structures on the left side of Old Route 15 in White Deer. (Jack Fisher.)

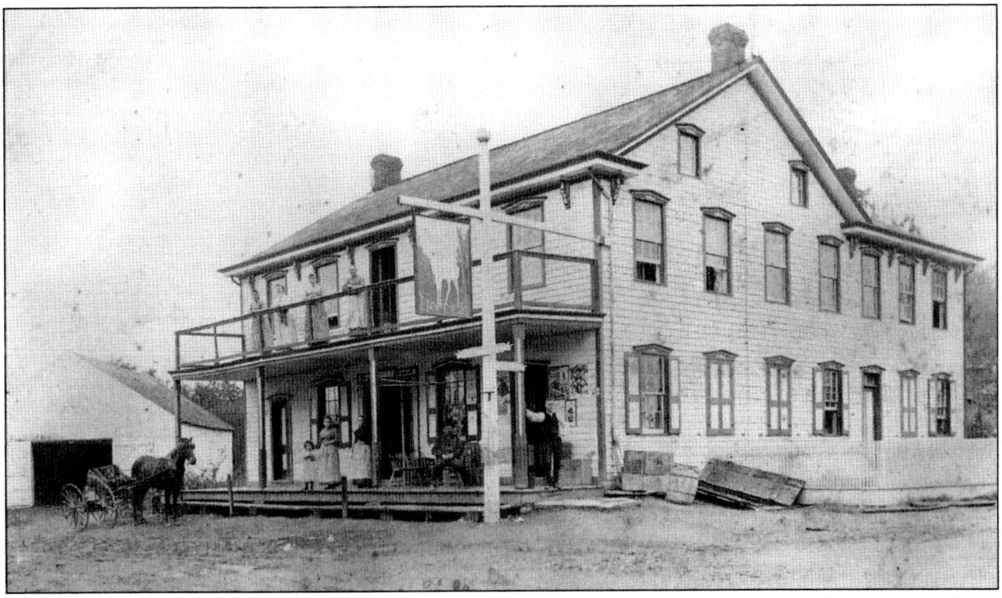

In 1889, White Deer's hotel and general store was owned by Michael Fisher of Allenwood and was operated by the Brintzenhoffs (pictured above). On the top porch, from left to right, are sisters Lil (born 1874), Stella (1873), Ellie (1862), and Lizzie (1861) Brintzenhoff. On the porch, from left to right, are Flavia (1884–1965), her mother, Katherine, and grandparents Mary and Fred. The Britzenhoff's son, Fred (born 1860), leans against the post. A postcard from 1908 (below) shows the Barbers and Hageys, the hotel proprietors from 1903 to 1939. Public accommodations were on the second floor and the family quarters and store were on the first floor. Frank Elias Barber (1872–1949) and his wife, Jane Eberhart Barber (1870–1948), stand with daughter Alice (1905–1991) at the right side of the porch. In the center, the Barbers' eldest daughter, Mary, (1891–1967) sits next to her husband, Fred Hagey (1886–1972), with his hand on his hip. (Above, Katherine Reitz; below, UCHS 2001.62.1.)

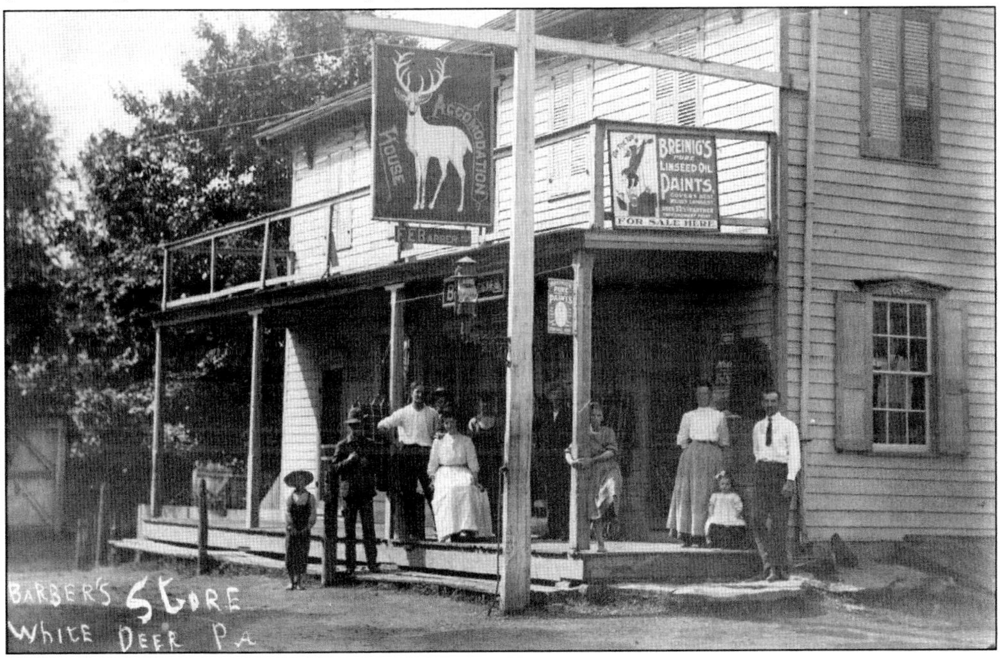

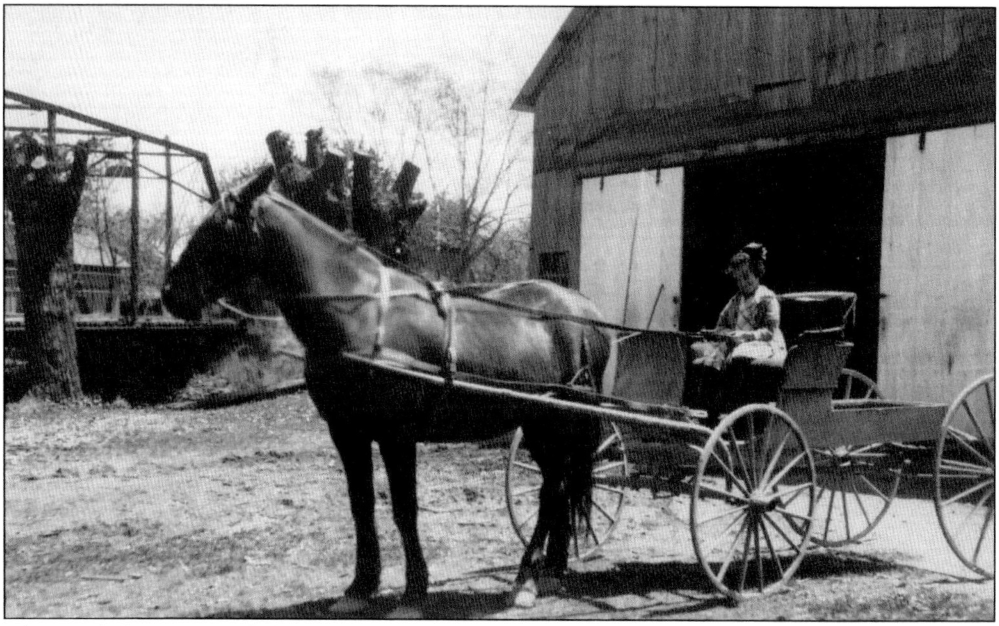

These real-photo postcards from the 1920s by Mary Barber Hagey include one of her daughter Dorothy (1914–1995) on a buckboard in front of the Hagey barn. The iron bridge over White Deer Creek is in the background along with heavily pollarded trees—a customary local practice for trimming back large trees like sycamores. The barn served as the hotel's livery. Below, Betty Jane (Hagey) Herald (1922–2008), and her mother, Mary Barber Hagey, are on the porch of their store and home around 1925. The sign above them is for Sheffer's Ice Cream from nearby Dewart, which started as a branch of the Sheffer Creamery of Muncy in 1900. In 1946, the Dewart Creamery was bought by Penn Dairies and remained in business until 1966. (Both, Sharon and Bill Herald.)

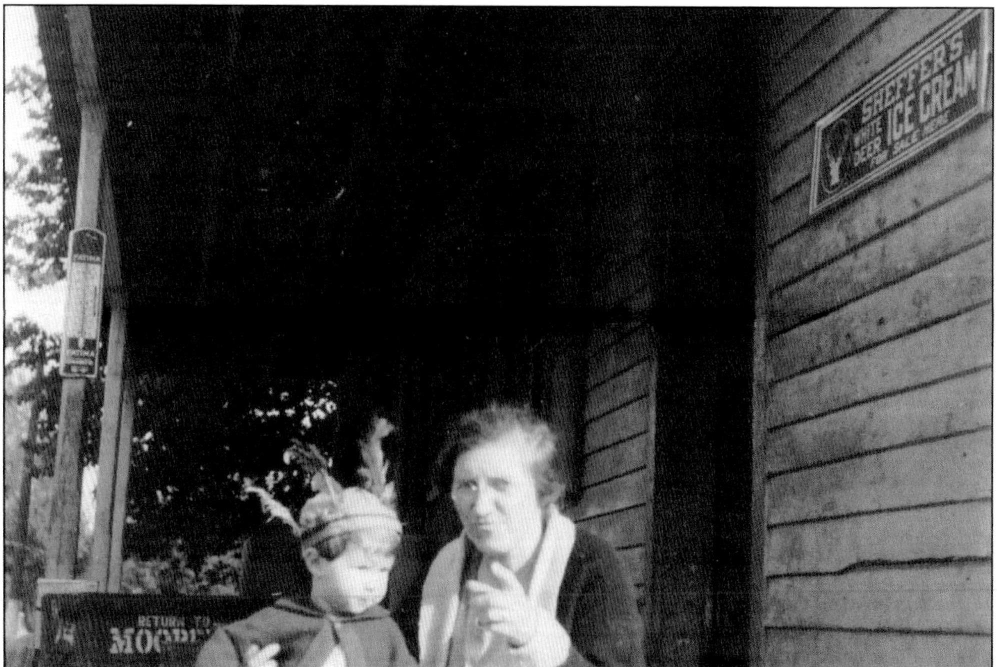

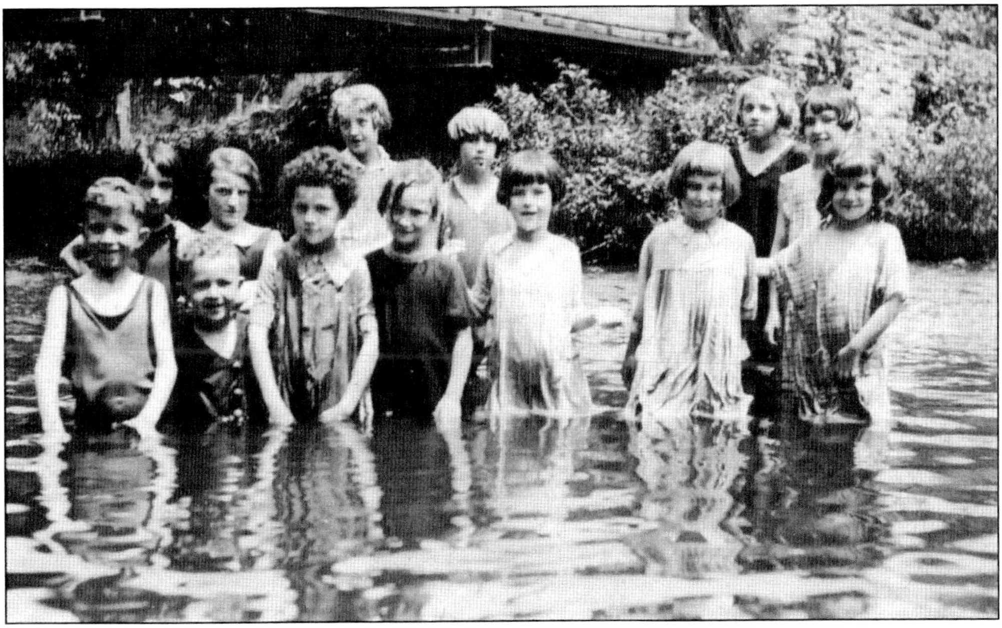

Above, Fisher, Bergenstock, Hagey, Hurst, and Koch children went swimming in White Deer Creek by the iron bridge in the 1920s, while wearing their play clothes. Pictured below around 1942, another generation has summer fun swimming near the cement bridge across Old Route 15. They are, from left to right, Donald Muffly, Richard Muffly, Linda Shaffer Snyder, and Kay Shaffer Golfieri. (Above, Sharon and Bill Herald; below, Kay Golfieri.)

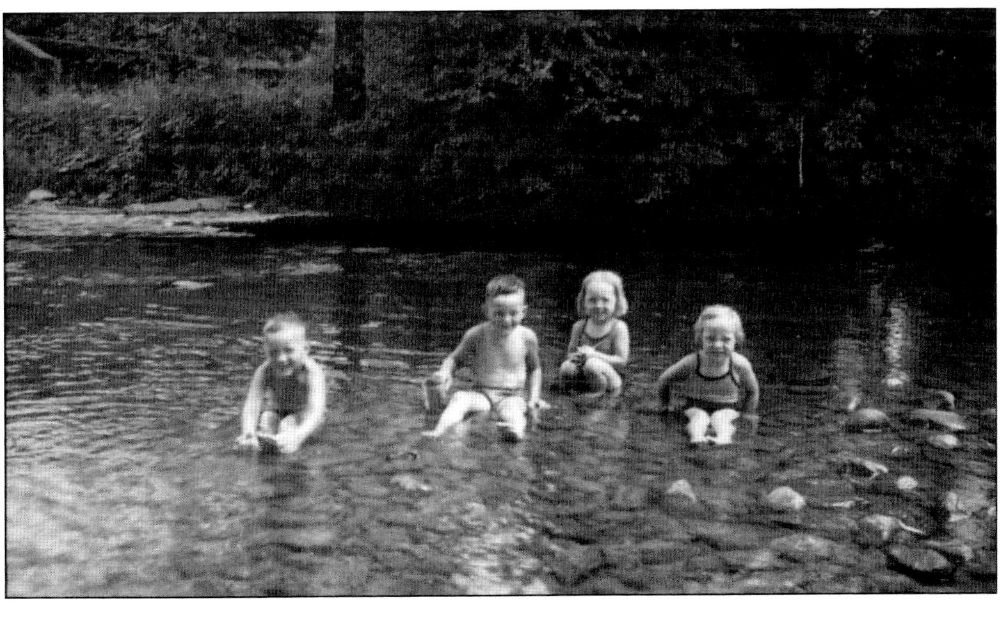

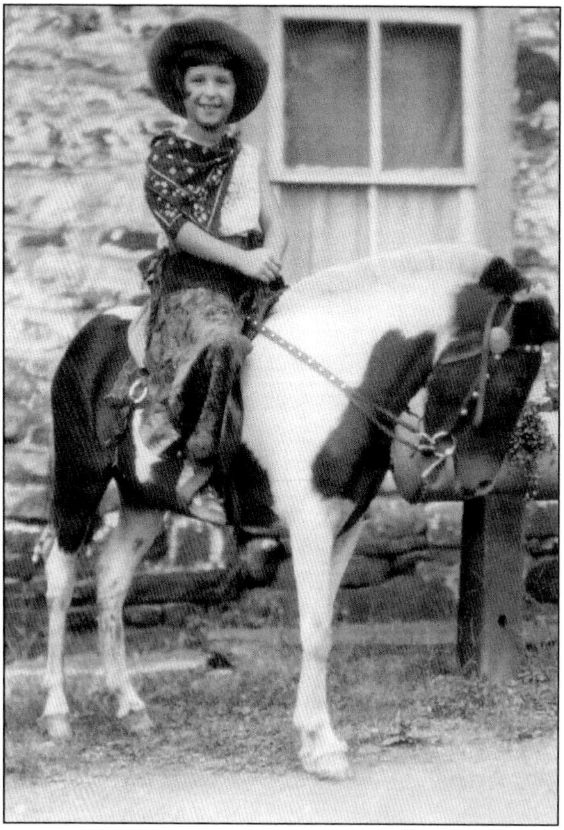

Youngsters in both the White Deer and New Columbia areas were photographed on the same pony. Here, Betty (Hagey) Herald is in front of Wagner's store in White Deer around 1929. On the back of the photograph is written, "Star on the corner/$2 Hagey." Presumably, Star is the pony and the real-photo postcard cost $2. (Sharon and Bill Herald.)

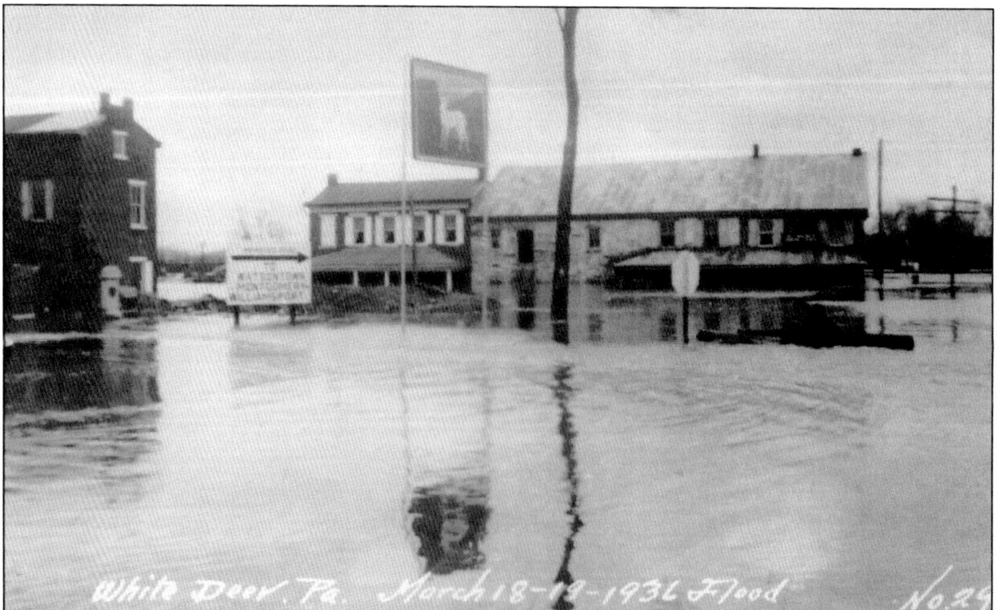

The 1936 flood in White Deer is captured in a candid photograph of White Deer's square with the Wagner store building and the iconic White Deer sign. It is not known what happened to this sign, which was still in the square in the late 1950s. (Ardith Wilkins.)

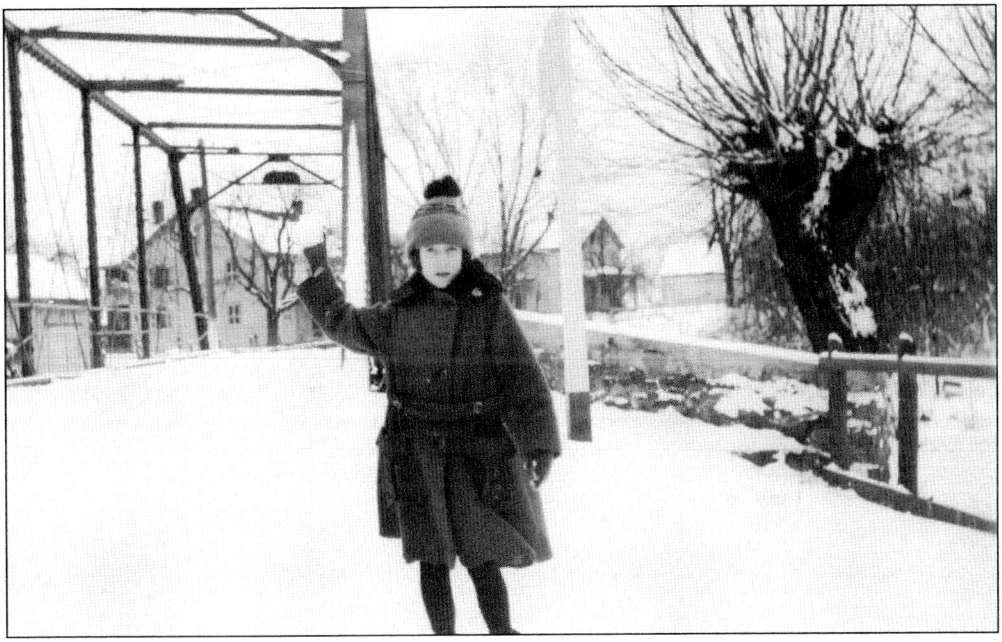

Winter meant snowballs for Dorothy Hagey Boop, who stands on the south side of the iron bridge in White Deer in her long woolen coat and leggings. The pier from the bridge was washed out by the 1972 flood, necessitating its removal. Dorothy's mother, Mary Barber Hagey (1891–1967), also took several real-photo postcard views of costumed Halloween revelers in White Deer in the 1920s. Halloween at that time was an event celebrated by roving bands of young children. (Both, Sharon and Bill Herald.)

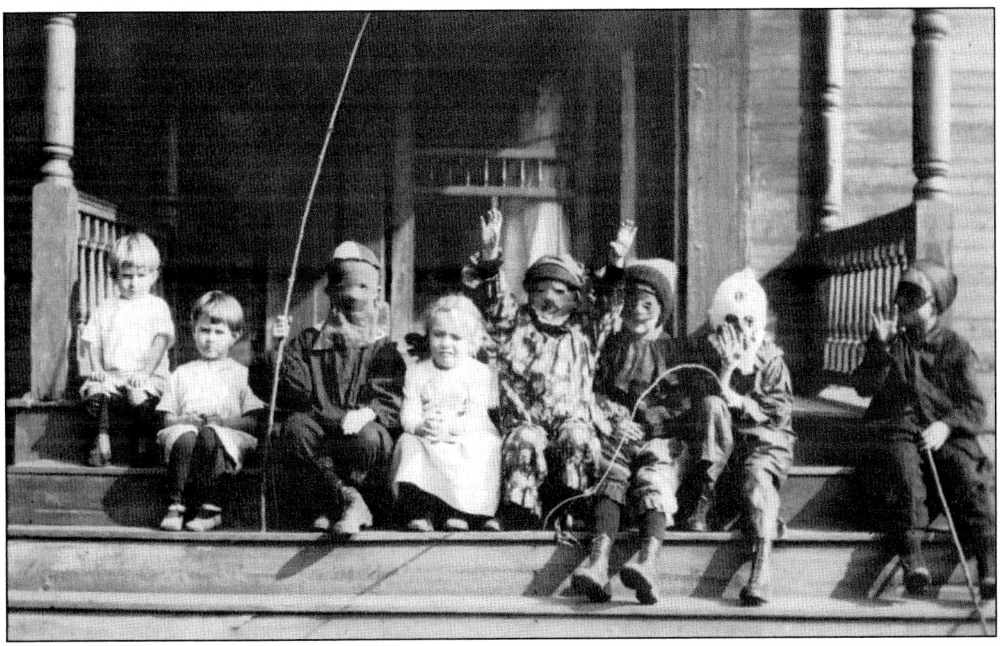

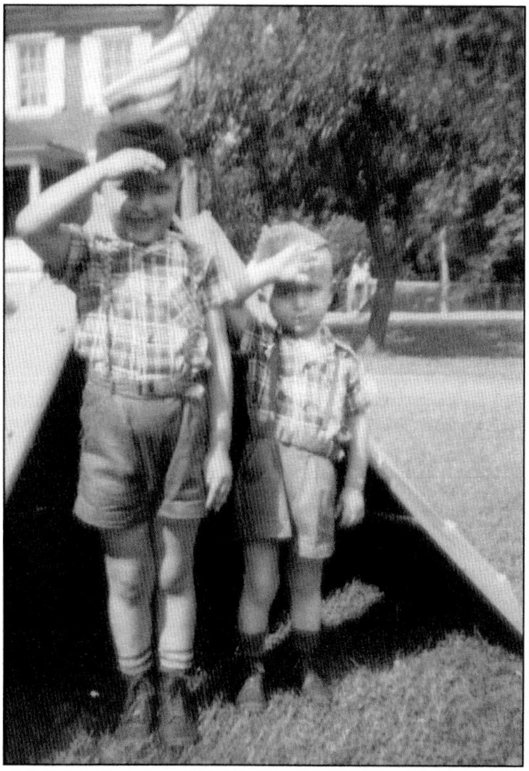

Saluting with patriotic fervor in their front yard in White Deer are William Hagey Herald (born 1940), left, and his brother Robert Archiel Herald (1943–2000). Their parents were Betty and Paul Herald. Betty's parents were Fred and Mary Barber Hagey. In 1945, the Heralds and Hageys lived on the first floor, north and south sides respectively, of the former White Deer Hotel and general merchandise store. (Sharon and Bill Herald.)

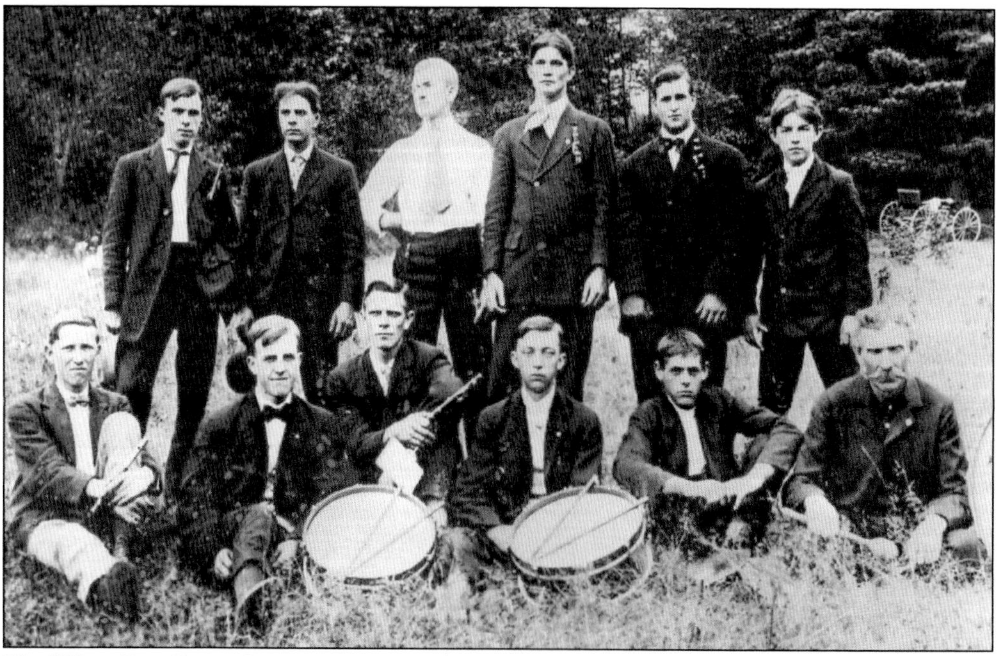

The White Deer Drum Corps was composed of percussion and woodwind players in 1906. Pictured from left to right are (seated) Joe Ranck, Bill Ranck, Floyd Huff, Ivan Bingaman, Lewis Bobb, and Oscar Huff; (standing) Adolph Ranck, Roy Rider, Joseph Ranck Sr., Clyde Harrison, Alfred Buck, and Delbert Rearick. (Donald Wilver Sr.)

Millard "Penny" Koch (1909–1984), son of Floyd and Flavia (Brintzenhoff) Koch, was first photographed in his christening dress. Pictured below many years later, Penny was photographed with his catch, a nice-looking trout, on the iron bridge over White Deer Creek. Millard was given the nickname "Pennypacker" or "Penny" by Fred Hagey, who gave colorful nicknames to many of the locals. Penny worked on the ferry, in a Civilian Conservation Corps camp, at a Works Progress Administration project in Allenwood, and in the shipyards of Philadelphia. He served with Gen. George S. Patton in World War II and retired from ACF Industries (originally the American Car and Foundry Company) in Milton. He hunted and fished all of his life, concentrating on fly-fishing in White Deer Creek after his retirement. (Both, Ardith Wilkins.)

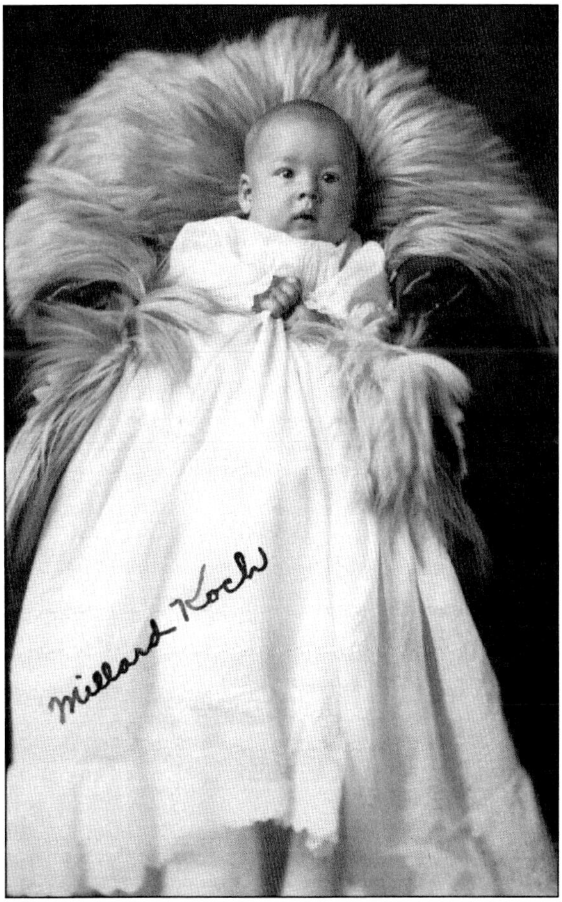

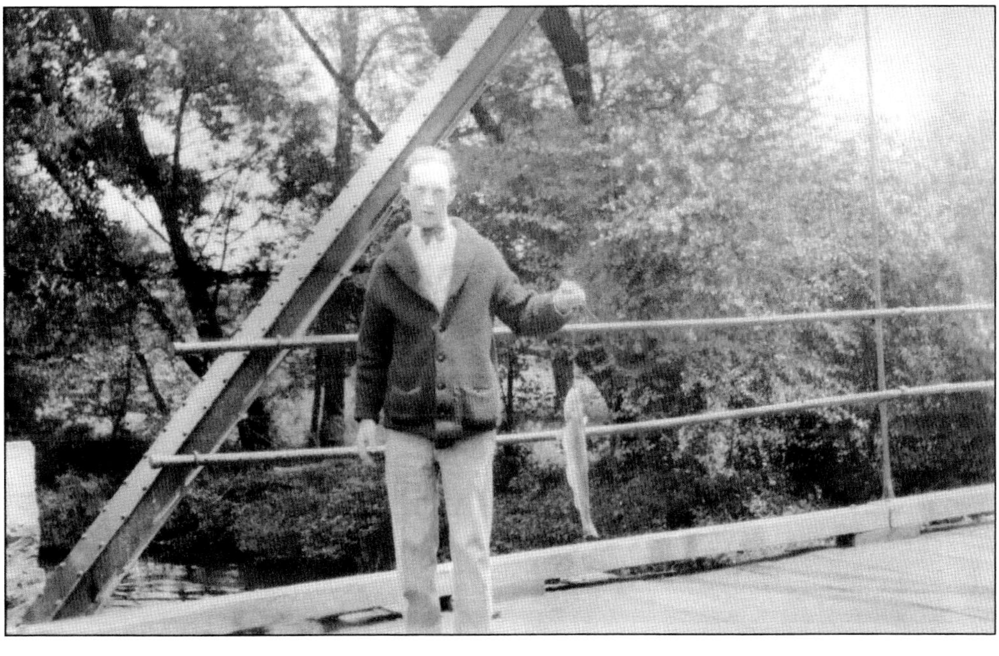

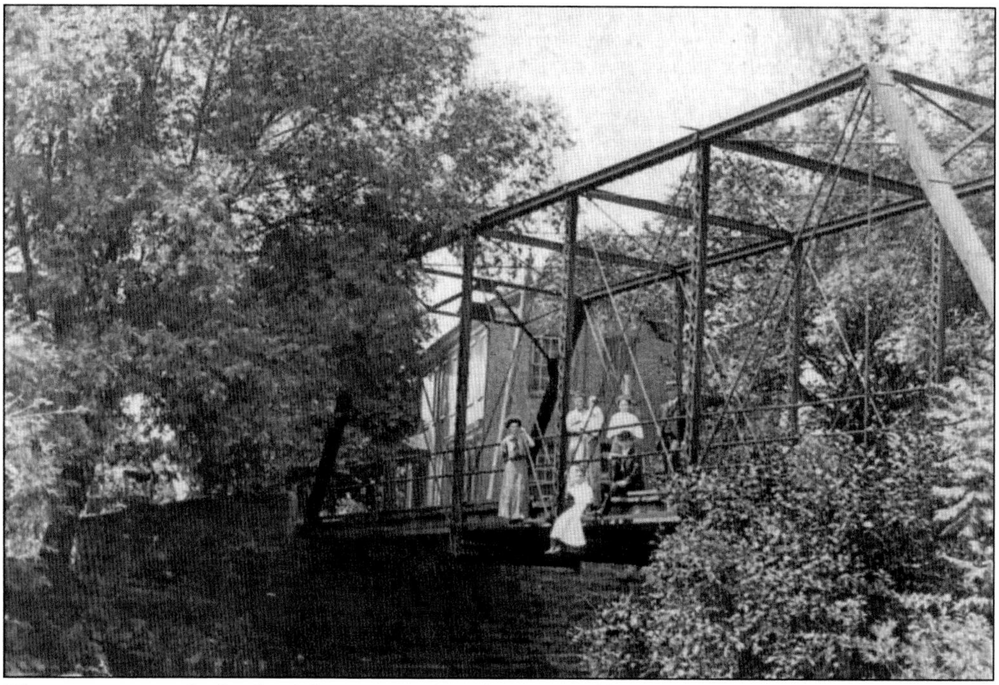

The notation on the back of this postcard reads, "View of bridge across White Deer Creek near old hotel." The bridge was on the old road to New Columbia, now named Leiser Road. Pictured are, from left to right, Flavia Brintzenhoff, Jane Barber with young Alice, Edna Kahle, Mary Barber, seated below, and Frank Barber, wearing a straw hat. The postcard was addressed to Floyd C. Koch (Flavia's future husband) but was never postmarked. (Ardith Wilkins.)

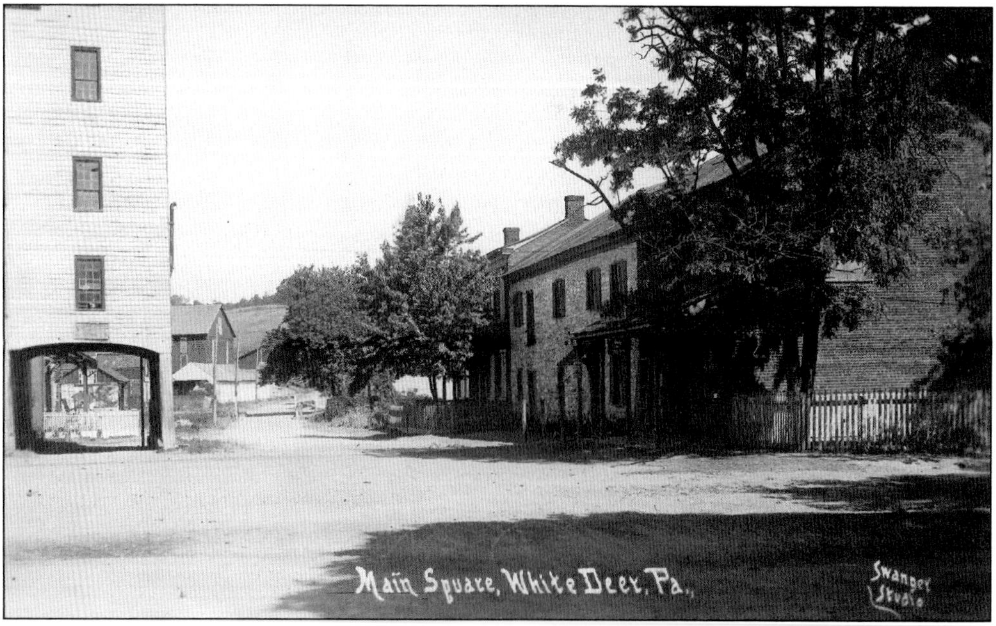

"Main Square, White Deer" shows a section of the White Deer Mill across from the masonry buildings that formed the Leinbach warehouse and store. The millrace actually ran under the stone warehouse and the square to the mill. (Ronald Nornhold.)

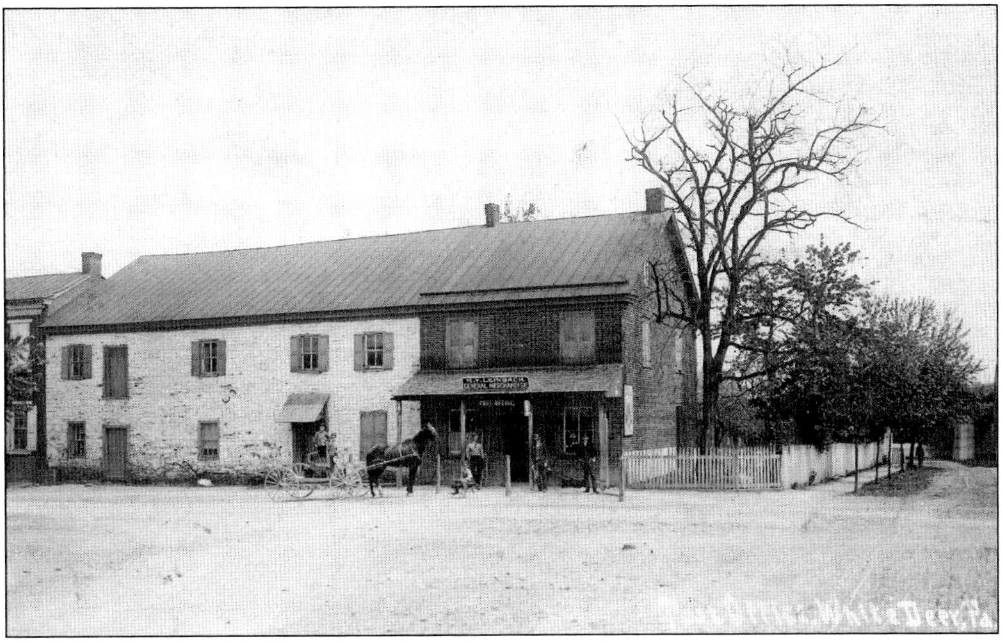

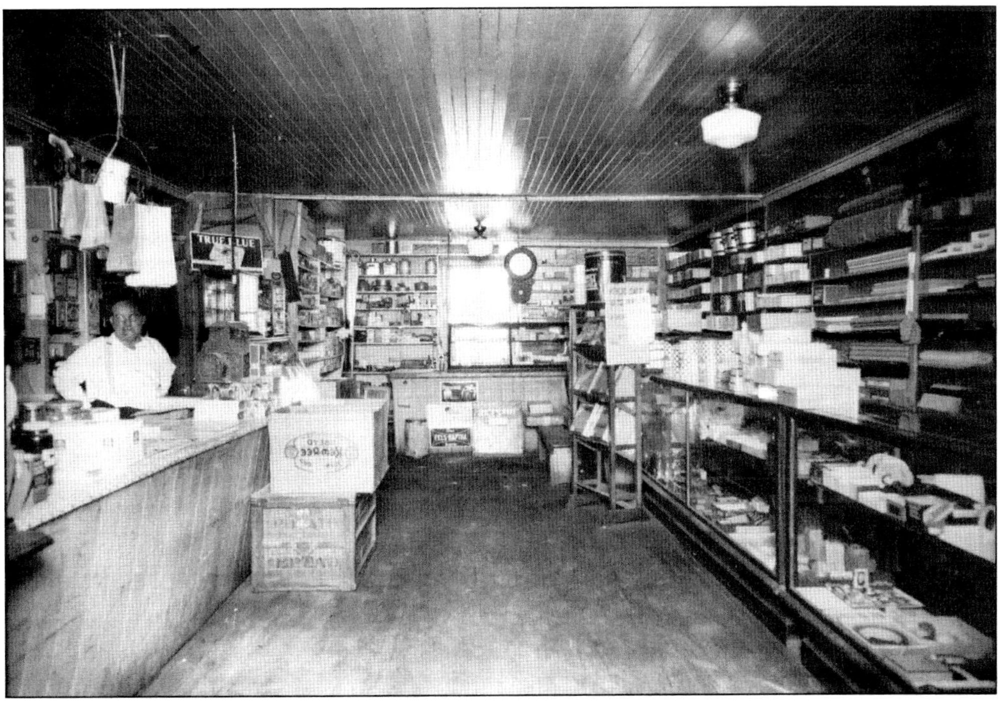

This 1908 real-photo postcard shows M.Y. Leinbach's General Merchandise Store located on the northeast corner of the square. Leinbach was a son-in-law of Moses Yoder, the original proprietor. The photograph below of the interior of the store dates from when it was later owned and operated by Frank Wagner (pictured) and his wife, Mabel, the daughter of Cyrus Leinbach. This was also the White Deer Post Office for many years. The building was purchased by George and Marie (Dutrow) Sampsell in the early 1960s and was demolished. (Above, Paul Prowant; below, Sharon and Bill Herald.)

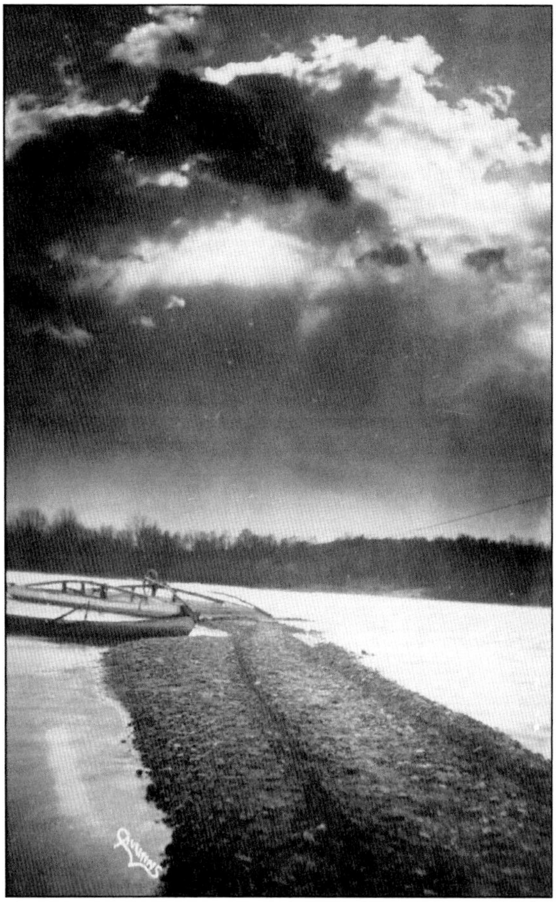

The White Deer–Watsontown ferry across the Susquehanna was first operated in 1801 by Daniel Caldwell. In 1854, it was purchased by John Bly and John L. Watson. A metal cable purchased from John A. Roebling of Trenton, New Jersey, greatly improved the efficiency of the ferry and was in use until the ferry was abandoned in 1927, when the White Deer–Watsontown Bridge was opened. The real-photo postcard below looks northeast on the old road to Williamsport, now Leiser Road, Calvin Yocum's home sits in front of Flavia Koch's house and barn. The old road to the ferry (since abandoned) ran along the south side of the Yocum home. The Yocum home is now a two-family dwelling owned by Joe Barraclough. Katherine (Koch) Reitz lives in her mother's home. (Left, UCHS 82.2.32; below, Katherine Reitz.)

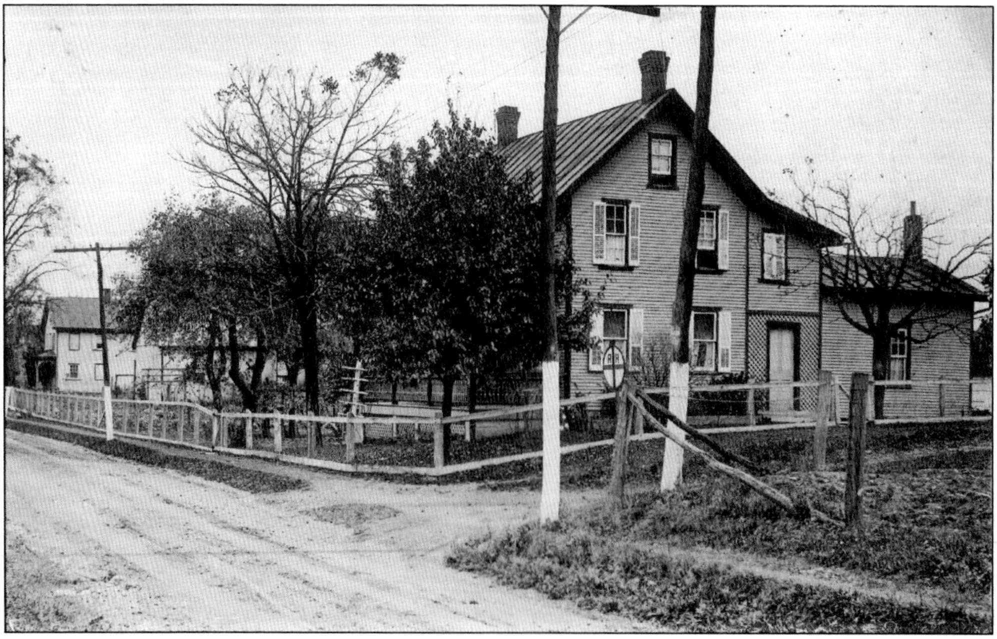

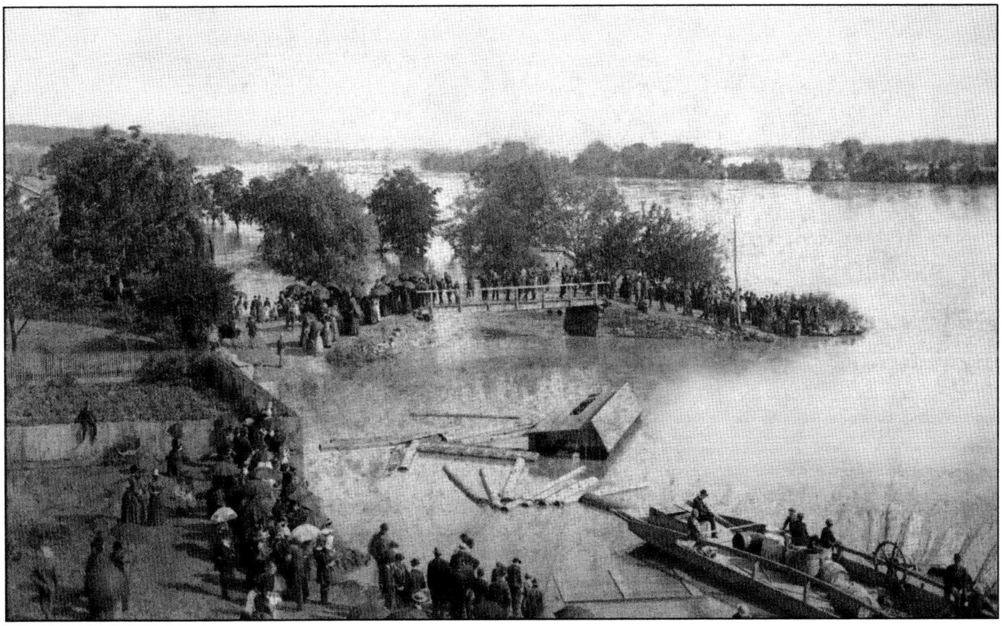

The White Deer–Watsontown Ferry (above) was photographed on June 2, 1889, on the Watsontown side of the Susquehanna after the Johnstown Flood. Pictured below around 1918 or 1920, White Deer residents at the ferry boathouse on the Watsontown side of the Susquehanna are, from left to right, (first row) Clarence Ranck, George Shutt, Yoder Leinbach, Millard Koch, Mart Bergenstock, Emmett Ranck, and Harry Richart; (second row) Pharos Ranck, Joe Walter, Aaron Plummer, Simon Kuhns, Oscar Huff, Adolph Ranck, and John O. Smith; (third row) unidentified, Owen Bergenstock, Clyde Harrison, Joe Negley, Sam High, two unidentified, Frank Wagner, Tom Koch, and Reid Kling Sr.; (fourth row) Floyd Koch Sr., Jim Koch, Floyd Huff, unidentified, Dick Huff, Will Plummer, Sam Koch, Dave Bly, and unidentified. (Above, Sharon and Bill Herald; below, Minnie Troxel Koch.)

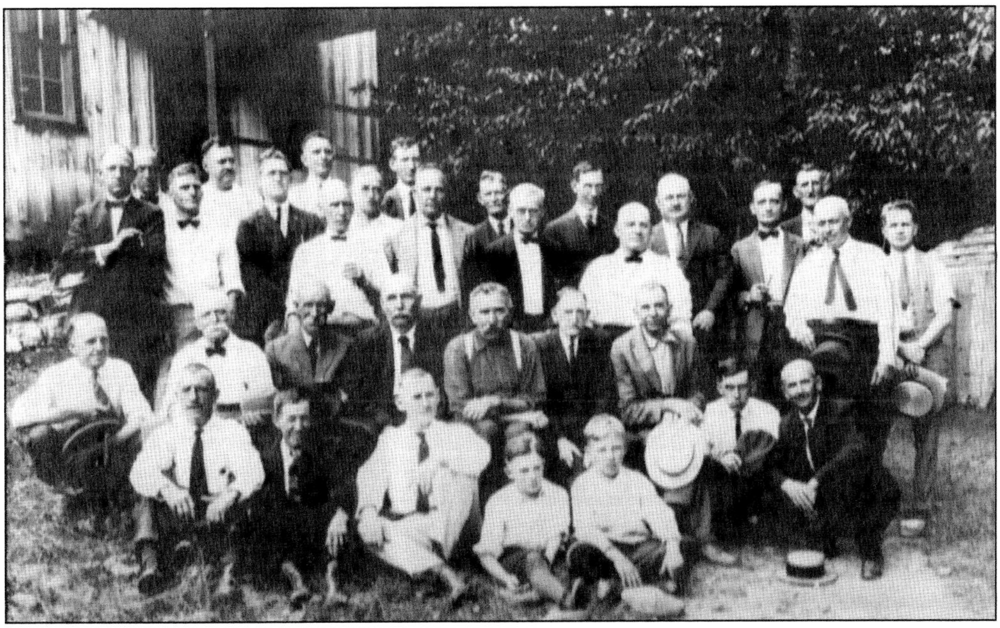

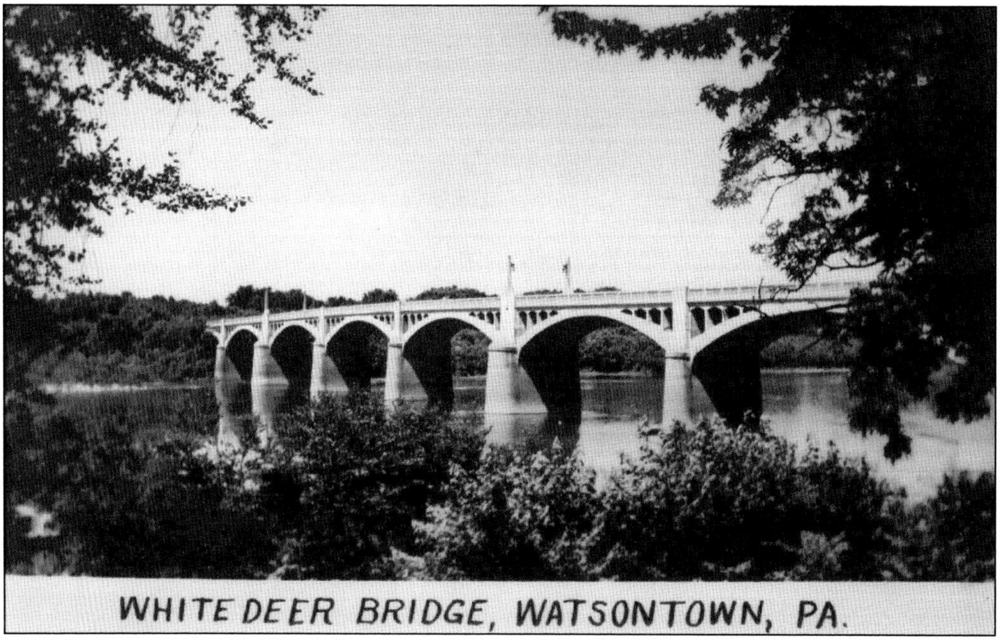

A real-photo postcard of the new Watsontown–White Deer Bridge was issued when the span officially opened on July 4, 1928. The first concrete was poured nearly a year earlier on July 12, 1927. The new bridge meant the demise of the ferry between White Deer and Watsontown. The Millersburg to Liverpool Ferry then became the last one operating above Harrisburg on the Susquehanna River. (Sharon and Bill Herald.)

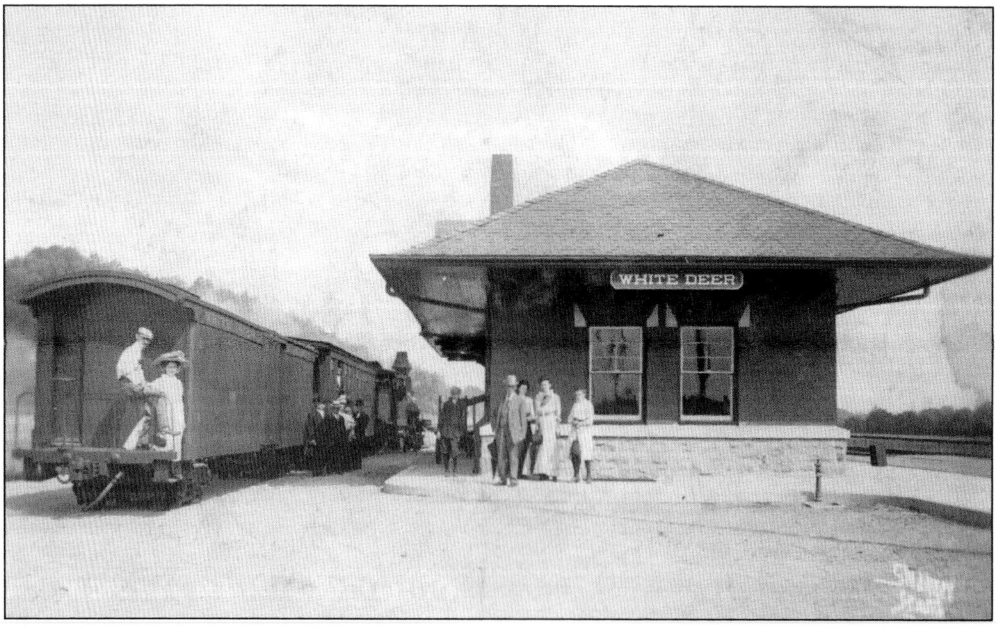

The White Deer passenger and freight station is pictured around 1910. Since the 1980s, the station has been home to the Central Pennsylvania Chapter of the National Railway Historical Society. It is open to the public in the summer months. (Sharon and Bill Herald.)

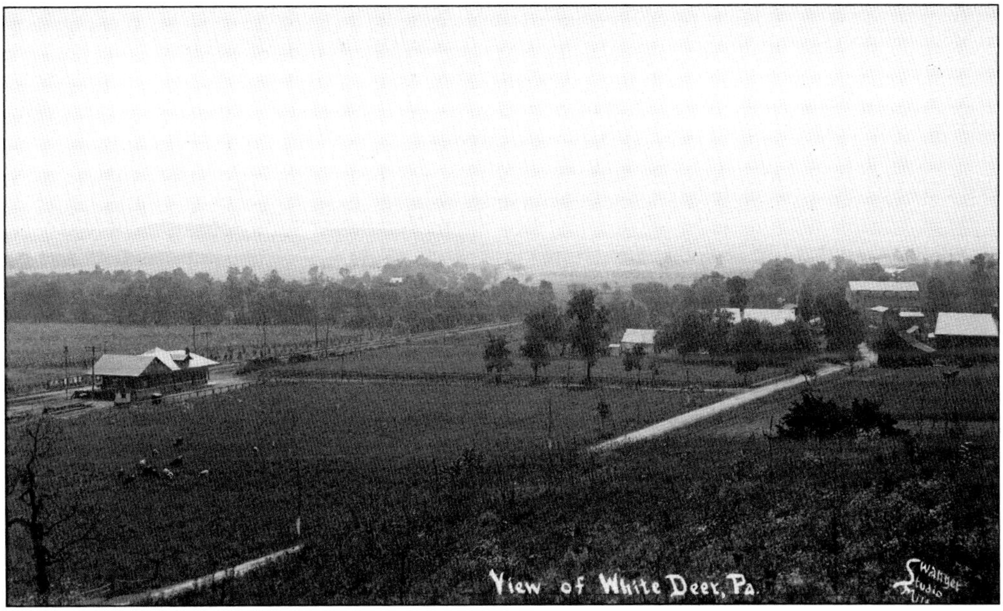

The real-photo postcard above from 1920 reveals the distance between White Deer and its train station. Before it burned in 1928, the White Deer Flouring Mill, operated by Jerome Hornberger, was the highest building and dominated the town. The mill was built on the location of the widow Catherine Smith's 1775 gristmill and sawmill. She was noted for rifle-boring mills and hemp mills that served the Colonials during the Revolutionary War. This area was abandoned during the Great Runaway of 1779, when Indians burned the mills. The gristmill was rebuilt in 1783 after "Widow Smith" returned from Lancaster. That mill burned in 1850. It was then reconstructed again. A historical marker, located in a park off Old Route 15 in White Deer, commemorates Smith. (Above, Ronald Nornhold; below, Paul Prowant.)

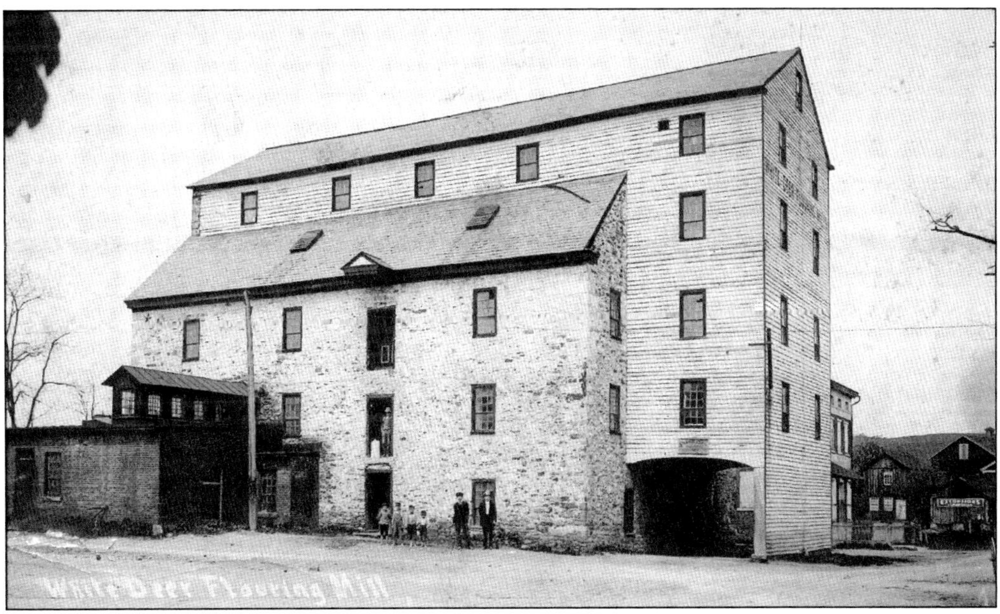

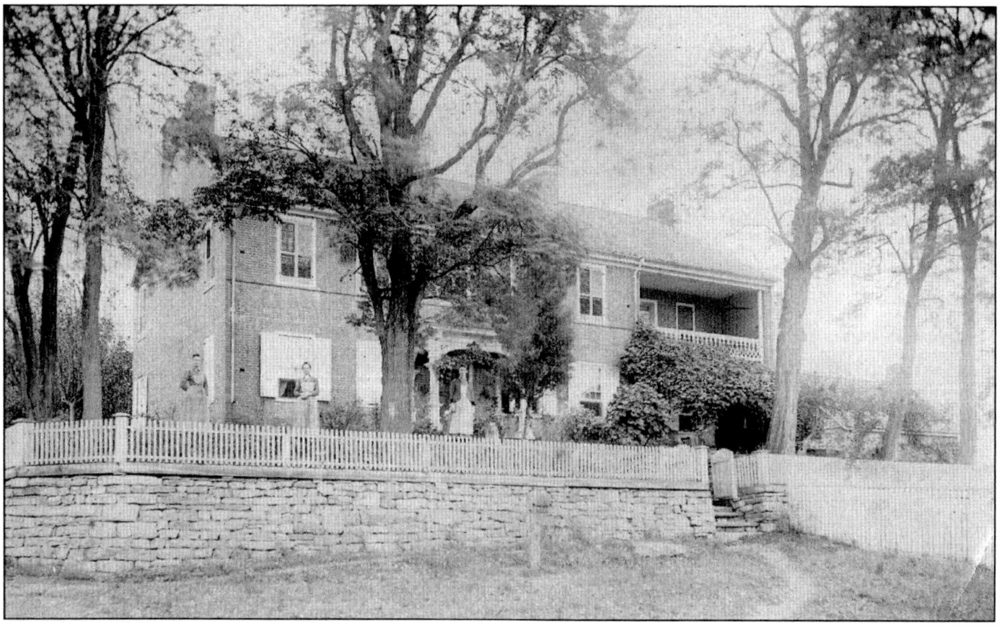

The northbound lanes of the new Route 15 ran beside the west facade of the Caldwell-Danowsky-Wagner house (above). Its stone summer kitchen may have been part of the home built by Catherine Smith and her husband when they relocated to White Deer from Lancaster in the 1770s. She lost possession of the home and other buildings in the early 1800s due to the lack of a clear title. The photograph below from 1959 is the White Deer Dairy Shop. Proprietors William and Lois Kocher lived next door at the site of Fort Menninger, which was built for defense during the American Revolution and was burned by Native Americans during the Great Runaway of 1779. The Kochs' home and shop were demolished in the mid-1960s for the construction of the new Route 15. (Above, UCHS 2002.14.16; below, Susan Snoddy.)

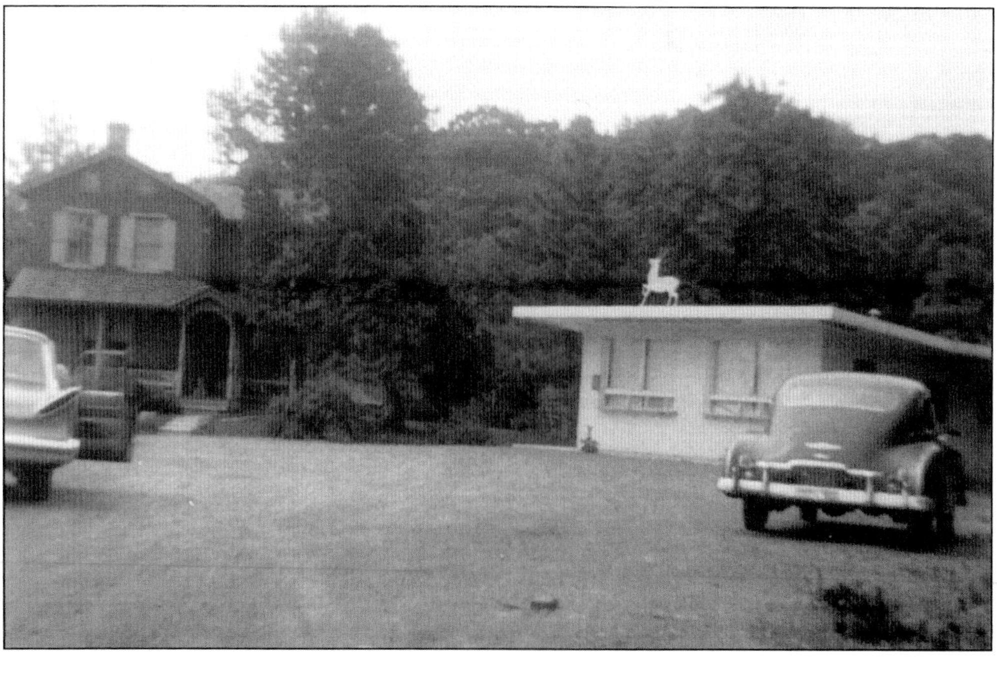

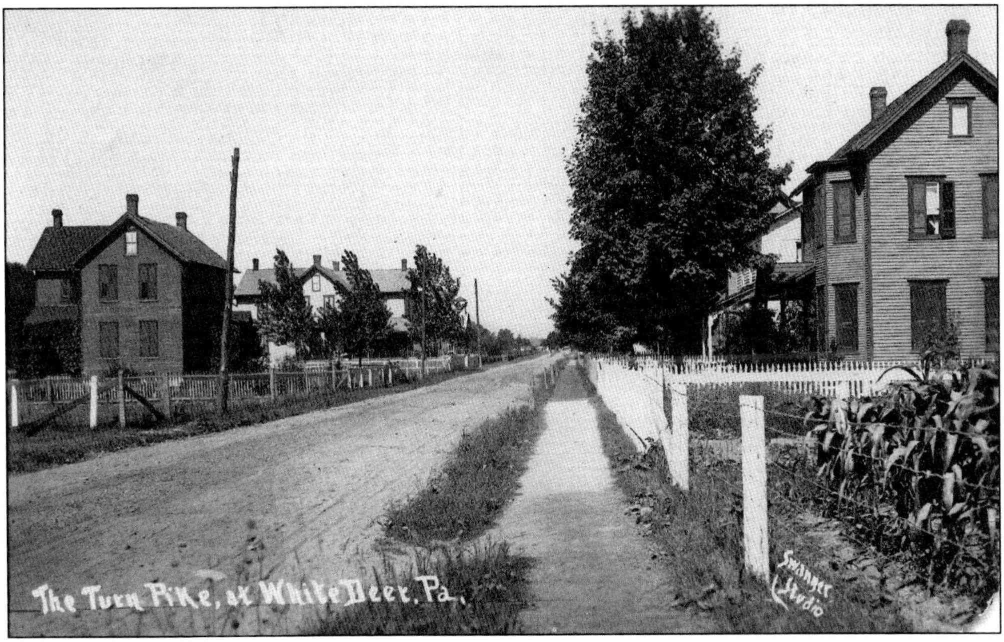

The White Deer Turnpike is in the real-photo postcard above by Swanger Studio from around 1908 to 1912. The first house on the left belonged to Reid Kling Sr. and the one at right belonged to Rev. Floyd Huff. The pike ran 20 miles due west to Carroll in Clinton County. Along the pike were an iron furnace, sawmill, oil and flouring mills, a woolen factory, and the one-room Factory School. Today, only the school and sawmill remain; there is also a community park. Located approximately five miles up the pike was the White Deer Dam, seen below around 1907. It supplied water to the White Deer, New Columbia, and Milton areas and was owned by the White Deer Mountain Water Company, then later by the Keystone Water Company. It is currently owned by the Pennsylvania American Water Company. (Above, UCHS 2008.53.30; below, Paul Prowant.)

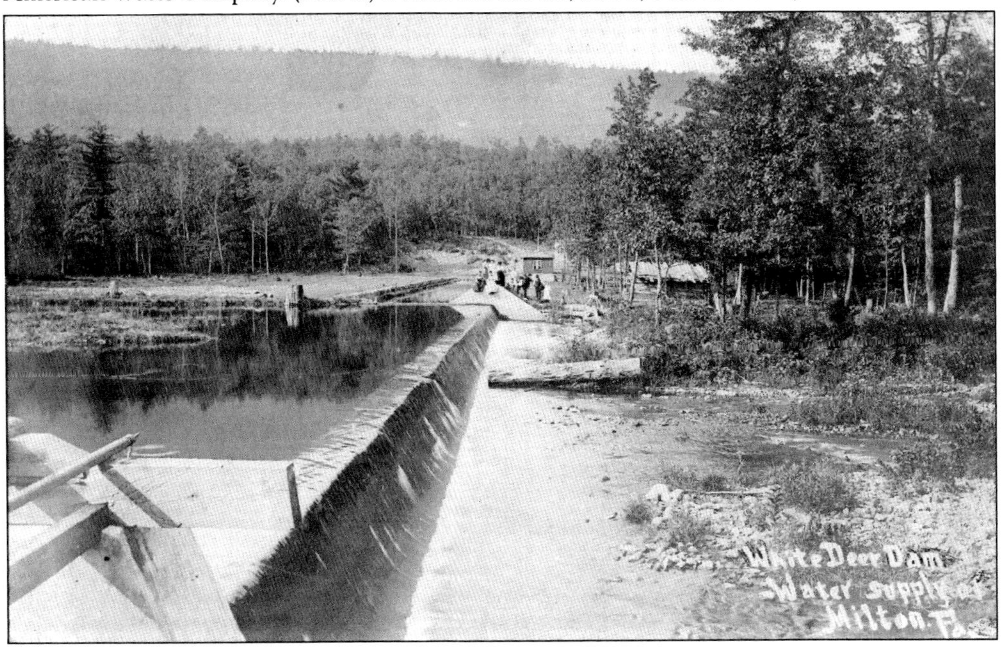

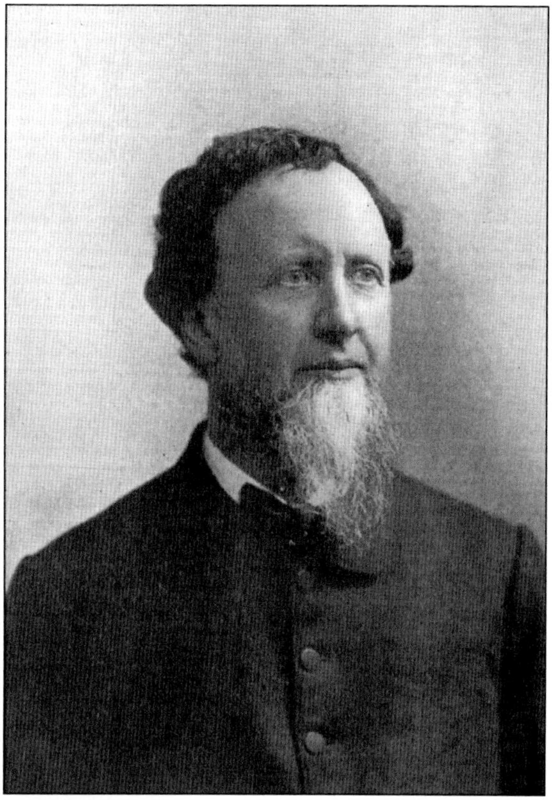

Rev. William Wicklein Clouser, a graduate of the Reformed Theological Seminary in Mercersburg, was asked to preach in English and German for the White Deer Reformed Church. In 1870, Clouser became a circuit-riding preacher for the four churches of the White Deer Charge—an area 25 miles by 10 miles. Delivering sermons until 1894, Clouser lived with his family in a brick home on what is now Leiser Road. (Ardith Wilkins.)

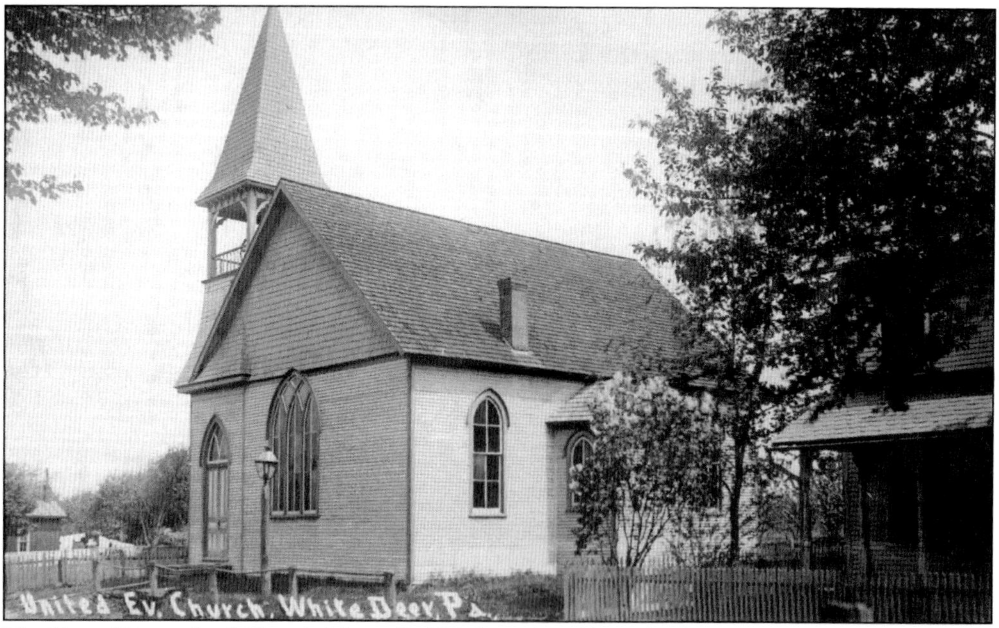

The United Evangelical Church (also called Walter's church) was built in 1896 after a split at the Mill Church in White Deer. In 1967, the church purchased a former Army chapel and moved it to its present location on White Deer Pike, naming it Faith Chapel. The old church building in White Deer was bought by Millard and Kathryn Koch and was demolished per the purchase agreement. (Ardith Wilkins.)

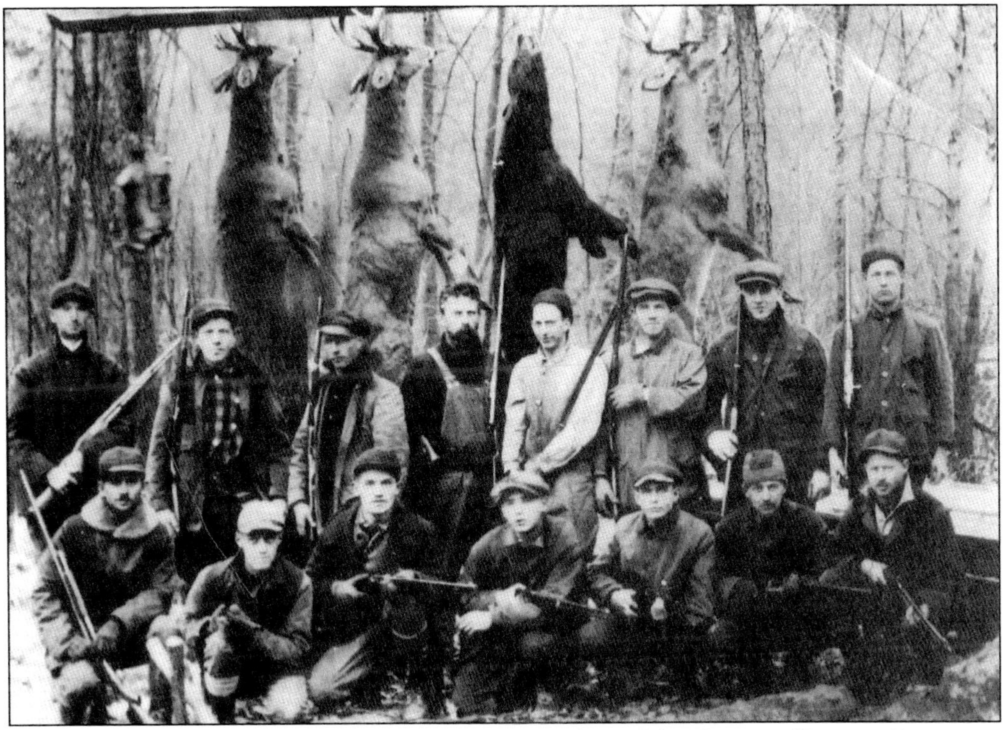

White Deer Township had many hunting camps. Members of the Keystone Hunting Camp pose with deer and a black bear in 1901. They are, from left to right, (first row) Russell Smith, Jay Koch, Ford Bergenstock, David Bergenstock, Myron Engleman, Rafe Koch, and Fred Merrill; (second row) Willard Simpler Sr., unidentified, Dan Wertz, Brigman Young, Ben Snyder, Dewey Fisher, Willard Simpler Jr., and Lee Yost. Taken in 1906, the photograph below of Camp Goodlander at Mile Run includes, from left to right, (first row) two unidentified, E. Huff, John Goodlander, Oscar Huff, and David Moore. Pictured in the second row, third from left, is William Huff. The *Lewisburg Chronicle* reported in November 1910, "Last Friday the members of Larry's Creek Hunting and Fishing Club shot the largest buck yet reported this season. He was a big albino, being pure white with the exception of a few brown spots along the back." (Both, Donald Wilver Sr.)

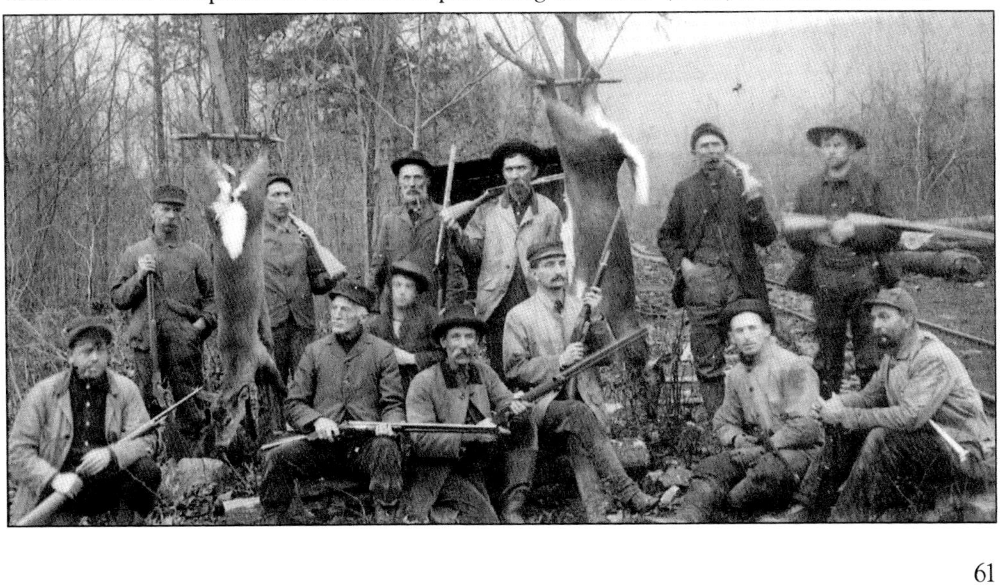

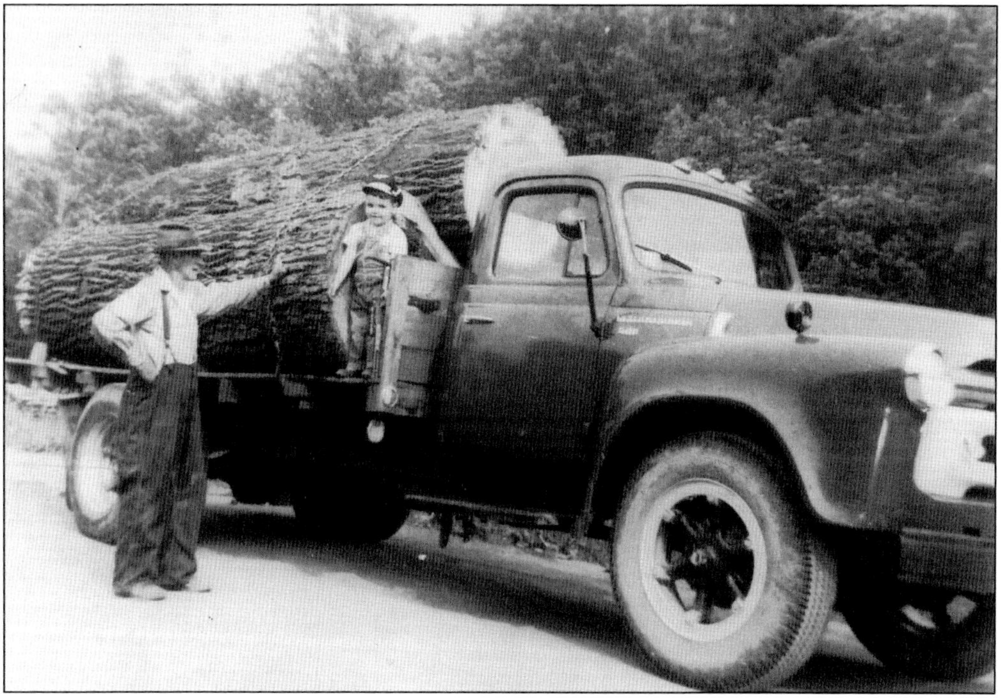

Joe Wertz and grandson Mike Wertz pose at the White Deer Lumber Company's sawmill, also known as Joe Wertz's sawmill. Notice the size of the logs being cut at that time, said to be as much as 36 inches in diameter. A real-photo postcard (below) shows an overview of the sawmill's yard. (Above, Sue Wertz; below, Kathryn Reitz.)

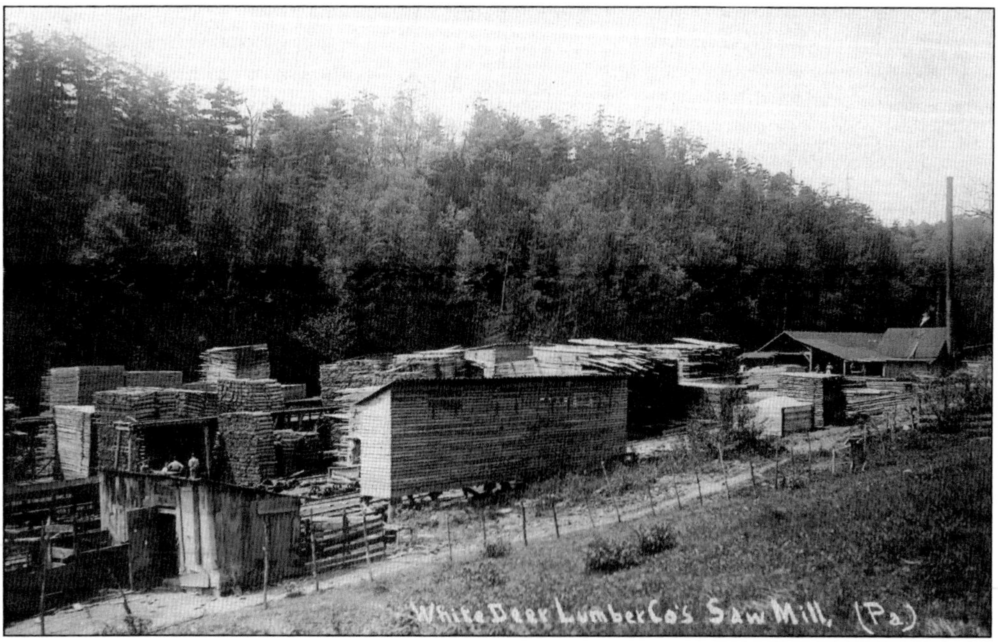

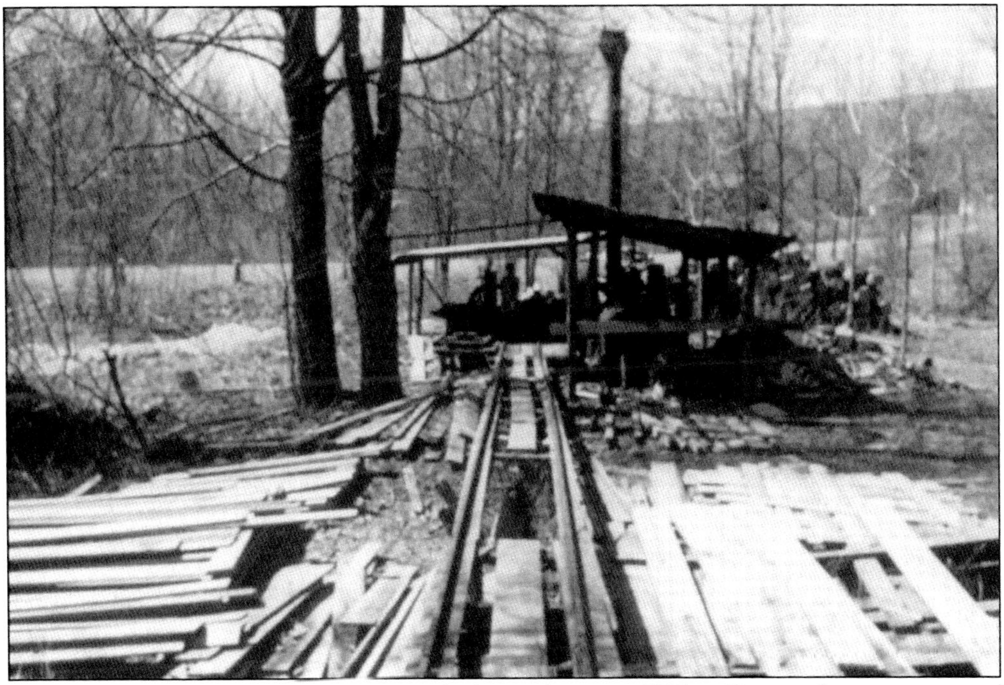

Dan Wertz's sawmill, located approximately four miles west of White Deer at the intersection of Dyer Road and the turnpike, is shown in the 1950s. This sawmill is presently owned and operated by Gordon Robert Wertz, Dan's son. (Jack Wertz.)

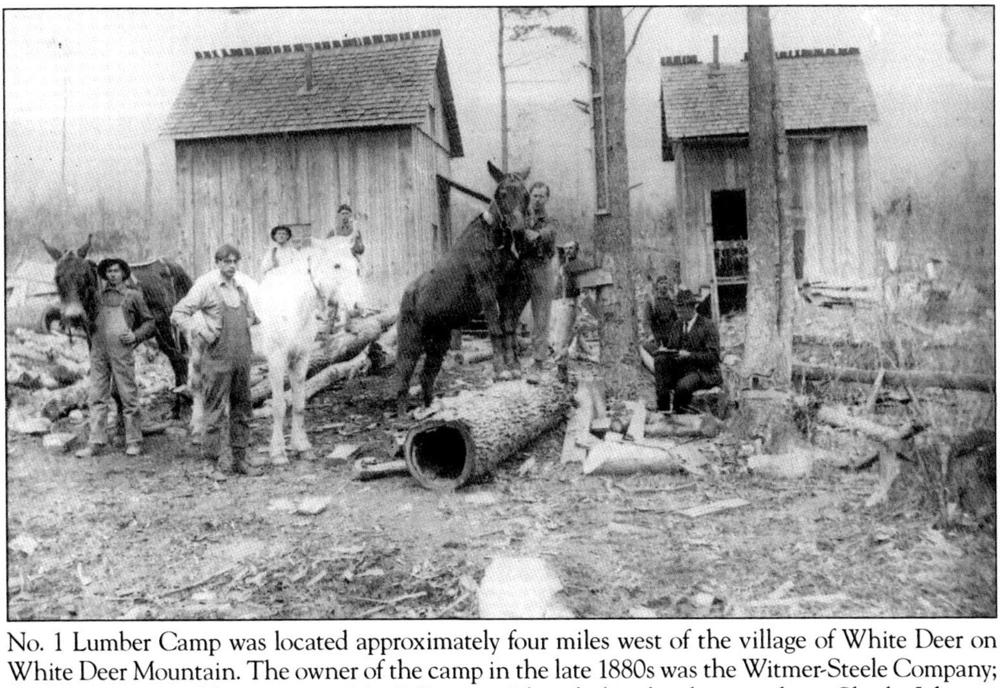

No. 1 Lumber Camp was located approximately four miles west of the village of White Deer on White Deer Mountain. The owner of the camp in the late 1880s was the Witmer-Steele Company; the former owner of the camp was John F. Duncan. Identified in the photograph are Charles Johnson (second from left) and Frank Jamison (standing on the log in the center). Johnson lived from 1882 to 1917. (Don Wilver Sr.)

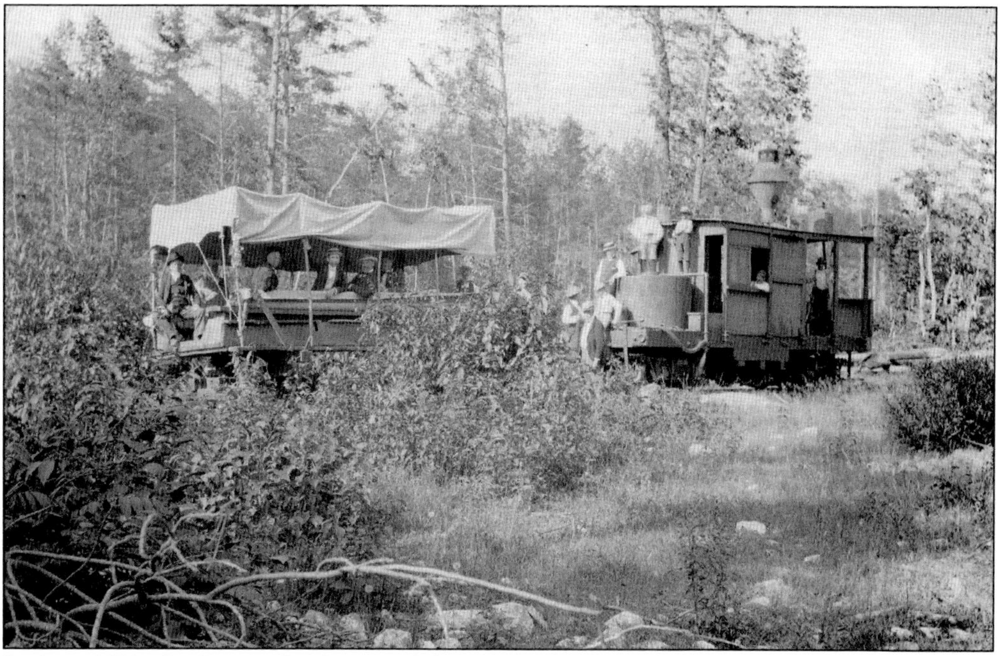

Built in 1889, the *Pot* was lumberman John Duncan's original locomotive used to carry both timber and passengers on the White Deer Valley Line, later called the White Deer–Loganton. Stops included Clam Bake Springs, the water reservoir, Lick Run, Mile Run, Zimmerman's, Tea Springs, Green Gap, Carroll, Brungard, and Loganton. The *Pot* ultimately was sold to the Watsontown Brick Company before being scrapped around 1918. (Both, UCHS 2010. 21.108.o and 2006.42.2.)

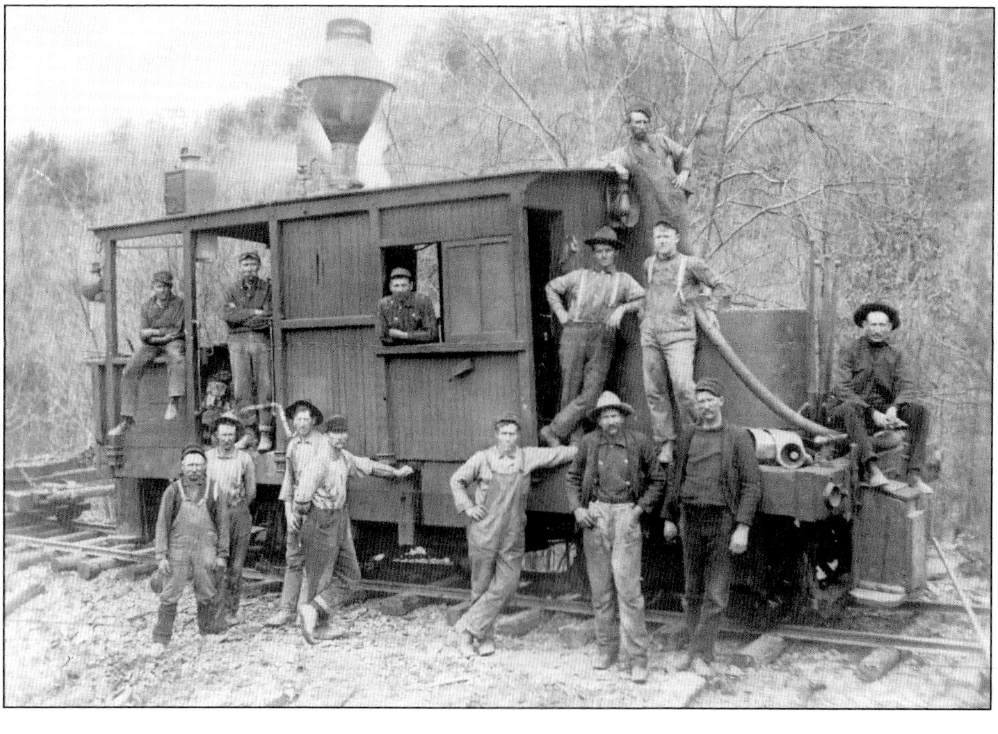

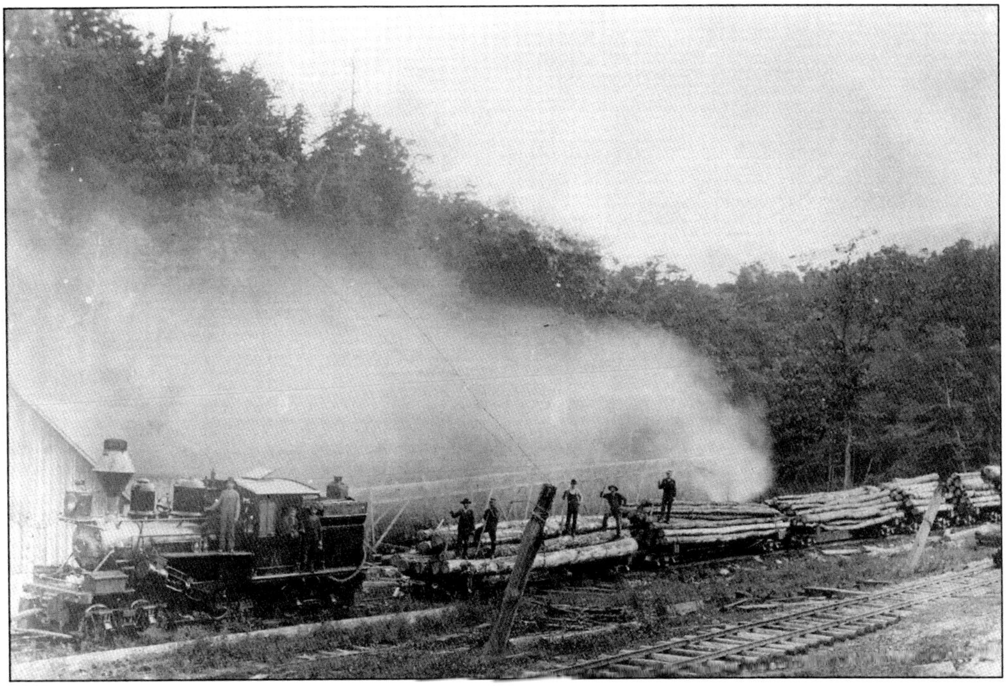

Aspects of the logging operation that John Duncan owned from 1900 until his death in 1904 were captured on film. Above, the log train is about to unload into the log pond. Smoke can be seen coming from burning bark, and the mill is on the left. Below, a winter scene shows the lumber train's narrow gauge tracks and a log landing in the woods. (Both, UCHS 2010.21.108.f and pp.)

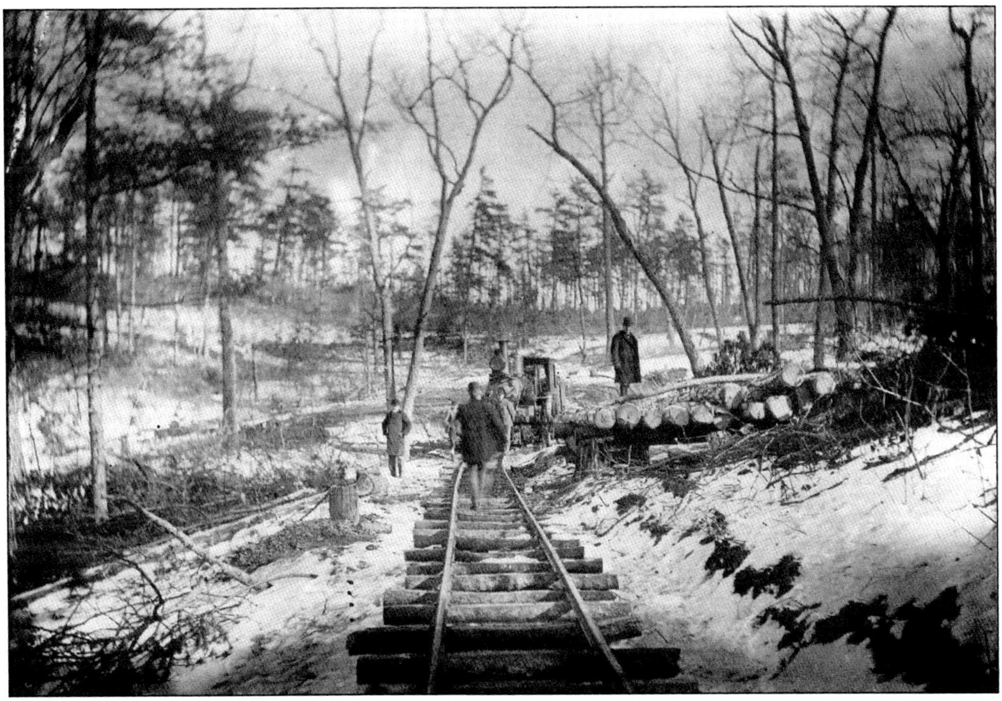

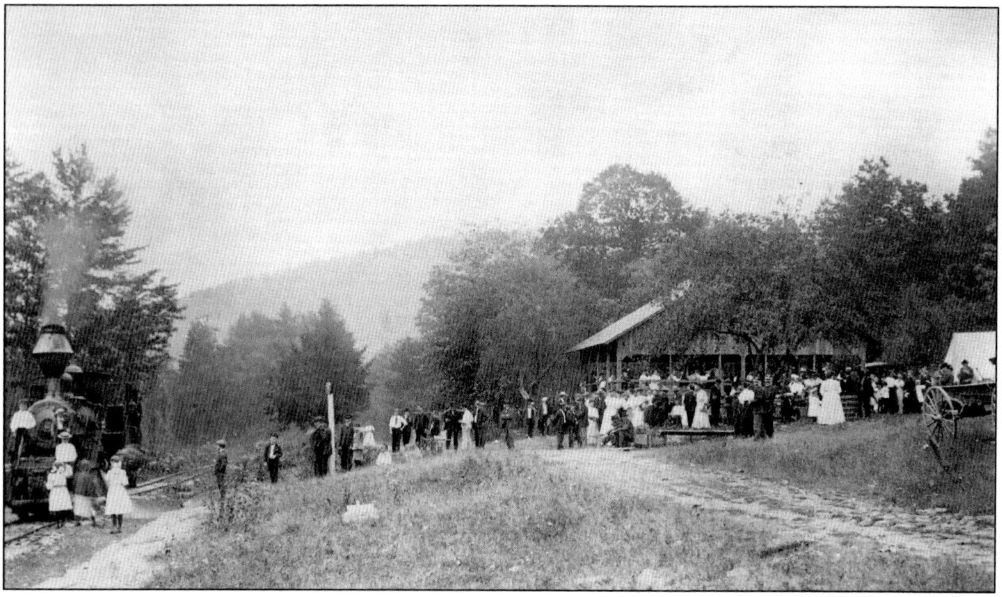

Passenger and open-air excursion cars are shown pulled by locomotive No. 1 at the Tea Springs pavilion (above) and at the Loganton station (below). From the late 1880s to the 1910s, the White Deer and Loganton Railway connected the Buffalo and White Deer Valleys in Union County to Sugar Valley in Clinton County. The run to Tea Springs was extremely popular from 1906 to 1916. However, the line was never profitable. Such an excursion was mentioned in the *Mifflinburg Telegraph* on September 8, 1911: "The White Deer and West Milton Sunday school picnic to be held Sept. 2 at Tea Springs, has been postponed until Sept. 9th on account of the wet weather." (Both, UCHS 2010.21.108.n and r.)

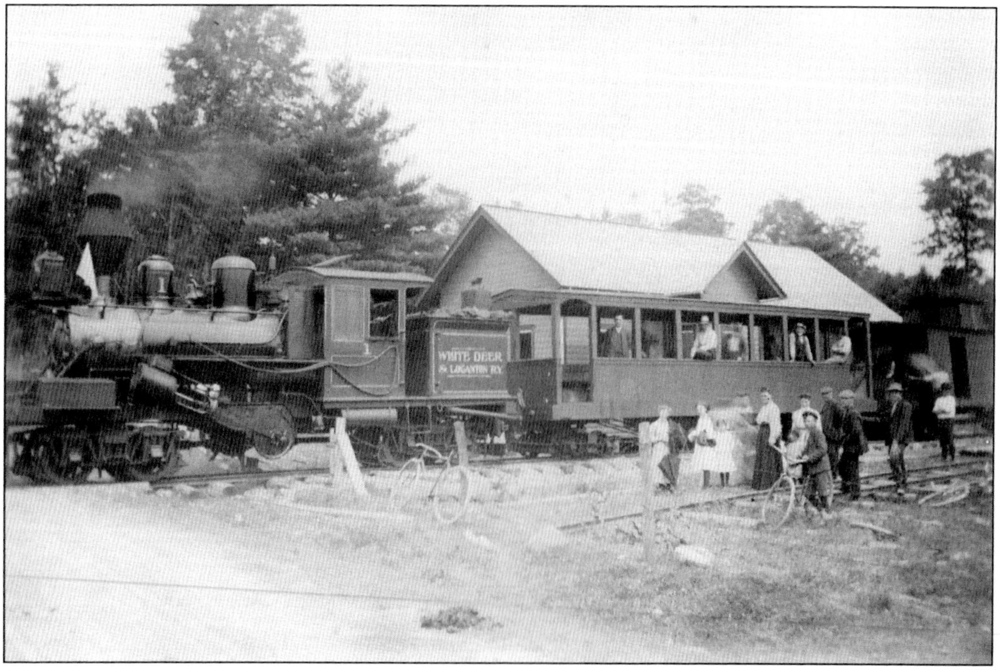

Three

New Columbia

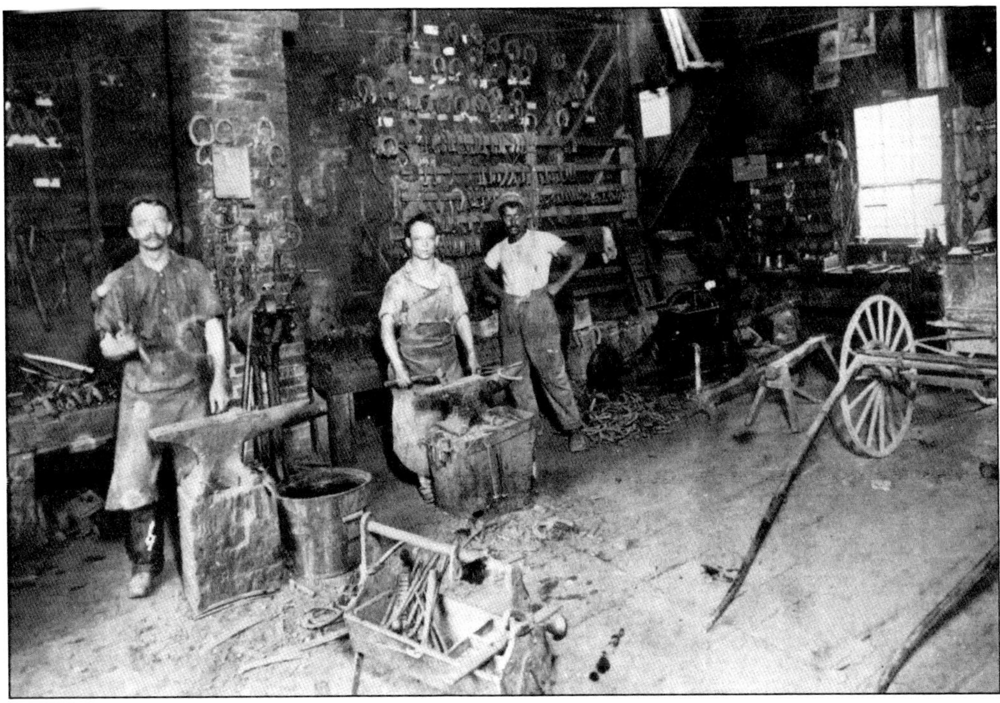

Pictured around 1895 in John Jefferson Ranck's blacksmith shop at the west corner of Main Street and Mulberry Alley are, from left to right, Ranck, Alfred "Fred" Reish, and an unidentified worker. Ranck's brother, Samuel, and John's eldest son, Percival, also assisted in the shop. Another New Columbia shop was William Blind's, where Ranck apprenticed for two years making and repairing vehicles. Ben Huff had two different blacksmith shops in New Columbia. (UCHS 89.5.15.)

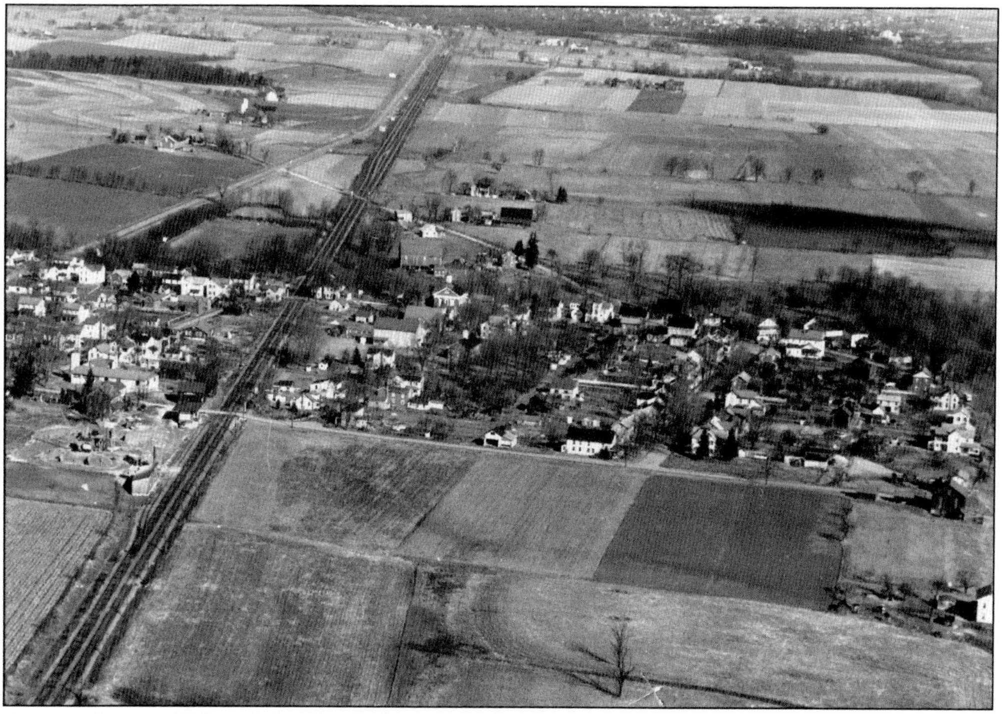

An aerial view of New Columbia before 1954 shows the town in its natural surroundings. This contrasts with the still sparse development of the community reflected in *Pomeroy's Atlas for Union and Snyder Counties* of 1868 (below). David Yoder and surveyor Henry Hertz laid out the town in 1818 with 132 lots on the south side of Main Street. Subsequently, lots on the north side of Main were added from what was formerly part of the John Fisher farm. In 1868, there were 59 homes and businesses, a sawmill on Dog Run, cabinet and blacksmith shops, a hotel, and a church. Along Main Street were the B & G lumber shop (owned by Benjamin F. Bostian and Samuel Gemberling), the William Blind carriage shop, and the Union Evangelical Lutheran Church. (Above, Bill Clemens; below, UCHS.)

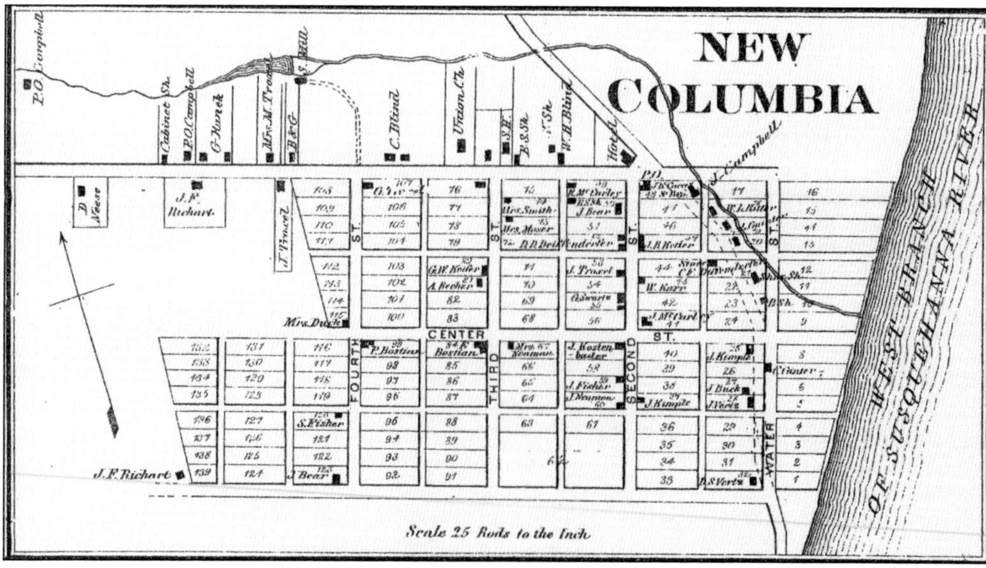

A photograph of Third Street shows one of the many two-storied log homes that once stood in New Columbia. The owner, Mrs. Chisolm, stands on the sidewalk, while Mr. and Mrs. D.A. Yost and infant Joseph Praser are on the porch of the frame house. The log home was razed, and the frame home still stands at 262 Third Street. It is currently occupied by Theresa and Ken Sampsell. (Terri Stump.)

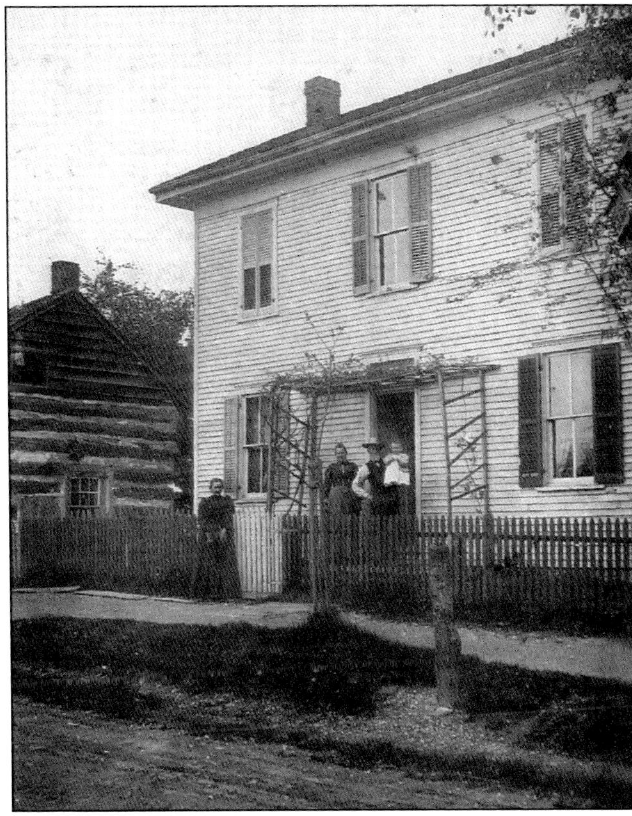

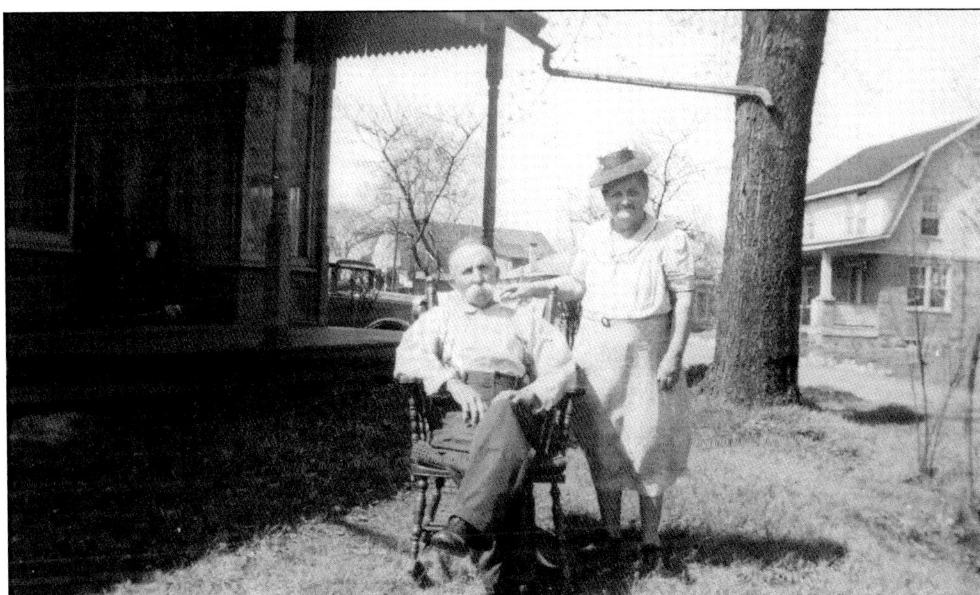

In the 1930s, Tom and Kate Huff were photographed sitting in front of their River Road. With its large store windows, the house was also the location of a bakery owned and operated by Addabelle Kimple and her daughter, Lisa. The Kevin Koch family currently owns the house. (Gilbert Bennett.)

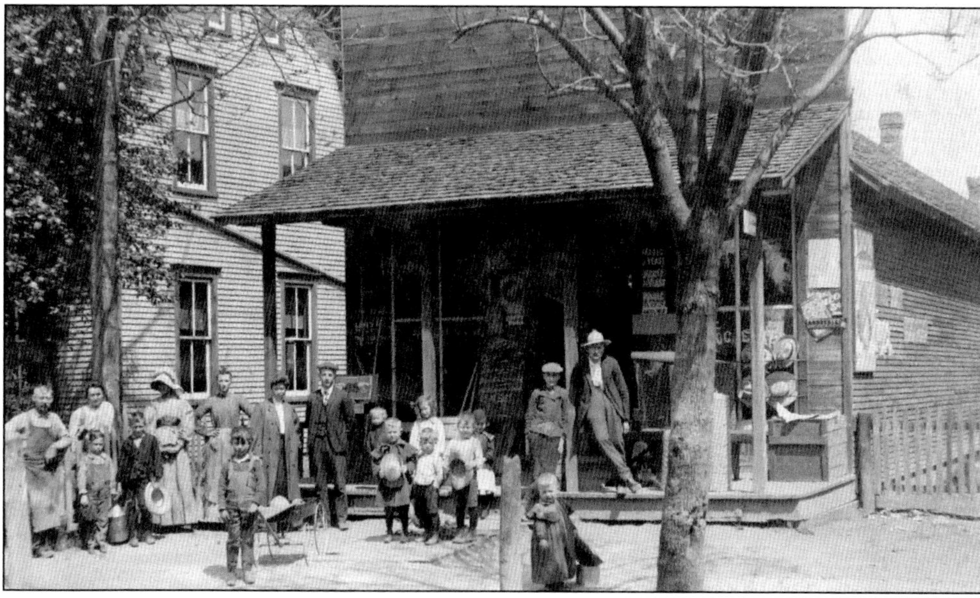

A 1907 real-photo postcard (above) shows Foresman's Store when William Foresman managed it for the Meek family of Allenwood. Foresman purchased the store in 1914, and it was family-operated until 1974. The adults are, from left to right, Charles, Flo, and Caroline Bostian, Minnie Reitmeyer, Iva Foresman, Roy Hummell, unidentified, and proprietor William Foresman. The children are, from left to right, Charles Bostian Jr., unidentified, Bruce Foresman (with wagon), Bertram Reitmeyer, Delbert Herman, Floyd Fisher, and the three children behind them are unidentified, as is the boy to the right of the post in the foreground. The c. 1960 real-photo postcard below shows Foresman's Store (left) and New Columbia's post office (with flag) on Main Street. Prudence Foresman and Sylbie Bennett were the owners at this time. Their aunt Bertha Foresman worked as a clerk from as early as 1910 until 1972. (Both, Terri Stump.)

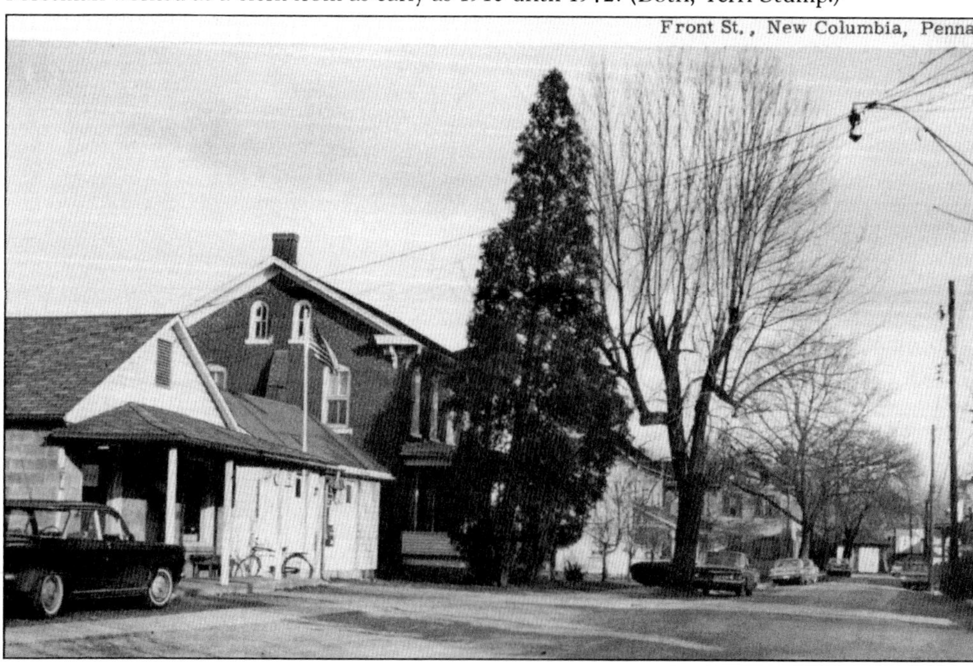

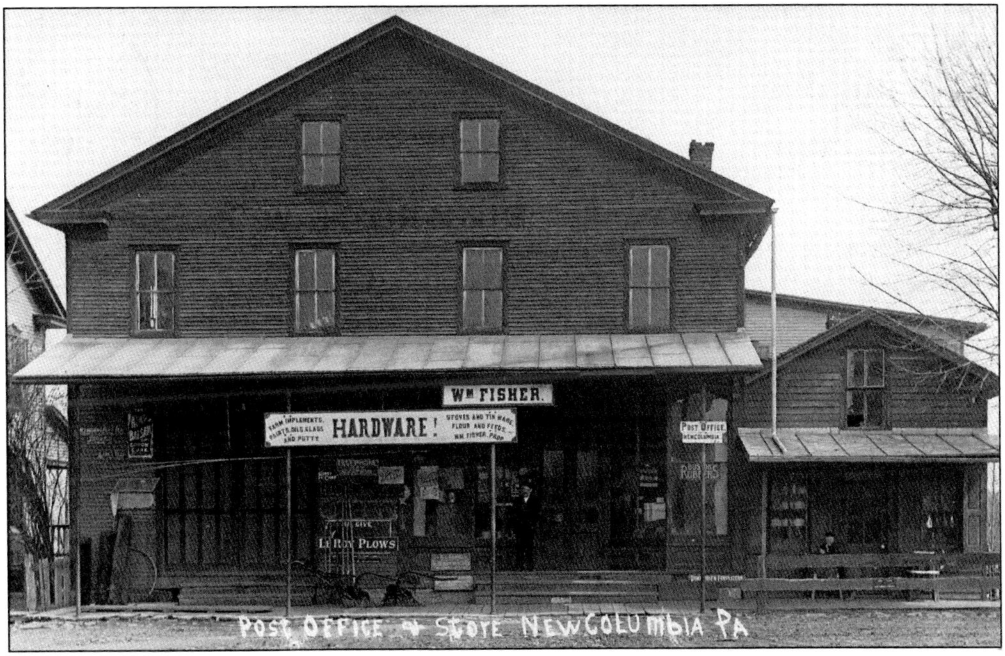

When Willam Dennis died in 1889, employee William "Billy" Fisher took over the business at River Road and Main Street. He sold farm implements, paints, stoves, tinware, flour, and feed. Fisher huckstered stoves and hardware in the countryside. Later, sons Floyd "Mike," Herman "Pete," and Delbert "Debs" retained the business. When Pete died in 1966, his wife, May, continued the enterprise along with Mike and Debs. George Cawley followed in operating the business. New Columbia's post office was here for about 17 years. At right, Kathryn Finck stands behind the counter of Finck's Store, which she and her husband, Blair Finck Sr., owned on Main Street from around 1945 to 1957. Finck's sold Peterman shoes and had a wide selection of clothes, including jeans and shirts. Finck's no longer stands and a mobile home is now at the site. (Above, Ronald Nornhold; right, Kathryn and Blair Finck Sr. family.)

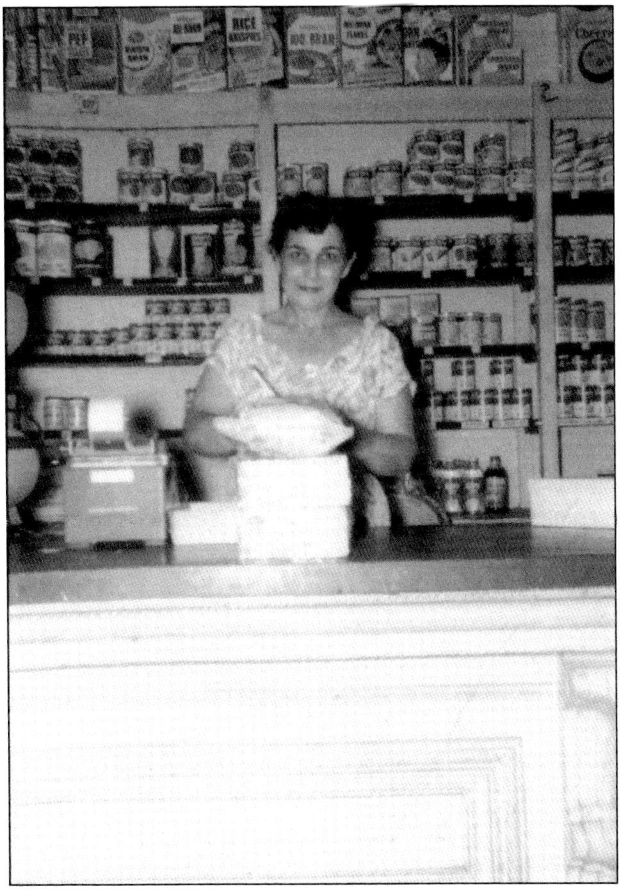

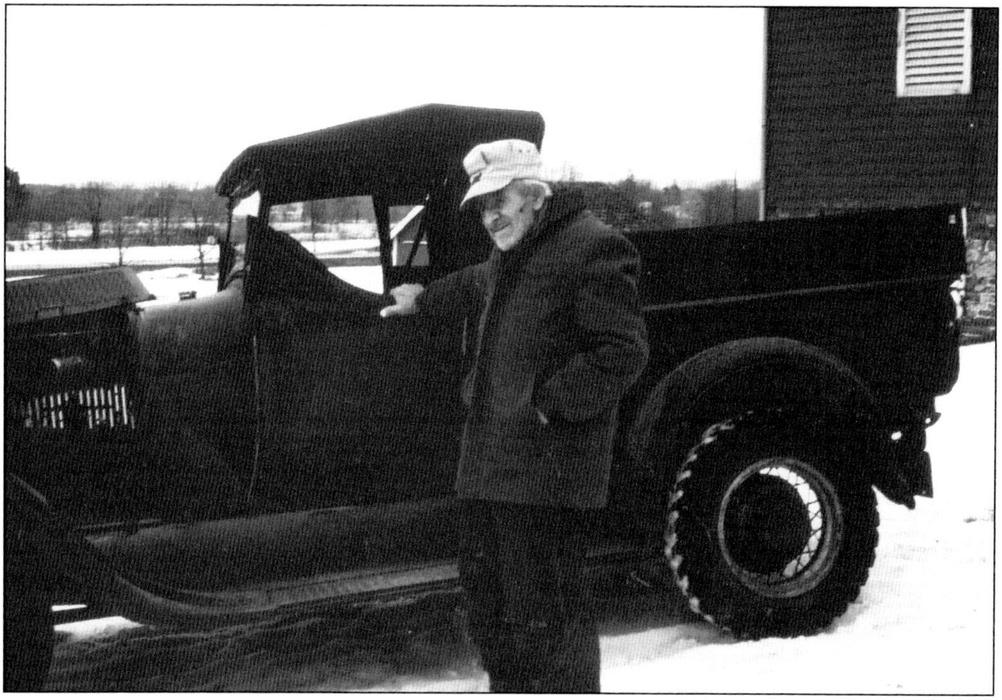

Foster Ranck (1899–1985), a farmer and gunsmith who lived on Old Route 15, just south of the railroad tracks, stands by his truck (above). The 1929 Ford Model A Roadster has been restored by owner Donald Wilver Sr. of New Columbia. Harrison Ranck (1864–1956), father of Foster and a farmer on Old Route 15, stands next to his Model A Ford sedan (below). (Both, Donald Wilver Sr.)

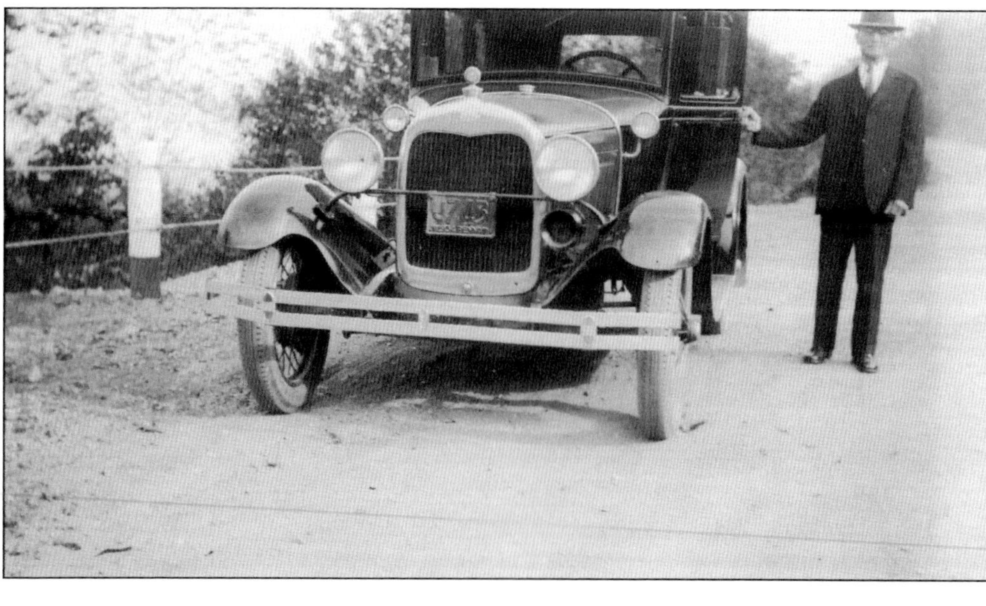

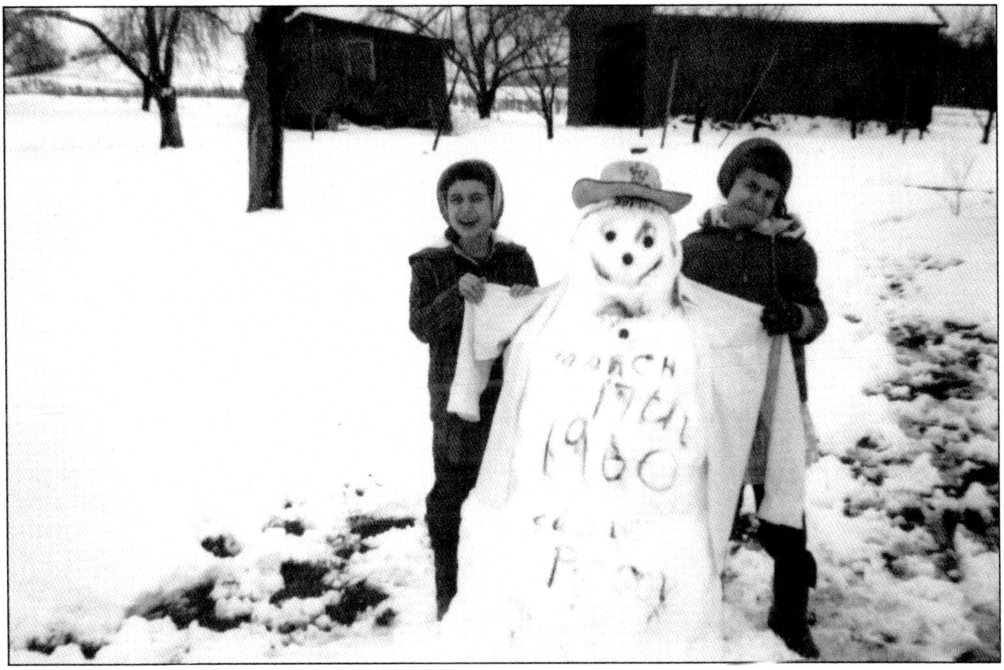

Susan (left) and Peggy Berkheimer pose with a snowman they made on March 17, 1960, at the Ario Showers farm. Before it was used for the Route 80 cloverleaf at New Columbia, the Showers farm relocated to what is now 10500 River Road, owned in 2011 by Jan Heckman Hanlon. (Susan Berkheimer.)

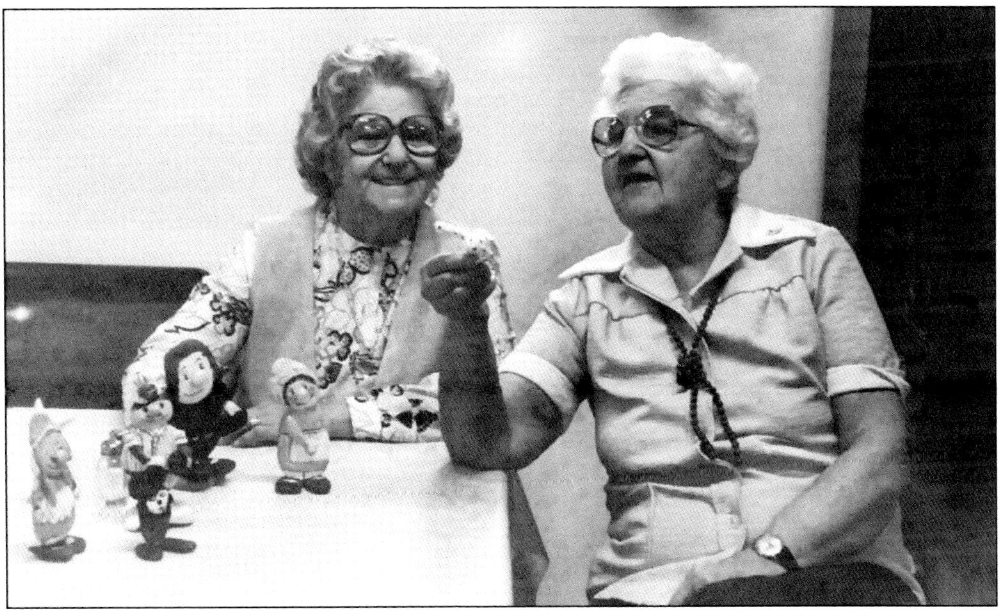

Julia (Hixon) Anderson and Pauline (Hoffman) Hause, pictured at New Columbia's Senior Action Center, admire their "stone people." This lively senior center was one of three in Union County and was started in 1974 by the Union/Snyder Area Agency on Aging under the Older Americans Act. The New Columbia Center brought local senior citizens together for midday meals and activities from 1974 to 2010. The seniors met at the former Foresman's Store and at the Grange hall. (Bill Clemens.)

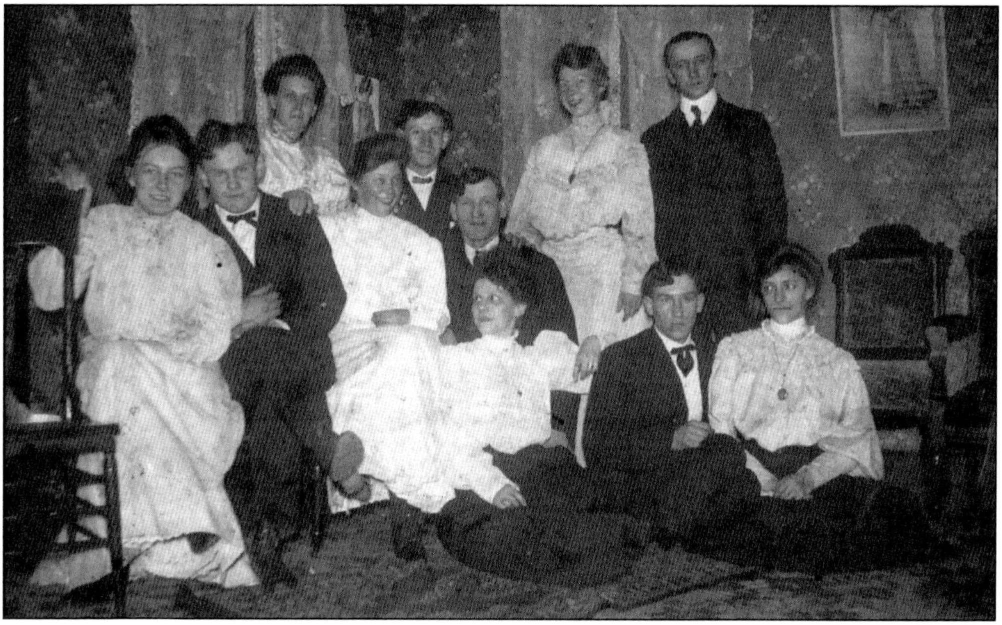

Patterns predominate the wallpapered ceiling and walls, carpeted floor, and thin curtains in this rare home interior. The women are, from left to right, Bessie Foresman, unidentified, Iva Foresman, unidentified, Bertha Foresman, and Kate Foresman. The Foresman home was close to where the New Columbia Short Stop is currently located. The Foresman barn was razed to make way for the ramp off the new Route 15. (Bill Clemens.)

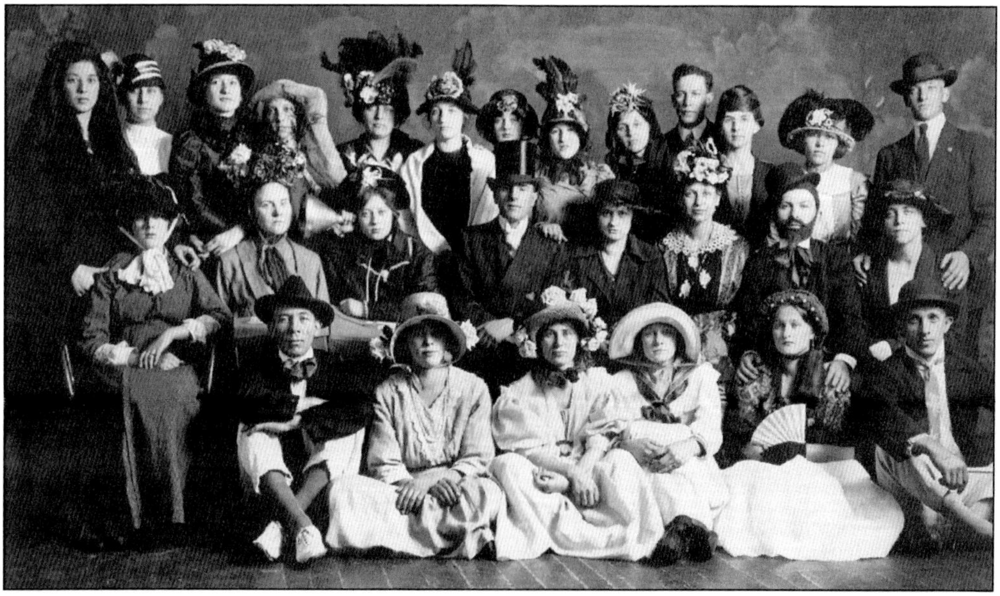

Players at the Patriotic Order Sons of America are, from left to right, (first row) Stewart Prowant, Ina Ranck, Florence Clemens, Harriet Reitmeyer, Sylbie Foresman, and George Jows; (second row) Hazel Keefer, Hazel Fisher, Geraldine Lagerman, Harry Bostian, Prudence Foresman, Margaret Ranck, Proctor Hoffman, and Viola Showers; (third row) Zita Tanner, Sara Lynn, Millie Fisher, Florence Ranck, Nell Jows, Ethel Tanner, Florence Keefer, Vera Ranck, Mary Moore, Howard Reitmeyer, ? Farley, Lucille Ranck, and Tilse Tanner. (Bill Clemens.)

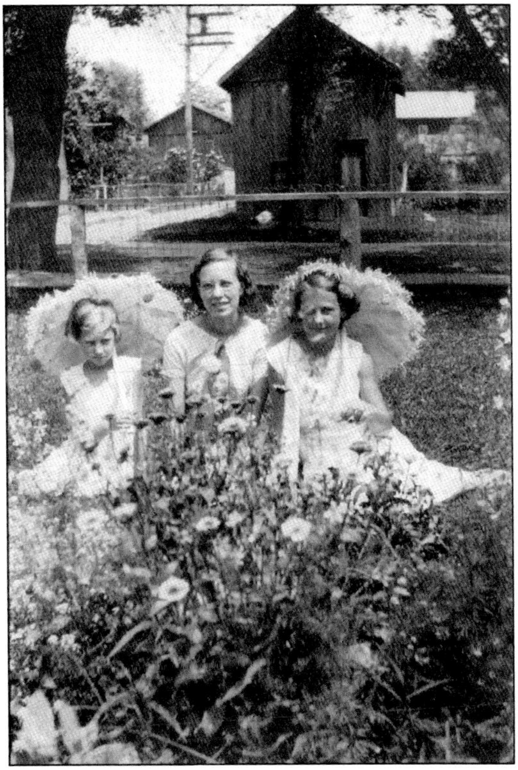

Pictured in the early 1930s, sisters Dorothy (born 1923), left, and Pauline Ranck (1920–2003) flank sister-in-law Viola Smith Ranck (born 1913) at 243 Second Street. The Trutt house is across the street but has since been razed. Below, Walter "Doc" Ranck (1910–1974) tends his chickens at the Ranck home with the Trinity United Methodist Church in the background around 1930. This was an era when small farm animals were in town. (Both, Dorothy Ranck.)

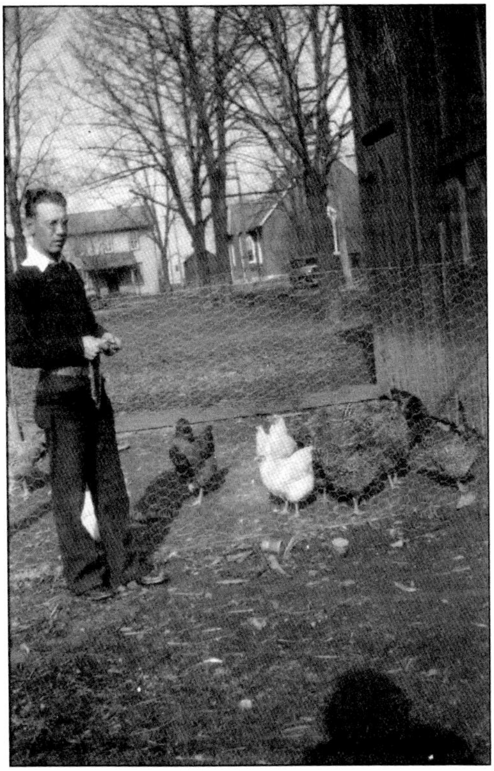

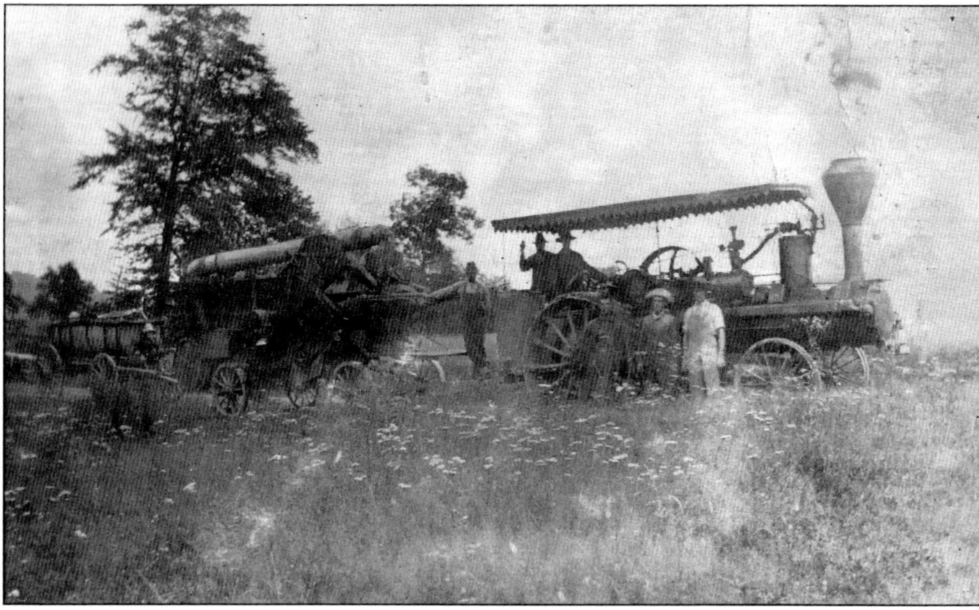

A steam-driven thresher is pictured in a field on the Yocum farm (above) and back at the barn (below). Below, from left to right, are hired hand Jim Wertz, Ira Bowersox (seated); Charles, Rosie, May, Anna (Charles's wife), and William Yocum. Calvin Yocum is on the thresher, and Clarence Yocum is in the foreground. Charles lived from 1865 to 1928, and Anna lived from 1862 until 1931. Both the house and barn located on Showers Road outside New Columbia have burned. (Above, Paul Prowant; below, Donald Wilver Sr.)

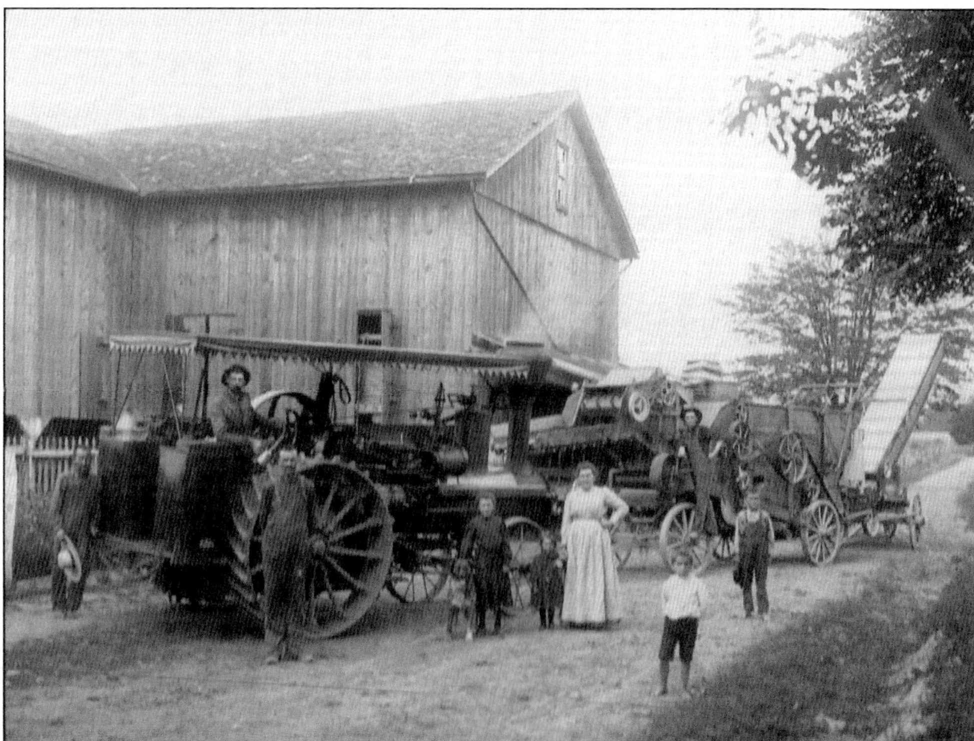

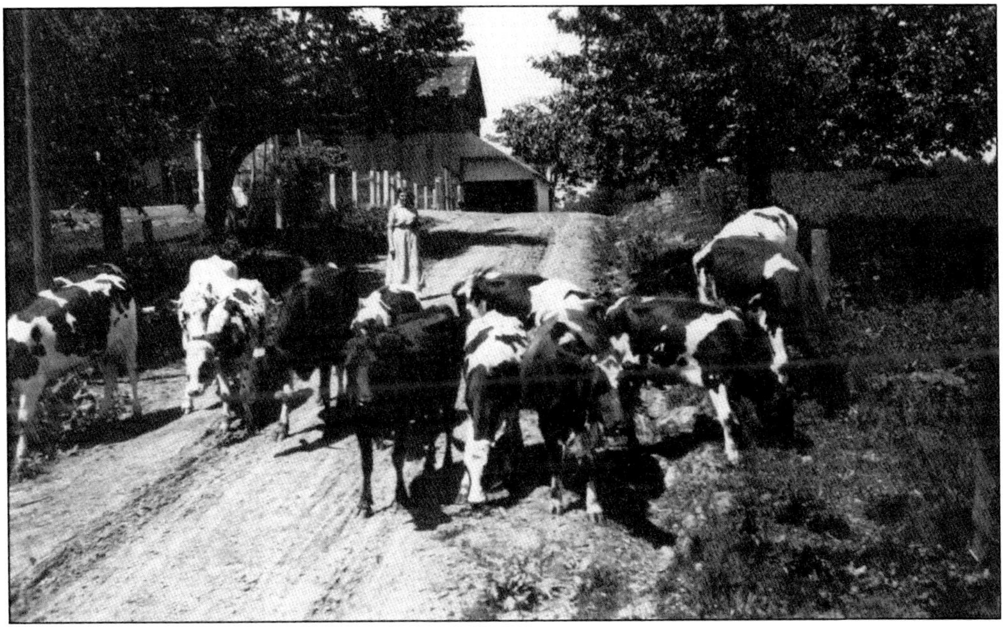

Rosie Yocum, the sister of Charles Yocum, is shown with her brother's cattle. Below, in a colored photolithographed postcard from the early 1900s, oxen pull a wagon full of hay on Main Street east of the railroad tracks in New Columbia. (Above, Donald Wilver Sr.; below, Terri Stump.)

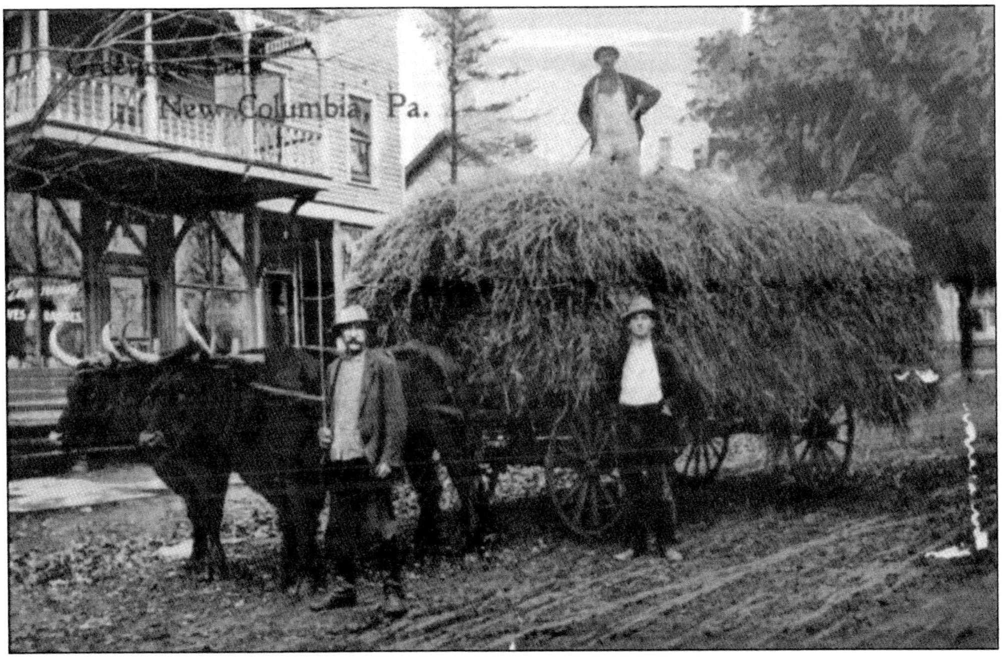

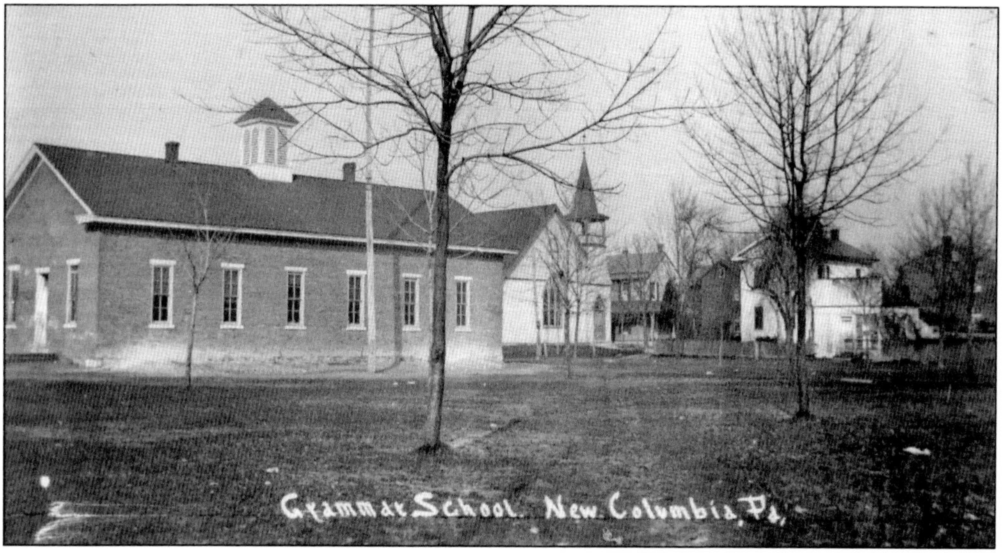

In 1882, New Columbia's school housed both primary and grammar students. Primary students in 1950–1951, from left to right, are (first row) Peter Hause, Ronnie Shearer, Kenny Keefer, Harold Herman, Billy Prowant, Bud Hoover, Chuck Keifer, Carl Herman, Orison Culver, and Harry Walker; (second row) Patsy Miller, Bonnie Jean Dershem, Dottie LeBard, Dolly Fenton, unidentified, Linda Miller, Sue Fisher, unidentified, Dorothy Trutt, Beverly Goodwin, and Rochele (Cookie) Marks; (third row) Charlotte Hause, Patty Clemens, Betty Jane Bennett, Diane Walker, Marty Mae Fisher, and Marie Reimensnyder; (fourth row) Robert Keifer, Ralph Goodwin, Allen Dershem, David Guyer, David Lynn, Bill Lebard, Wesley Reichard, and Lee Reedy; (sitting on porch) Phyllis Fink. After consolidation in 1955, this building was turned over to the New Columbia Civic Association; it continues to serve the community. (Above, Terri Stump; below, Susan Ohl Wirth.)

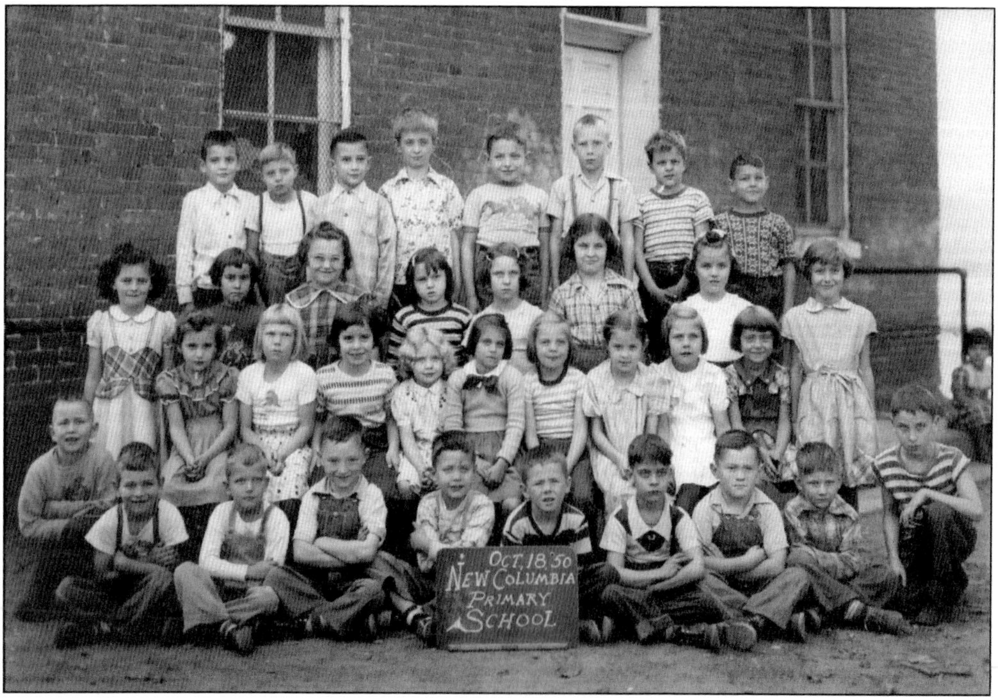

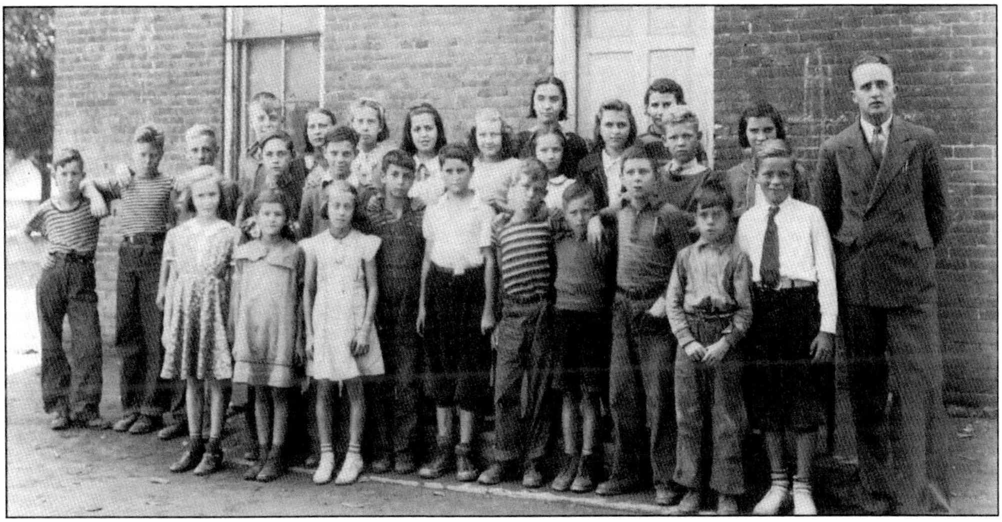

Above, a 1939 photograph of the grammar school students and teacher includes, from left to right, (first row) Janice Noll, Barbara Hause, and Marion Troxel; (second row) Gilbert Bennett, Jim Prowant, Cecil Ranck, Ned Kefer, Chester Hendricks, Rufus Baker, George Walker, Wilbert Bennett, Merlyn Huff, Ray Koch, Eldon Koch, Bob Rank, and Mr. Harmon; (third row) Bill Huff, June Trutt, Ida Mausteller, Leotta Shearer, Delores Marks, Grace Bennett, Nellie Armstrong, Voneida Ranck, and Hazel Trutt; (fourth row) Sis Delaney and Emmy Walker. Pictured below in 1955, fifth-grade students from the Beaver, Bennett, Blyer, Buck, Cawley, Earhart, Fisher, Funk, Hause, Hess, Hoover, Huff, Koch, Lilley, Metzger, Miller, Myers, Nunn, O'Fallen, Reynolds, Shively, Shreck, Smith, Swanger, Treibley, Thursby, Trutt, Walker, Ealtham, Welliver, Yoder, and Young families pose with teacher Randell Arbogast in the newly built consolidated White Deer School in New Columbia. (Above, Gilbert Bennett; below, Minnie Troxel Koch.)

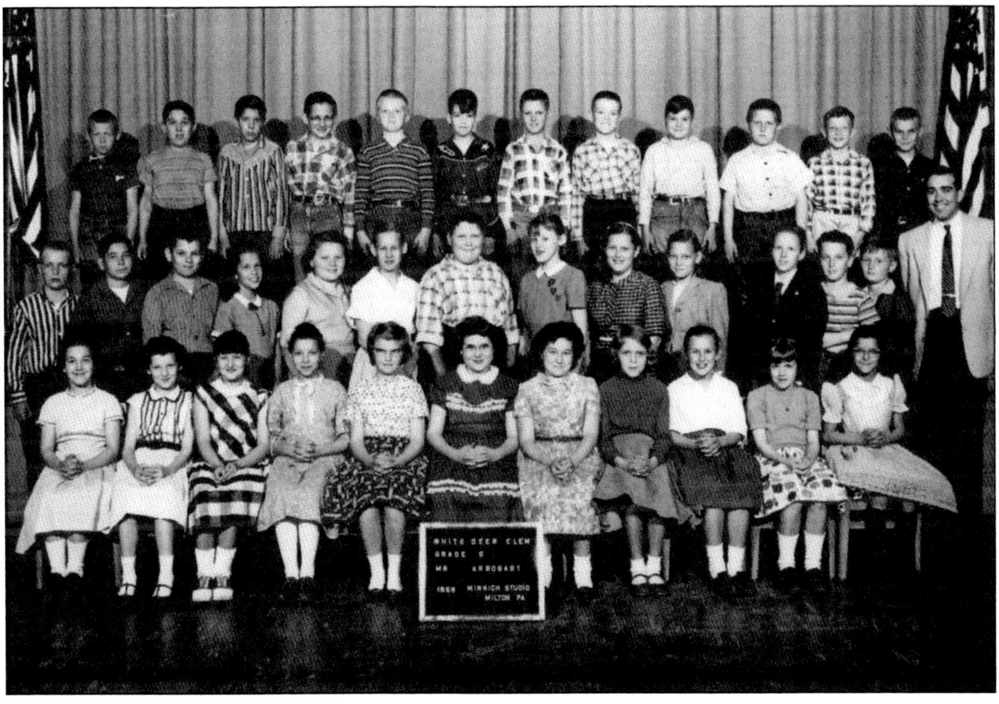

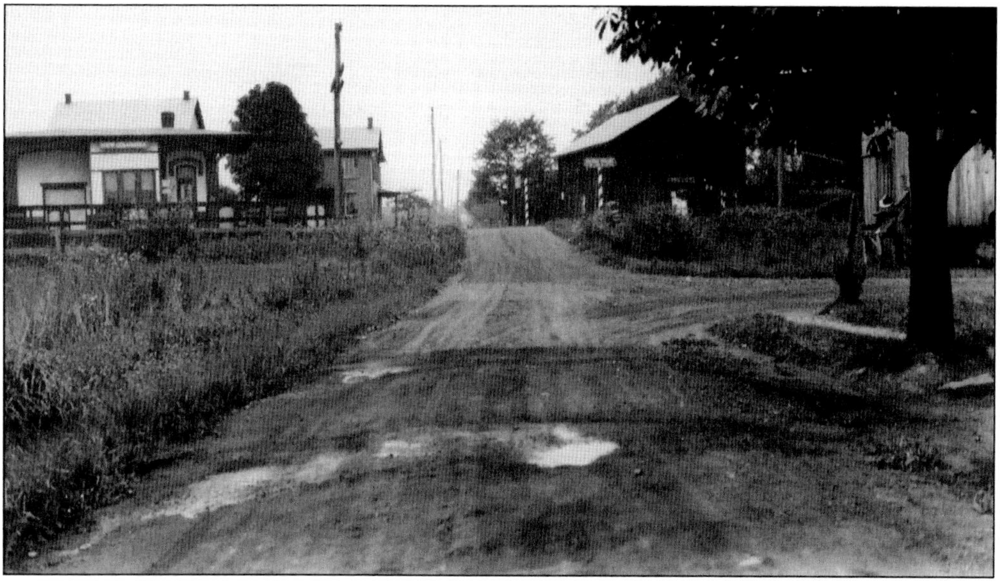

Photographs were taken of all the railroad crossings in New Columbia in September 1928. The image above of Crossing D includes the New Columbia Railroad Station on the left. The picture below shows the New Columbia School on the far left. (Both, UCHS 91.5.27 and .30.)

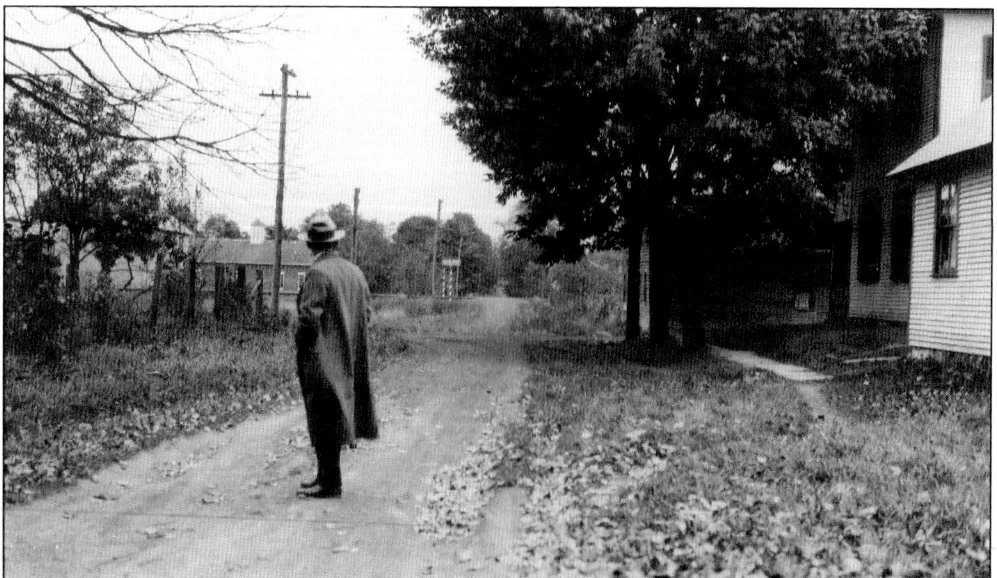

From left to right, twins Wilbert "Snake" and Gilbert "Gib" Bennett, born in 1927, were photographed around 1931 on a horse in front of the 1882 New Columbia School on Third Street. Their mother, Emmie Bennett, is holding them steady. (Gilbert Bennett.)

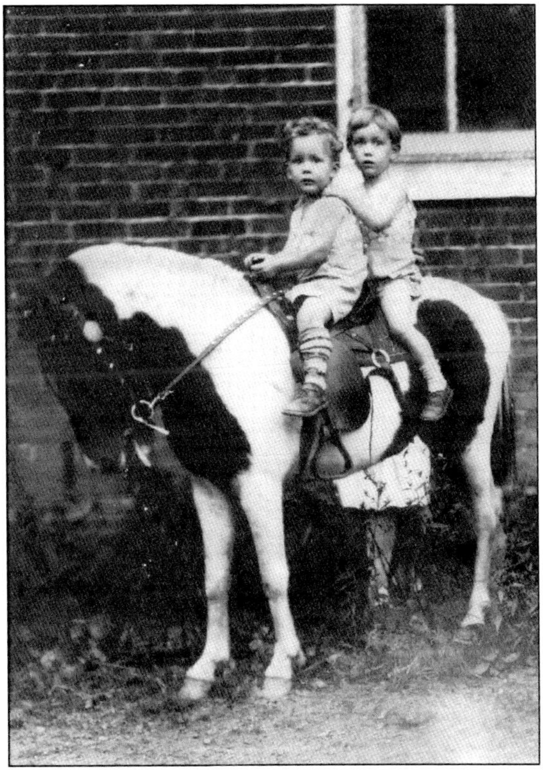

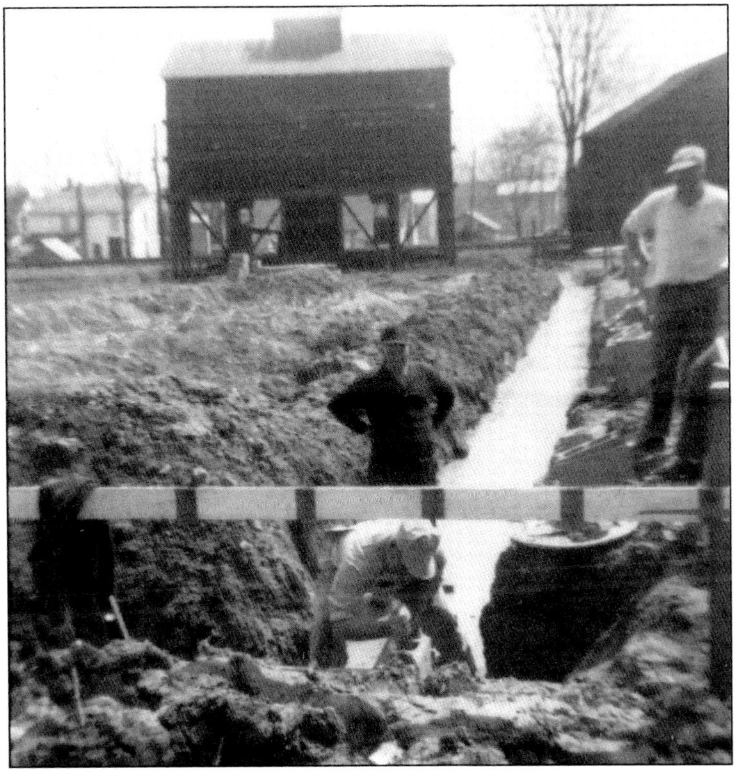

In March 1955, the first blocks were laid for the White Deer Township Fire Company located on the corner of Cemetery and Fourth Streets. Archie McNeer (left) and Boyd Koch stand by while Spencer Trutt works in the ditch. The railroad's coal dock and Ben Huff's blacksmith shop can be seen in the background. (Minnie Troxel Koch.)

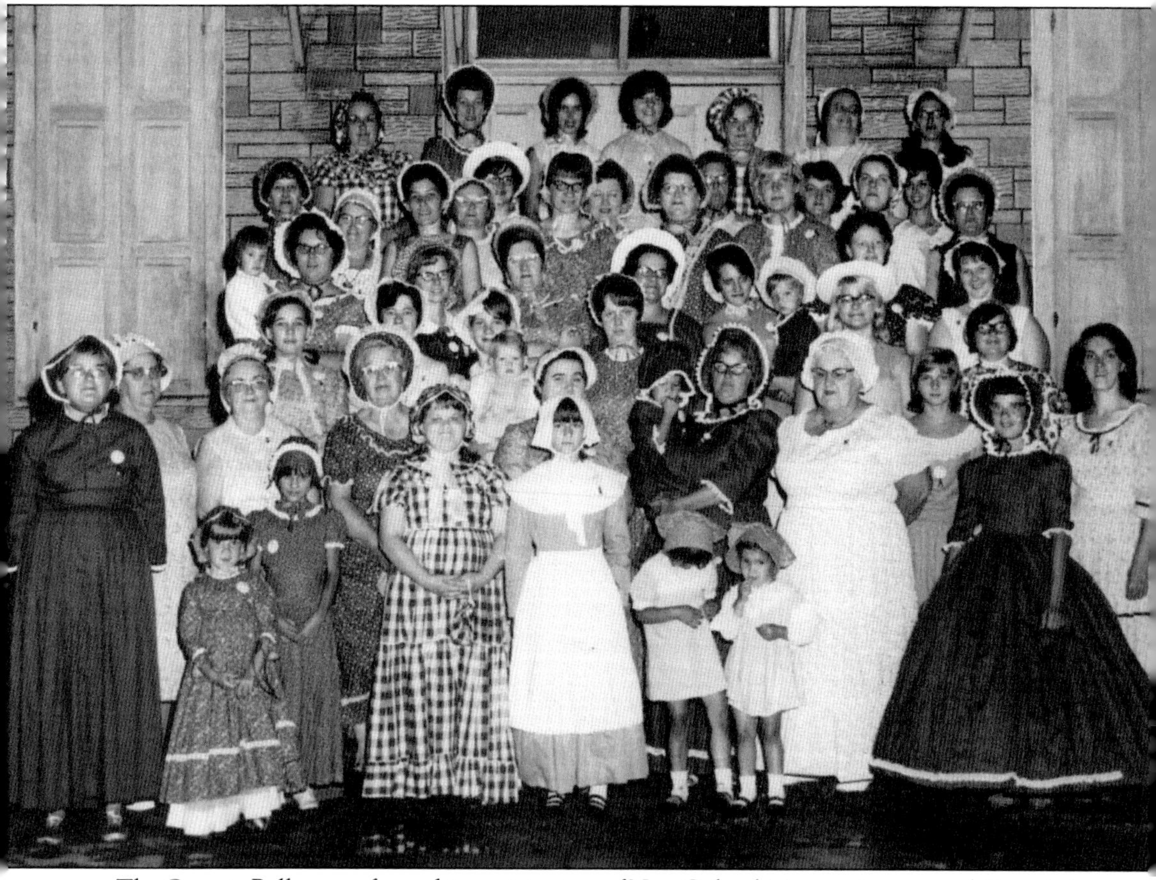

The Georgia Belles were formed in anticipation of New Columbia's sesquicentennial. From left to right are (first row) Sandy Shuck, unidentified, Charlotte Hovenstine, Lisa Ashenfelder, and two unidentified; (second row) Jeanette Hanlon, Blanche Huff, Helen Lynn, Margie Miller, Rachel Bittner, Marianne Snyder holding Candy Snyder, Madge Stewart, Terri Stump, and Sherry Finck; (third row) Esther Bennett, two unidentified (holding unidentified), Rosalie Shuck, Deb Herald, and Freda Ritter; (fourth row) Marsha Lawton holding unidentified, Minnie Koch, Freda Bennett, Carrie Younkin, Elaine Goodwin holding unidentified, Gin Bennett, and Shelvie Houtz; (fifth row) Dorothy Ranck, Hazel Snyder, Shirley Trutt, Ruth Showers, Marianne Cawley, Darlene Bennett, Delores Ocker, Beryl Gordon, Mildred Cawley, Dorothy Black, Donna Seebold, Sue Fisher, Nancy Hoover, and unidentified; (sixth row) unidentified, Barbara Ashenfelder, unidentified, Cheryl Rheppard, Betty Showers, Polly Heckman, and Audrice Walker. (Terri Stump.)

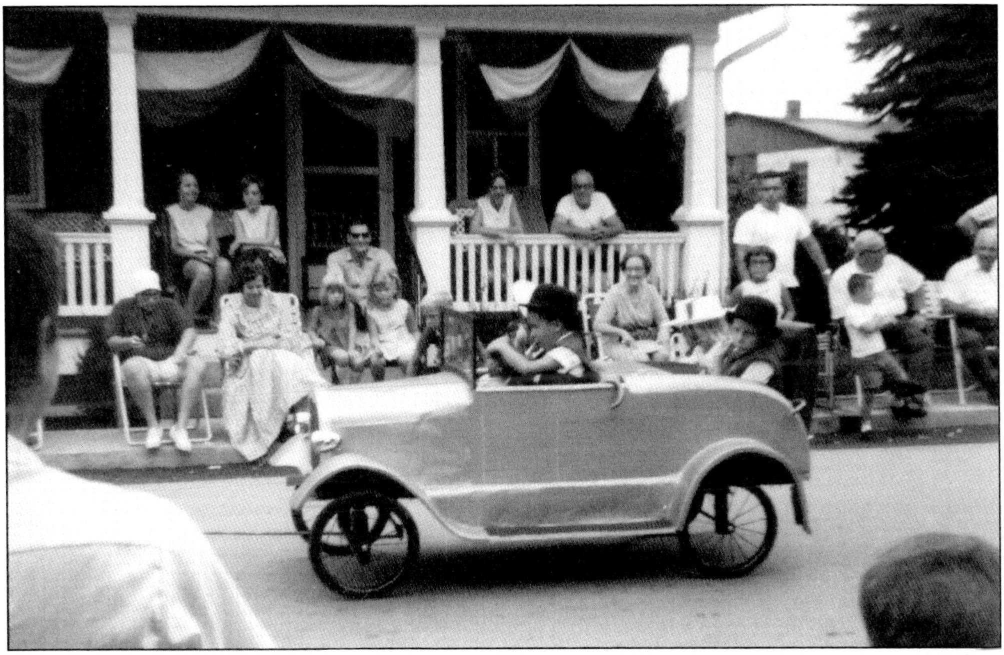

Robert Clemens Jr. and Yolanda Clemens (hidden), the children of Robert Clemens Sr. and Sylvia (Fair) Clemens, are in the front seat of a car built by their father. In the rumble seat are David Kreps, son of Mabel and Thurlow Kreps, and Tammy Fair Lawson, daughter of Richard and Lois (Klinefelter) Kreps. The car is being towed in a parade. (Clara Shearer.)

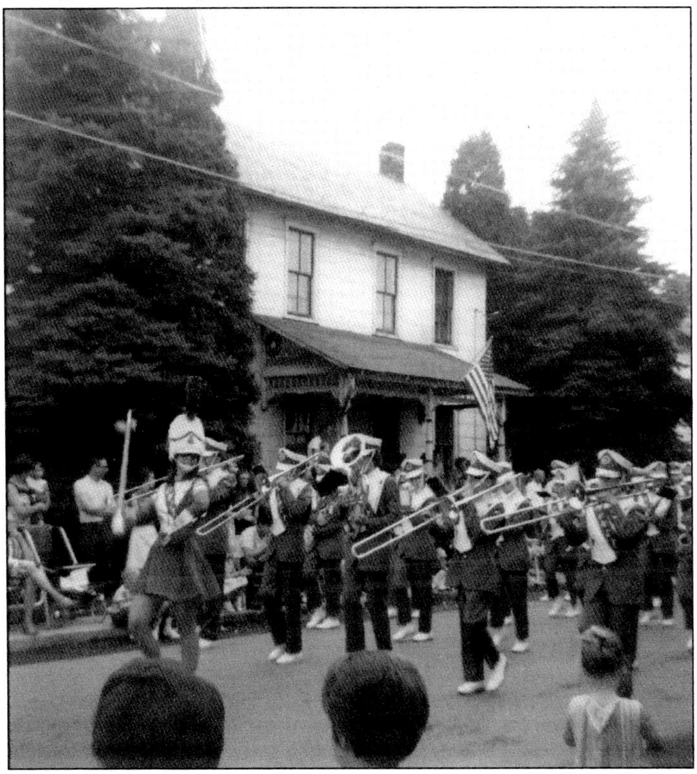

Muncy High School's marching band participated in New Columbia's Sesquicentennial Parade in August 1968 along with Beavertown's Drum and Bugle Corps, Lewistown's Sweetheart Drum and Bugle Corps, Mifflinburg High School's band, Milton's Commanchero Drum and Bugle Corps, Milton High School's band, Mount Carmel High School's Mounties sponsored by Snyder's Hoagie Shop, the Sunbury City Band, and Warrior Run High School's band. (Clara Shearer.)

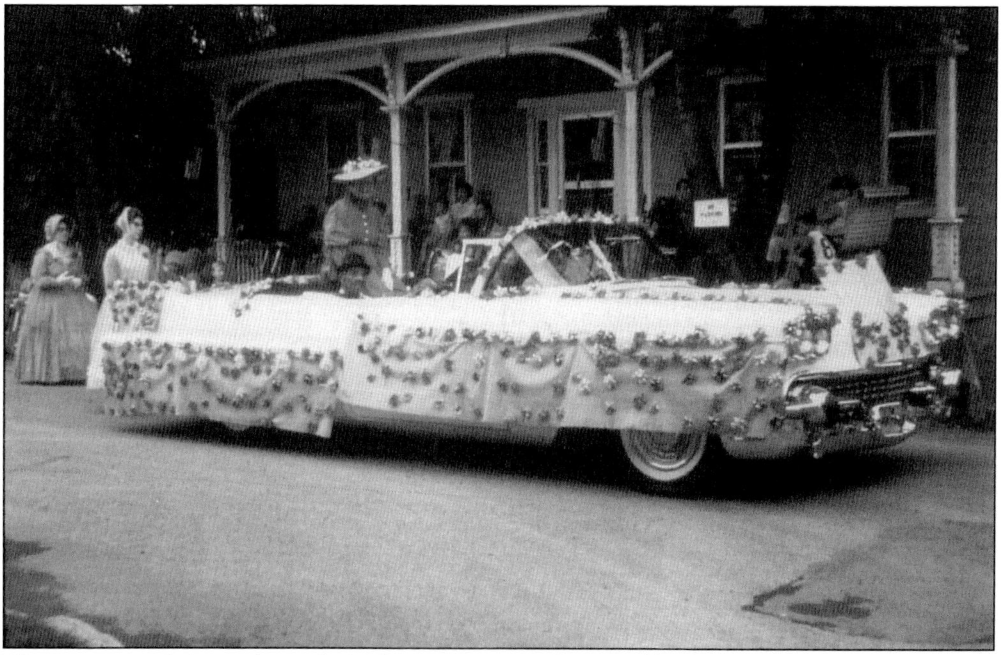

The car pictured above, driven by Nelson Keiser, was decorated by the Turbotville Fire Auxiliary. The Hans sisters are walking behind it while Jessie Reynolds, who was 62 at the time, sits in the backseat wearing her 1959 Turbotville Centennial dress. Elma Corderman is sitting to Jessie's right. In the photograph below, Susan Robinson, Miss Pennsylvania 1968, is among the distinguished guests at the event. (Both, Sherry Wolf.)

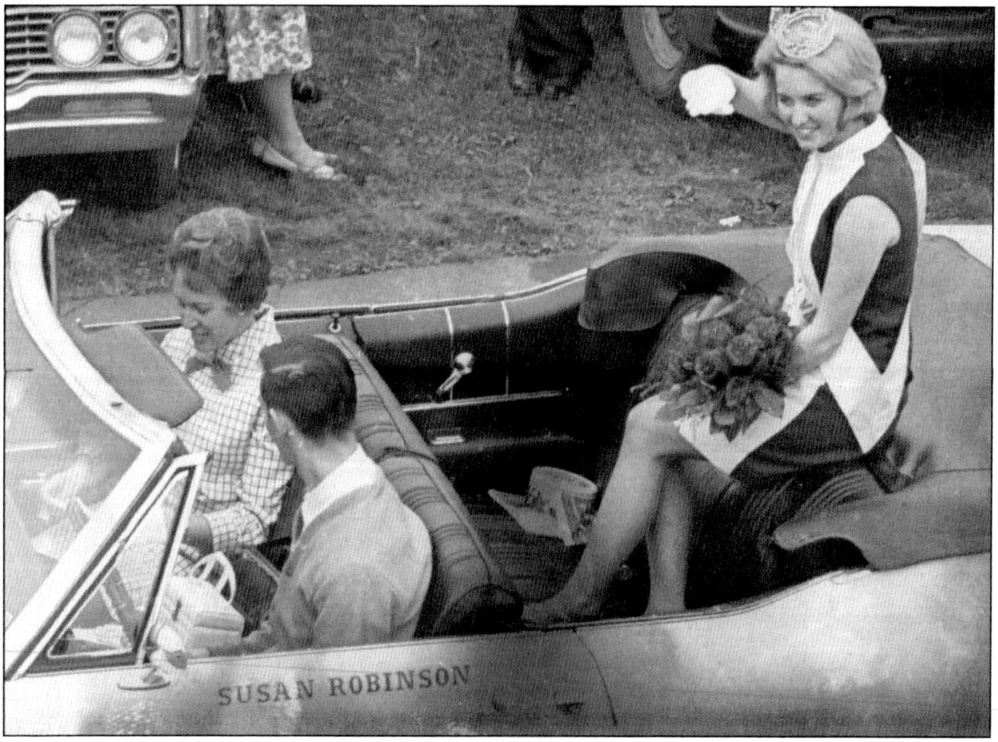

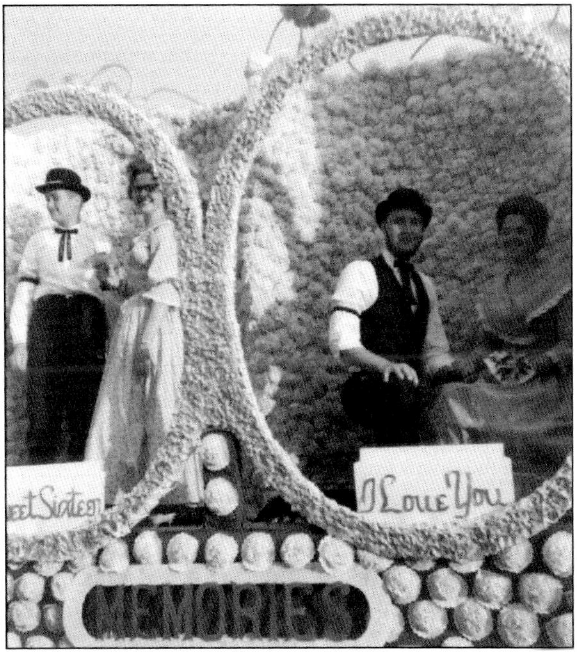

Pictured from left to right, Dave Shearer, Kay Ocker, and Van and Mary Marks ride on a float in New Columbia's Sesquicentennial Parade. Below, the Brothers of the Brush, or the "New Columbia Settlers," had a float that read, "Beautify America—Get a Haircut." The Brothers of the Brush were William Hause, Van Marks, Allen Pick, Davis Shearer, Allen Dershem, Annson Dershem, Roy Witmer Sr. and Jr., Dan Witmer, Jasper Ocker Sr. and Jr., John Snyder, William Shearer, Richard Starks, Kenneth Heywood, L.B. Snyder, William Derr, Clarence Billman, Charles Reynolds, Richard Winter, John Reichard, James Wilt, Richard Binder, Frank Yost, Richard Smith, Venin Yost, Barry Berger, Charles Beck, Harry Ross, Maynard Lahr, Wayne Starr, Dan, James, and David Snyder. (Both, Clara Shearer.)

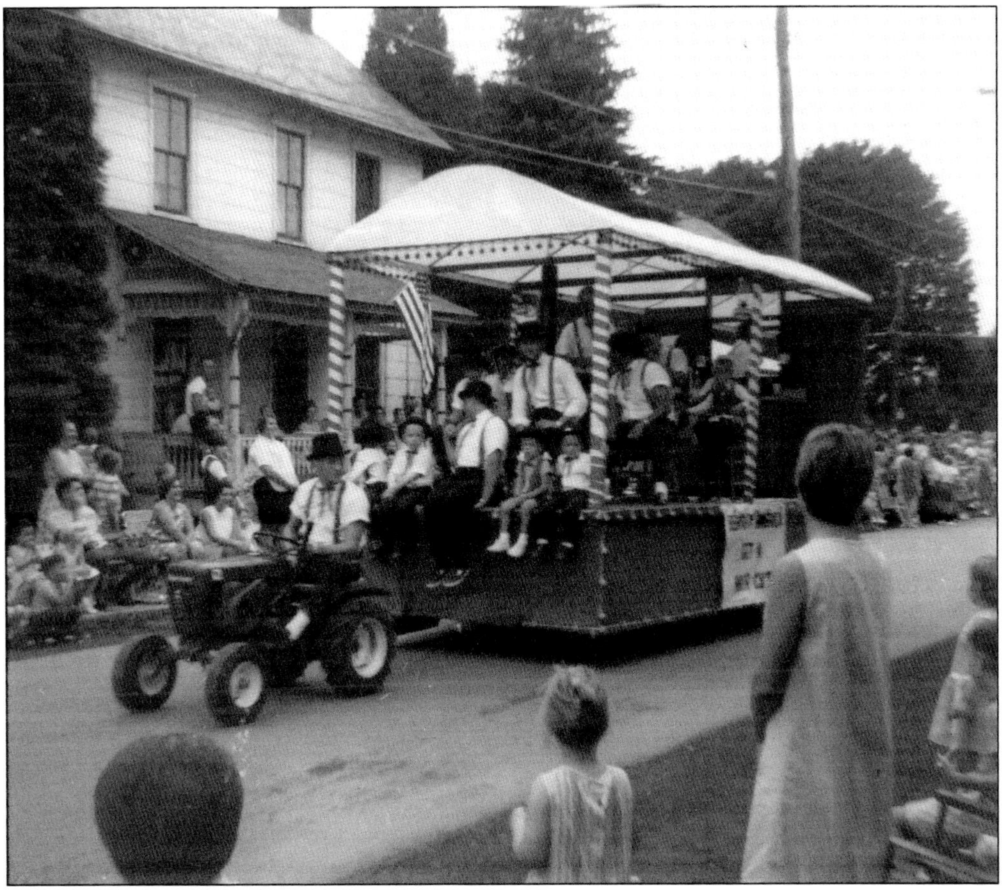

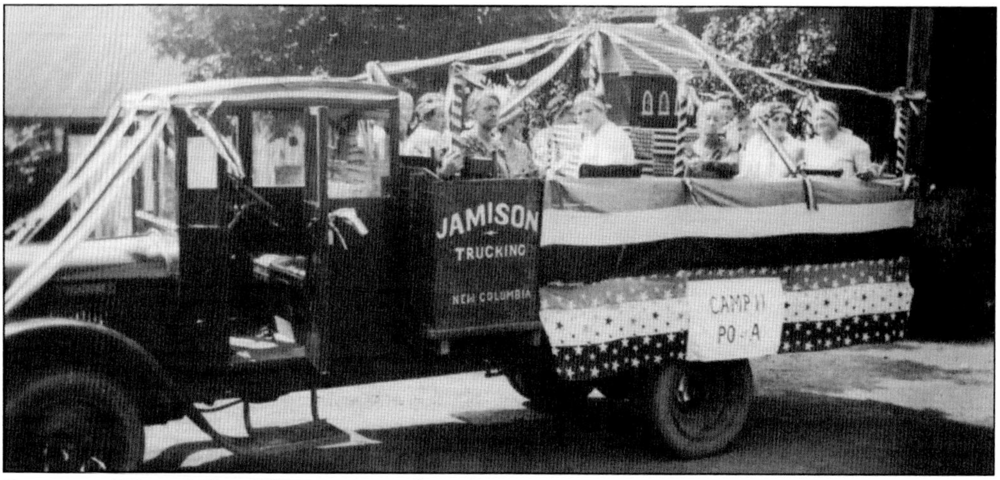

Sitting on Edward "Jinx" Jamison's truck at the sesquicentennial parade are, from left to right, Millie Fisher, Pauline (Mutchler) Prowant, "Little" Corey Neese, Grace Shearer, and Bessie (Foresman) Clemens. Jamison (born 1871) owned several vehicle garages in New Columbia and, with his son Clarence, operated a bus line from Milton to Danville. (Clara Shearer.)

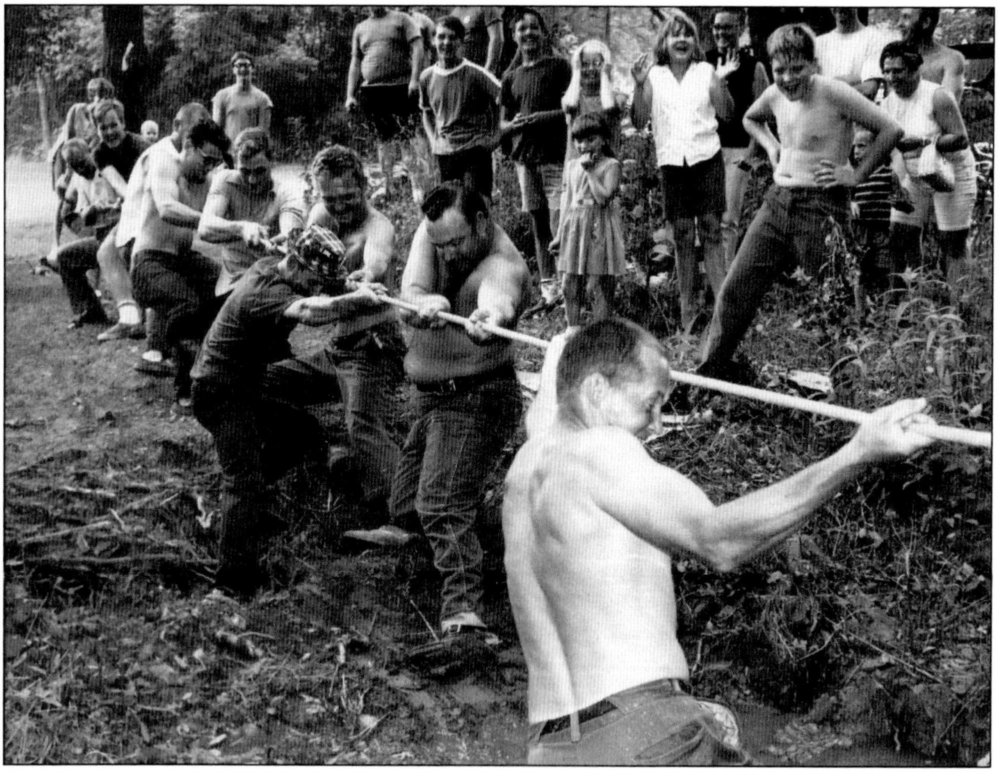

The sesquicentennial featured a tug-of-war contest across Dog Run, behind the River Road home currently owned by Betty Shemory. Pictured pulling the rope, from front to back, are Dick Smith (foreground), Ken Haywood, two unidentified, Mark Noll, two unidentified, and Dave Shearer. Spectators watching include Cheryl (Cawley) Rheppard, Don Shearer, Tina Haywood, Mrs. Ken Haywood, and Jack Ocker. These men pulled against the fire company men, who won the contest. (Clara Shearer.)

This three-generation picture, taken outside their home at 521 New Columbia Road, includes John Clemens (1848–1929), standing; William Agustus Clemens (1876–1958), kneeling; and young William Ned Clemens (1922–1994). The 20-foot-square house was a 1916 New Eden Aladdin Readi-Cut purchased for $596.60. The framing came by rail from Chicago and was erected by William Agustus with help from his father, John, a carpenter and sawyer. (Bill Clemens.)

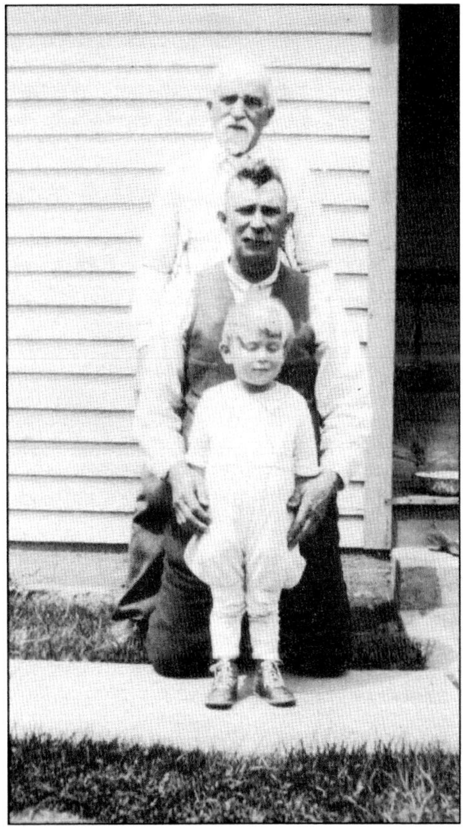

In 1917, the Hoffman Reunion (mislabeled Huffman), like others in Union County, often brought three and sometimes four generations together. In the last row are percussion and brass instrument musicians who were either family members or paid performers. Identified are the couple in the front center, John and Sarah (Hoffman) Foresman, and to their right are Lydia (Hoffman) Shaffer, unidentified, and Hester Hoffman. Directly behind Sarah is William Agustus Clemens and to his right is Bessie (Foresman) Clemens. (Bill Clemens.)

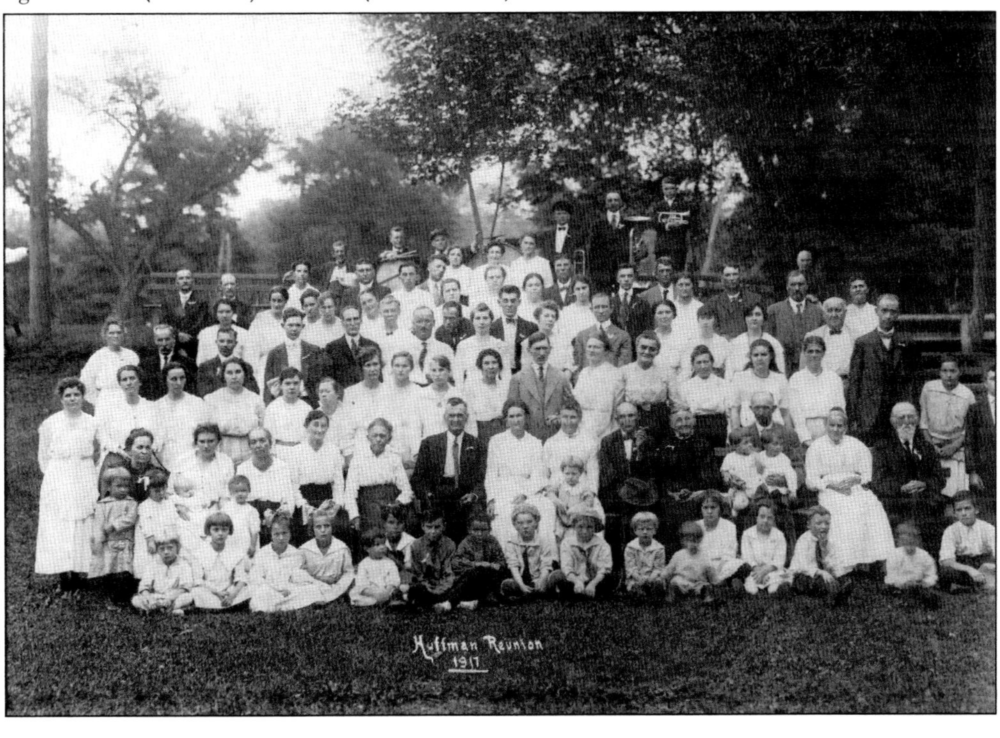

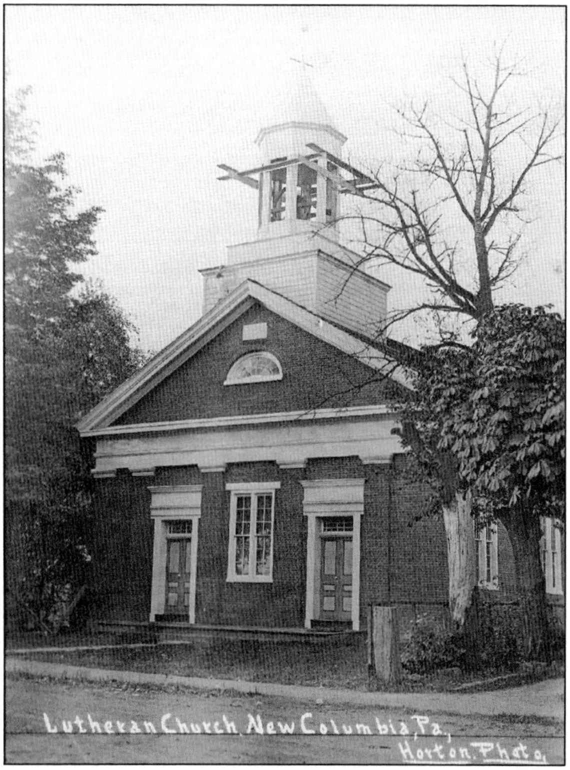

New Columbia's Lutheran church, first located on Main Street around 1843, is photographed here while undergoing repair or painting of its steeple around 1908 to 1911. The church building recently sold and was renamed the Spanish Mennonite Church. (UCHS 92.9.89.54)

Pictured in a cabinet photograph from the early 1900s is the Gleaners Sunday School Class of the Trinity United Evangelical Church. From left to right are (first row) Geraldine Lagerman, Florence Bennage, Ethel Tanner, and Etha Hoffman; (second row) Pauline Prowant, Nell Jows, Grace Prowant, Mae Stewart, Viola Baylor, and Prudence Foresman; (third row) Lois Lagerman, Rita Tanner, Leah Delaney, Millie Fisher, Marguerite Ranck, and Hazel Fisher. (Jean Showers.)

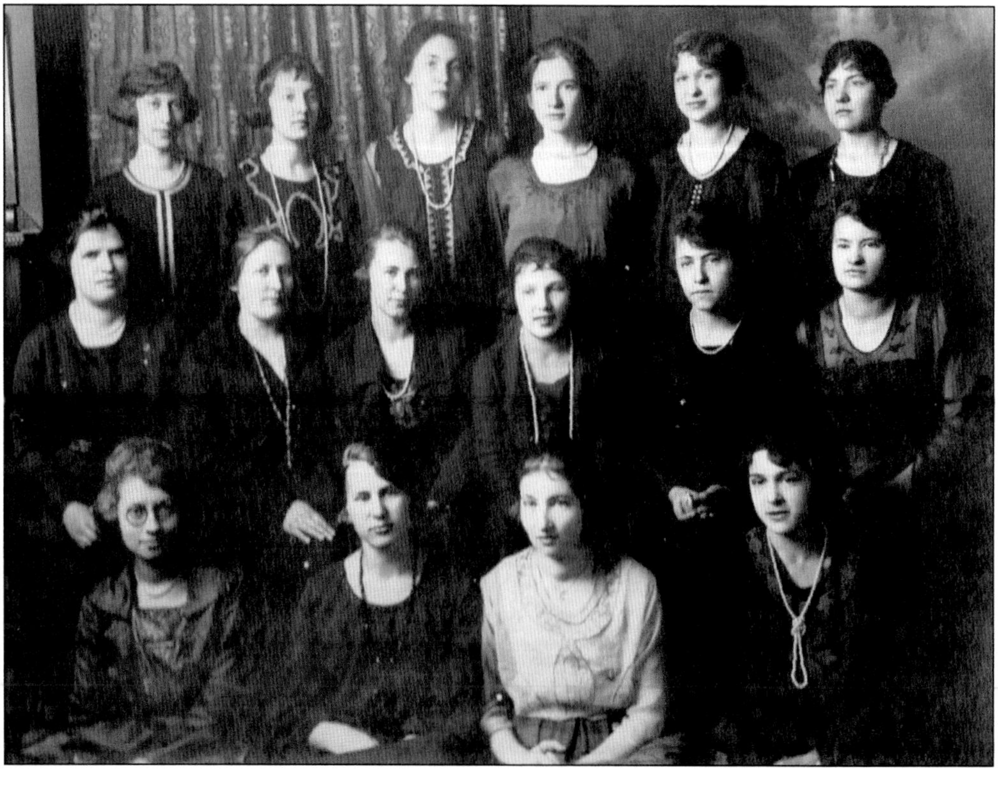

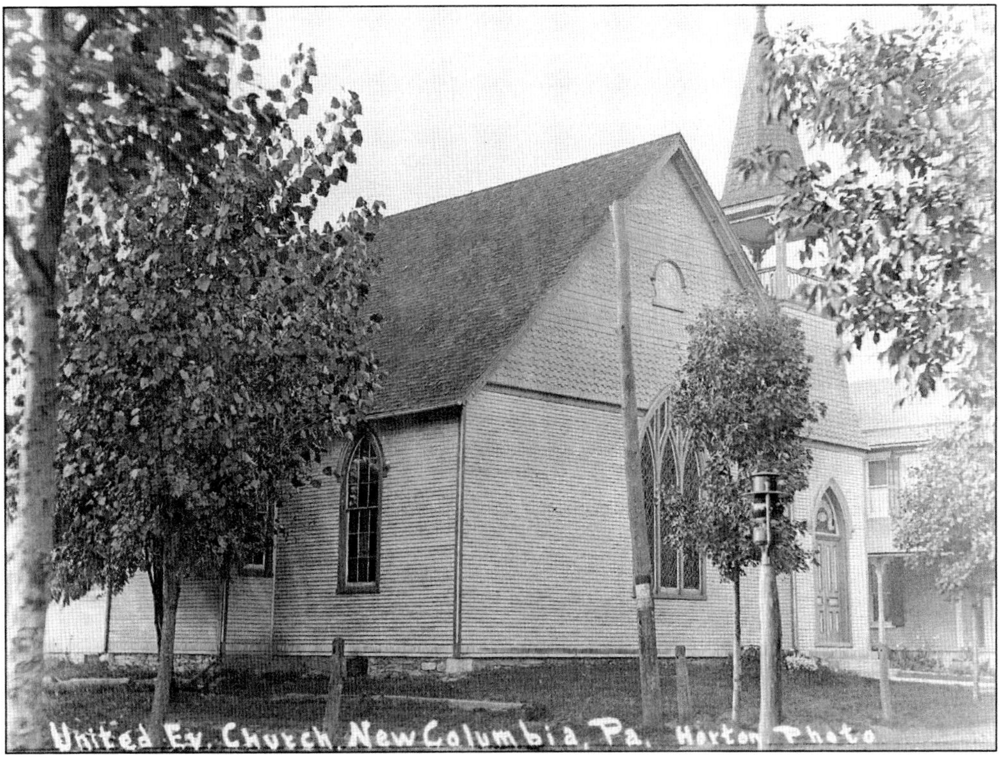

The Trinity United Evangelical Church on Third Street was built of wood in 1896 and was remodeled with brick veneer in 1927. West Milton photographer Stephen Horton illustrated its earlier exterior and interior in real-photo postcards in 1908. The postcard below of the interior notes that at age 10, Hazel Hile was baptized by Rev. H.C. Guthrie. In 1946, the church's denomination merged with the Church of the United Brethren in Christ, becoming the Evangelical United Brethren Church. In 1969, it became part of the United Methodist Church. (Above, UCHS 92.9 89.55; below, Patricia Longley.)

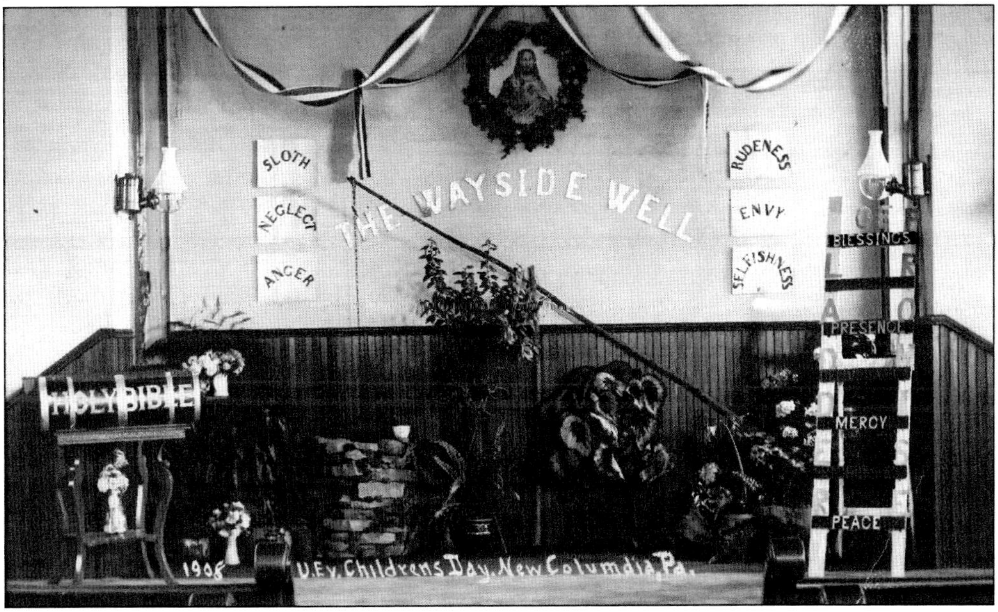

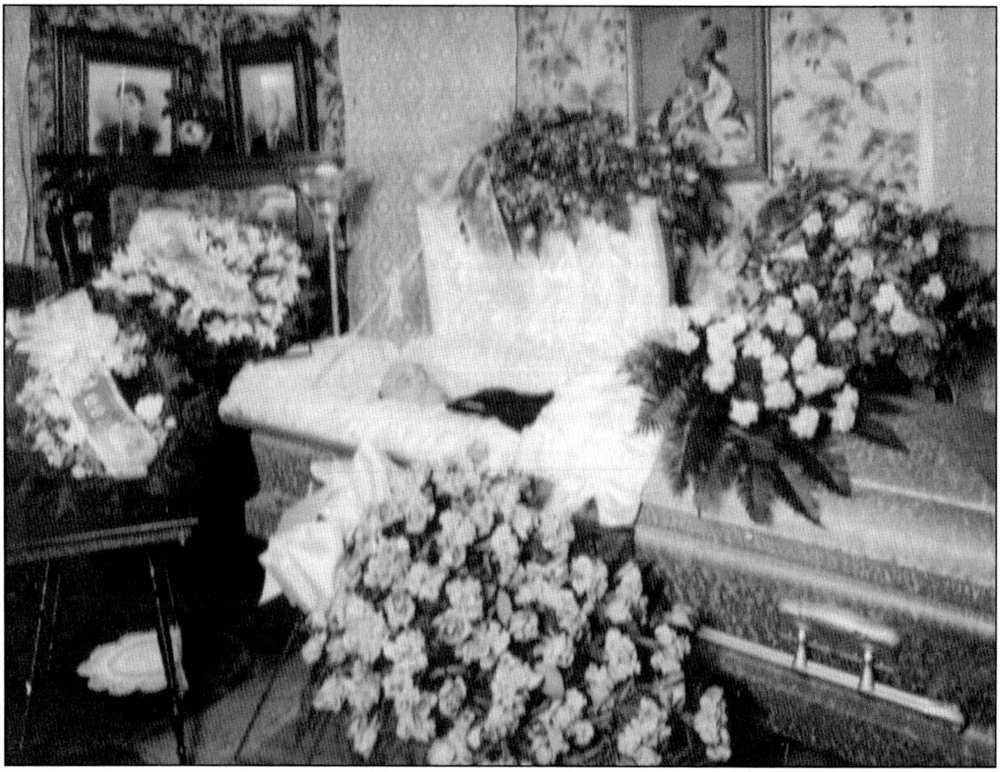

Allen "Doc" Erb's viewing celebrated his life (1867–1935) in his home at 162 Fourth Street. Erb had been the railroad section crew foreman, working at the small building located on New Columbia's Main Street, which the railroad tracks entered. The Highland Cemetery of New Columbia was founded by the John Jefferson Ranck family around 1887 and is seen below in a real-photo postcard around 1908. (Above, Minnie Troxel Koch; below; UCHS, 83.35.8.)

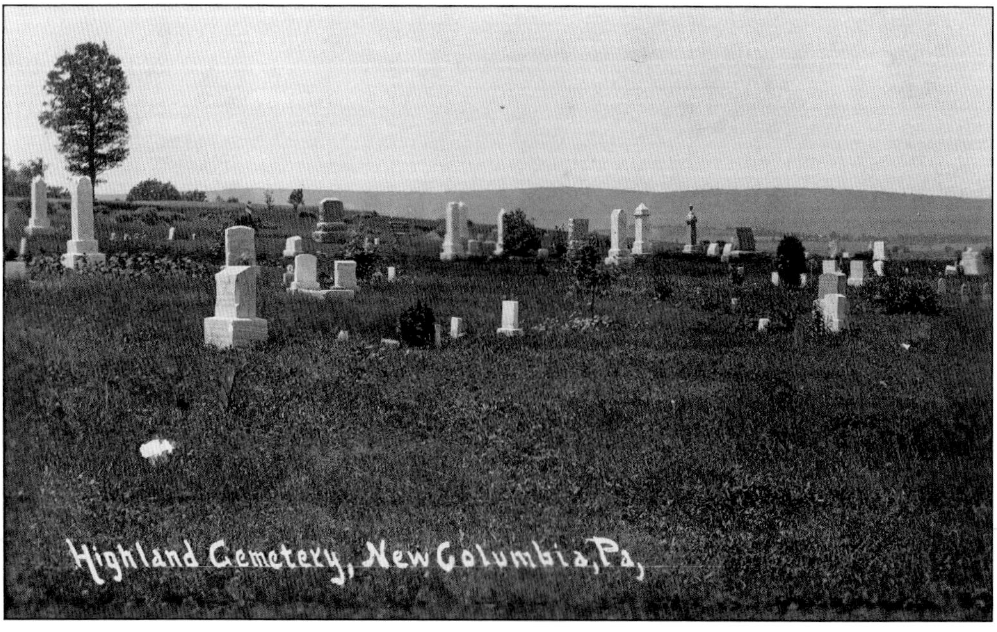

Four

West Milton and Central Oak Heights

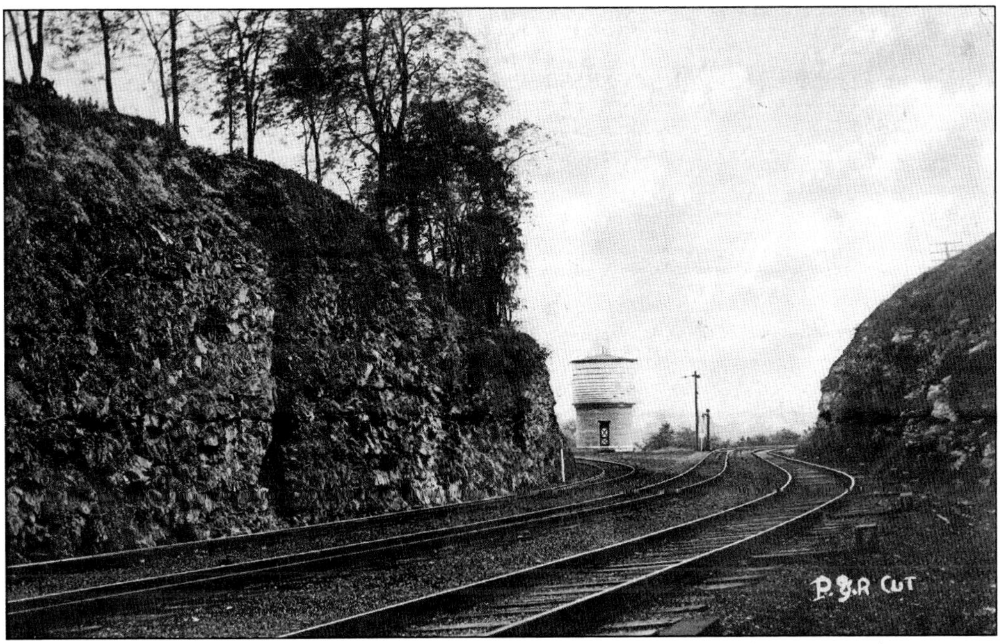

P&R stands for the Philadelphia and Reading Railroad. Since West Milton was at the junction of two Reading lines—the Catawissa-Danville-Milton-West Milton line and the Shamokin-Sunbury-Winfield-Lewisburg-West Milton line—it was a strategic location for the western end of the Reading Railroad. At the cut, the tracks seen here on the left went over the steel railroad bridge to Milton. This area was a stopping point for hobos. (UCHS 94.5.10.)

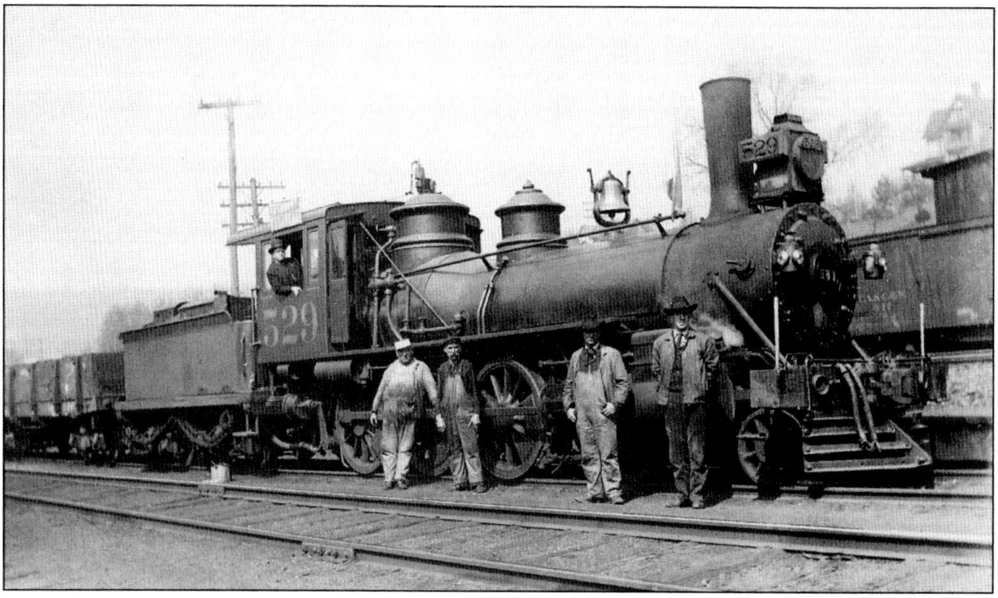

From 1901 to 1940, West Milton was a bustling railroad town with about 75 men employed as train gangs, yardmen, coal dock men, airmen, oilers, and telegraphers. This West Milton crew stands beside its train in 1906 as it stopped in Montgomery. Pictured from left to right (by last name only) are conductor Barrett, engineer Sedler, fireman Arssno, flagman W. Smith, and brakeman Kreisher. A rare interior photograph of a West Milton train crew in a work car around 1920 shows New Columbia resident William Agustus Clemens on the far left. He started working for the railroad by 1900, when he was a car shop laborer at age 23. Clemens became a fireman in 1910 and then was a steam railroad laborer from 1920 to 1930, when he was 53. (Above, UCHS 91.40.7; below, Bill Clemens.)

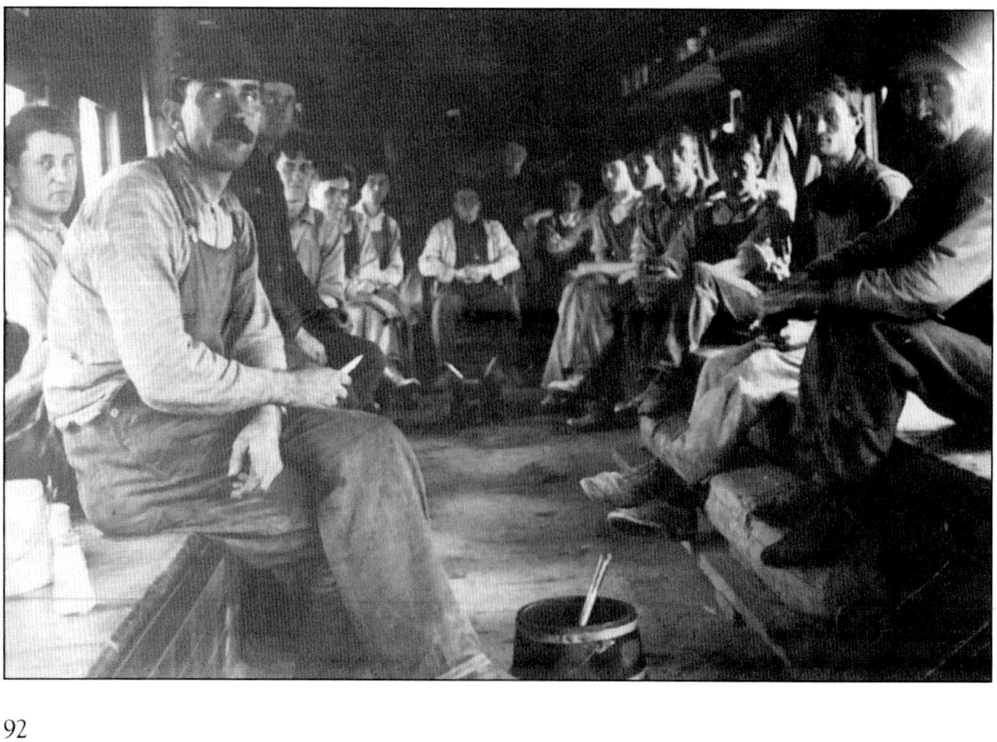

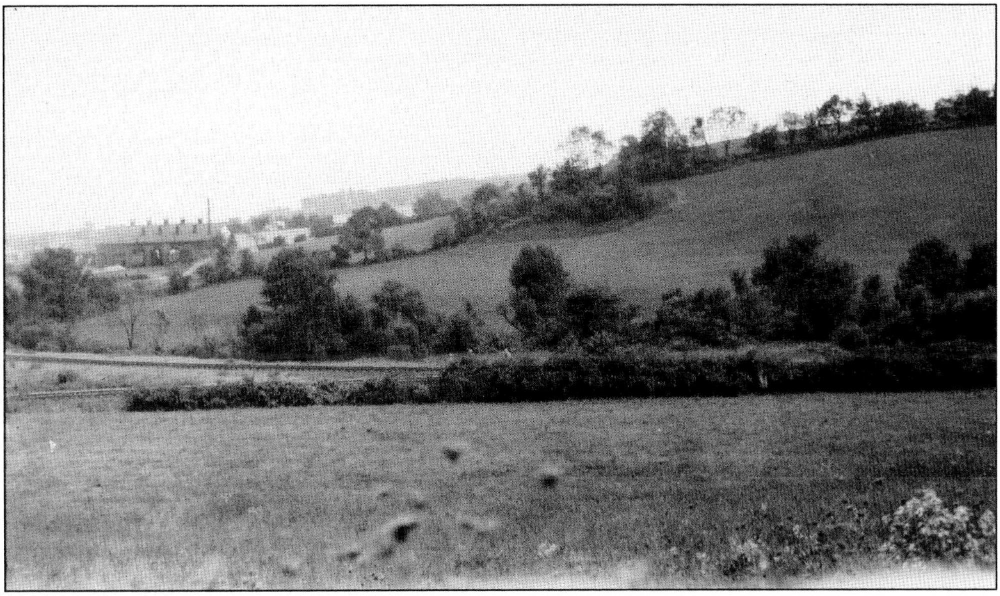

This view of "the Y" was taken at a vantage point on farmland looking over Old Route 15 and toward the large brick roundhouse just north of West Milton. The engines did not actually turn at or in the building, but rather used the Y to allow cars to go west on a track, back up, and then change engines. An average of 17 to 19 passenger trains, in addition to freight trains, were serviced each day at the roundhouse. Below is one of several real-photo postcards by Stephen B. Horton photographed between 1908 and 1911. (Above, UCHS 91.5.7; below, Ronald Nornhold)

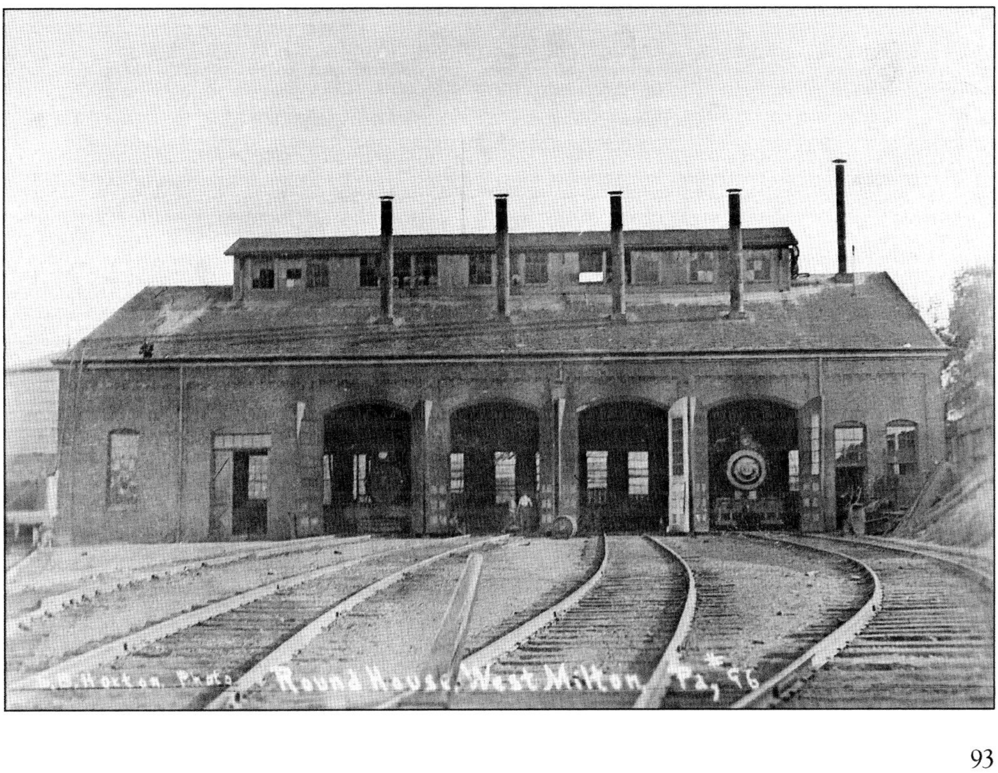

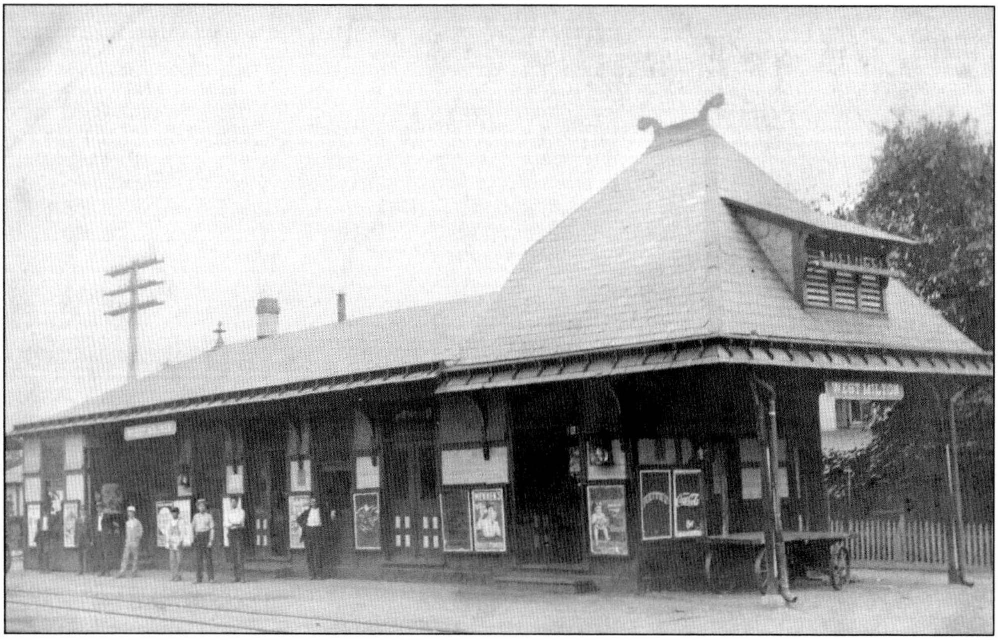

The passenger train station at West Milton is shown prior to 1907 (above). Notice the station's many corbels and interesting advertising posters for Bank's Business College, Acker's Bon Bons, Mennen's Toilet Powder, and Coca-Cola. The real-photo postcard below encompasses a larger landscape: the railroad tower to the west and an arriving steam locomotive. A watchman's shanty was also located at the station, since there were no gates or electrical signals at first. Mary Strine's father manned the position of watchman for many years. (Both UCHS 86.3.17 and 2007.14.1.)

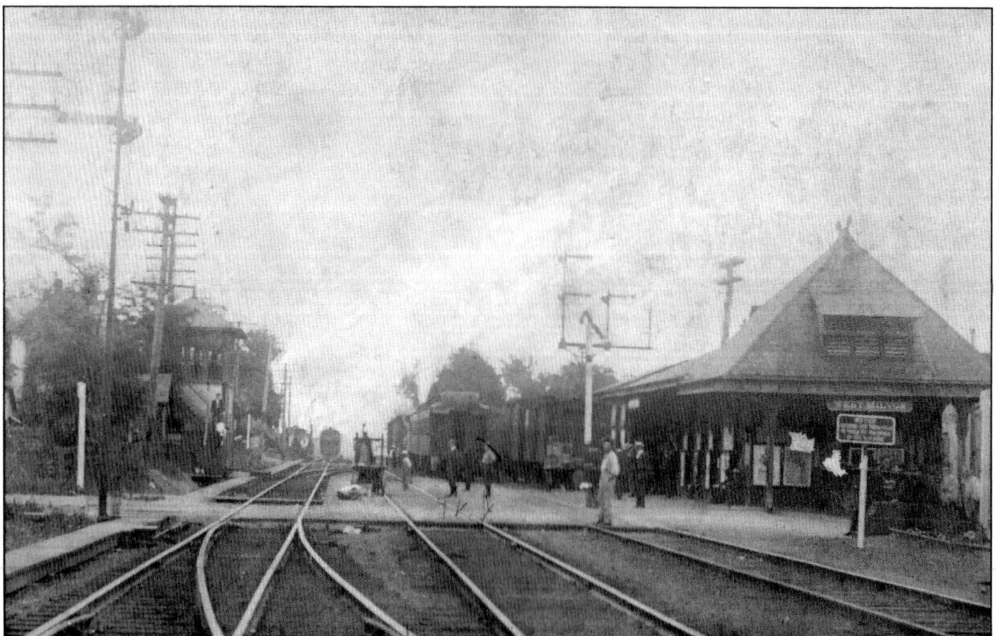

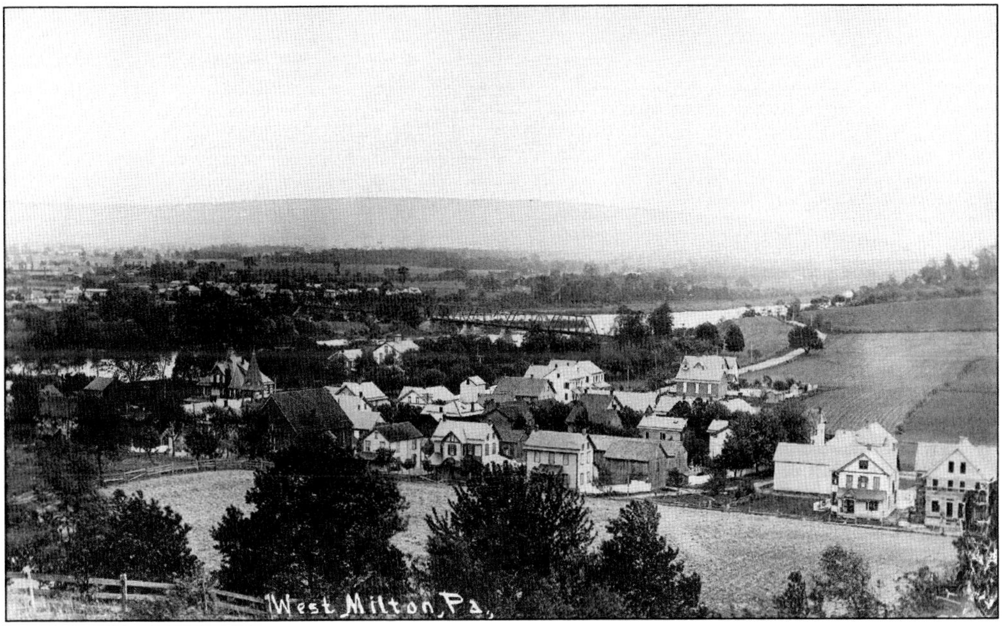

This bird's-eye view taken from the hill north of town encompasses buildings that reflect the architectural styles prevalent when Datesman's Station was renamed West Milton in the early 1900s. The railroad was the heart of the village for more than a generation. The Great Depression, then diesel engines, interstate trucking, and the addition of a new Route 15—built through the center of town—brought significant changes. The high ground on the far right was called Shikellamy's lookout, named for the Oneida chief who lived nearby in the mid-18th century. Below, West Milton and the Susquehanna River were photographed by John Swanger, who issued single- and double-width, black, and color lithographic postcards in 1919. The water tower just south of West Milton is seen at the junction of the Catawissa and Shamokin lines. (Above, UCHS 98.40.10; below, Alan Richard.)

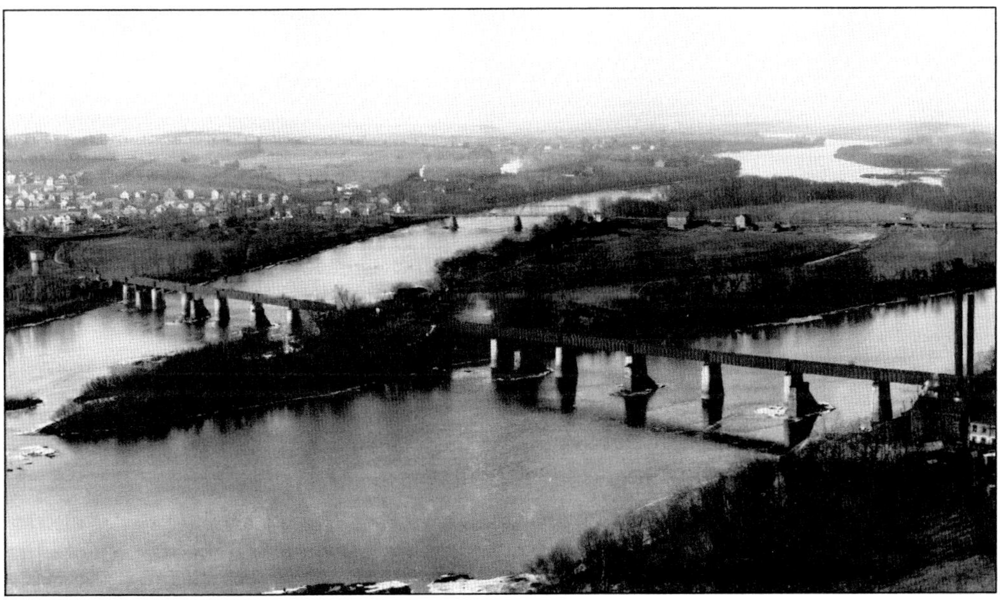

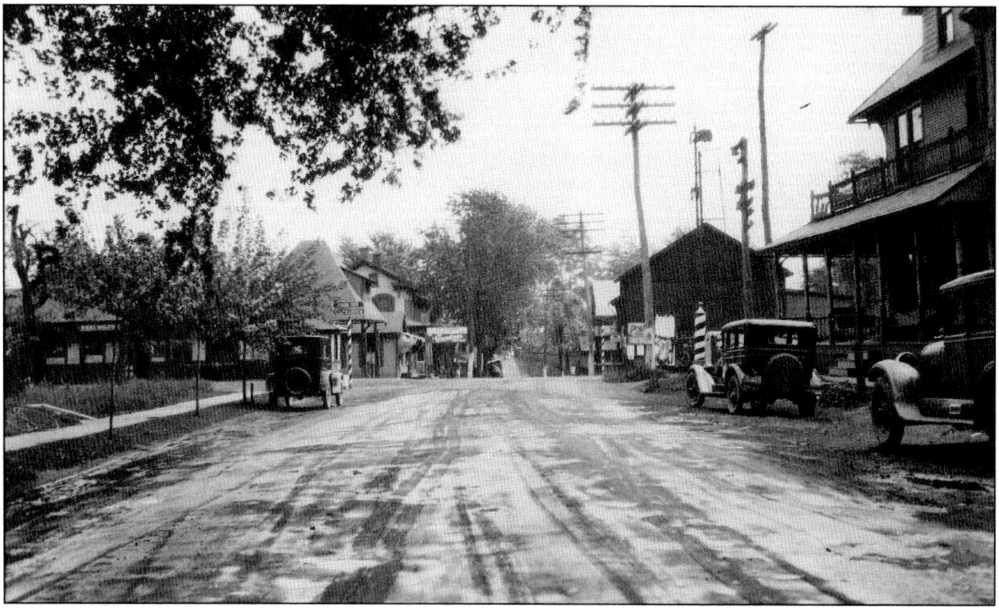

Looking east toward the bridge and Milton in September 1928, the photograph above shows a dirt Broad Street and the block beyond the railroad tracks. What remained of the block was demolished after the 1972 flood, with the exception of the hotel just before the tracks. The lodging was left to Bertha Keiser by A.E. and Benjamin Franklin Keiser. In the image below, looking left from the first block west of the bridge are a brick ice cream parlor, a wooden structure named Snyder's Confectionery Restaurant that later became a restaurant belonging to Al Moyer, then the railroad station, tracks, watchman's shanty, and John Pawling's home. The lower left shows the town's first hardware store, which was later made into apartments. The nearby barn was Larro Feed that later became a coal office and yard. (Both, UCHS 91.5.12 and 91.5.10.)

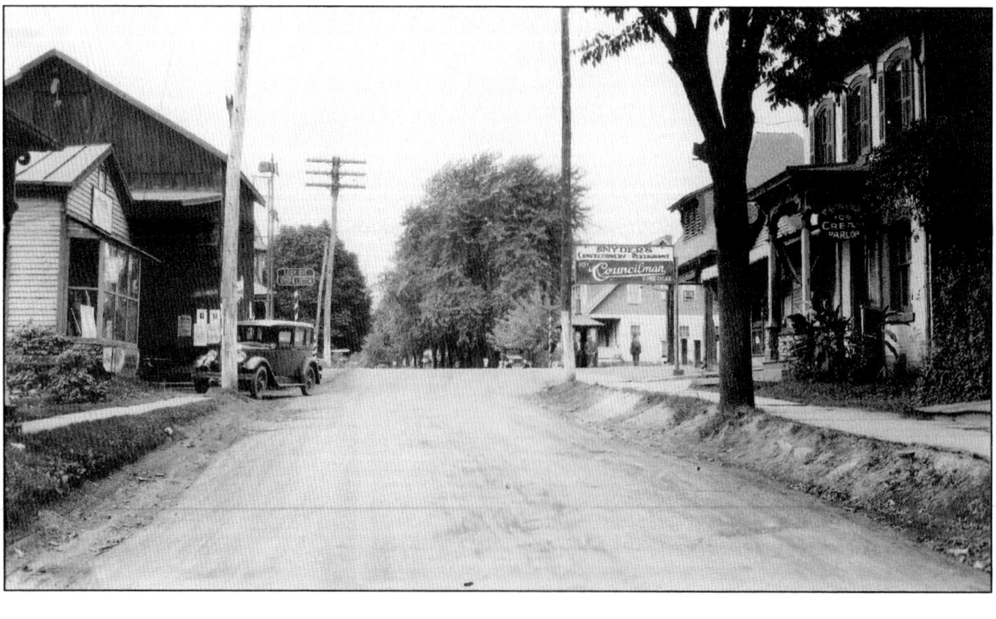

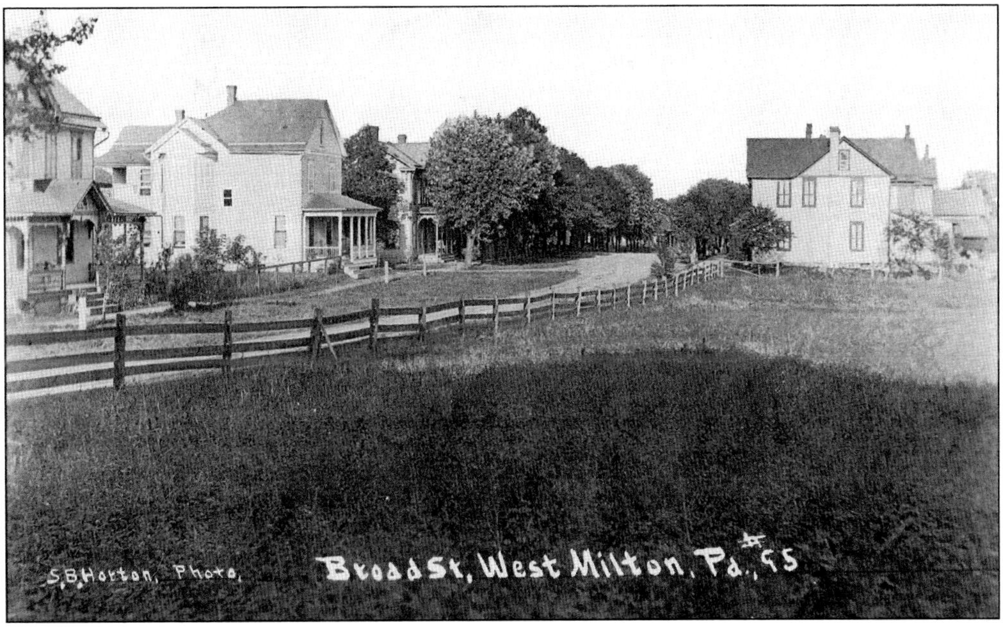

This 1908 postcard captures bucolic Broad Street, an area that saw many changes in the late 1950s, when several frame houses were demolished for the building of a new Route 15. Farther west is the parsonage for the Lutheran church of the "Twin Churches." It sits next to the Route 15 overpass. On the right is presumably the Kling farm, now the site of six brick buildings. (UCHS 2006.65.2.)

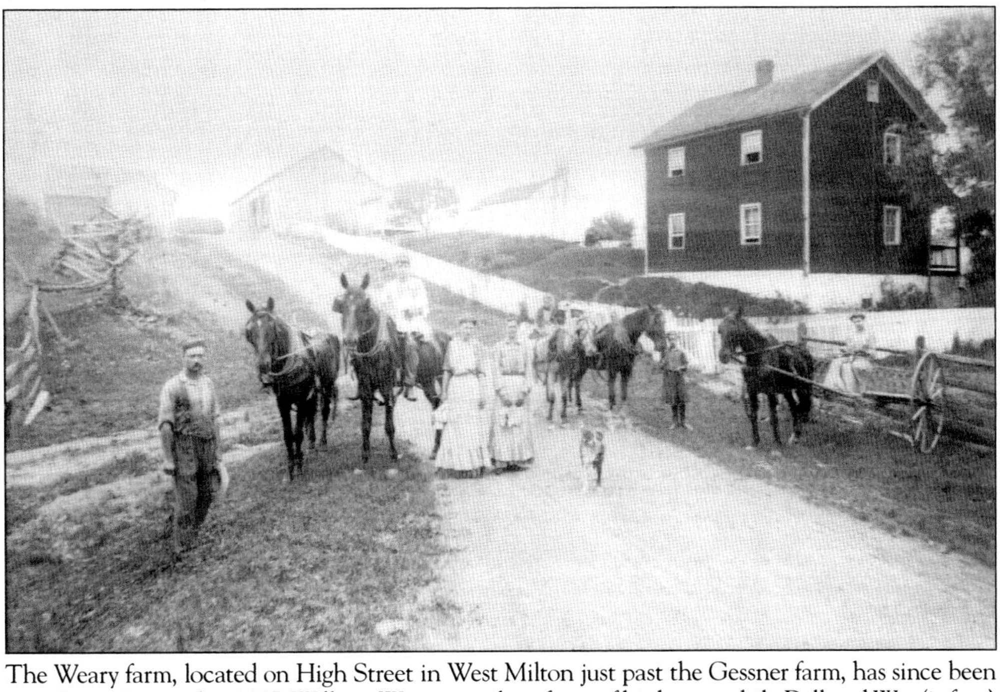

The Weary farm, located on High Street in West Milton just past the Gessner farm, has since been torn down. Pictured in 1907, William Weary stands in front of his horses while Dell and Wes (infant) Adams sit in the saddle. From left to right, Nora Adams and Annie Weary stand while Faye Weary is on horseback and Alma Snyder stands nearby. Martha Weary sits on the hay rake. (Doris Caris.)

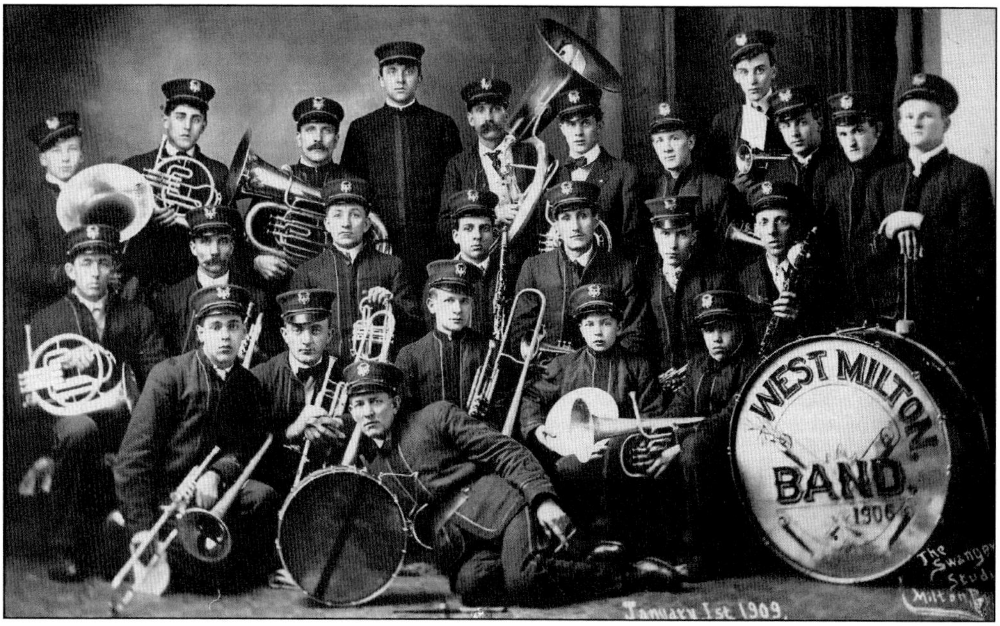

This 1909 New Year's Day photograph shows a sizeable West Milton Band. Founded in 1906, the band practiced on the second floor of Grove and Zimmerman's Well Drilling establishment located behind what became Byerly's Meat Market and later in what became the Byerlys' warehouse after the drilling business closed. In the 1920s, a band called West Milton's Little German Band was formed. (UCHS 2006.61.13.)

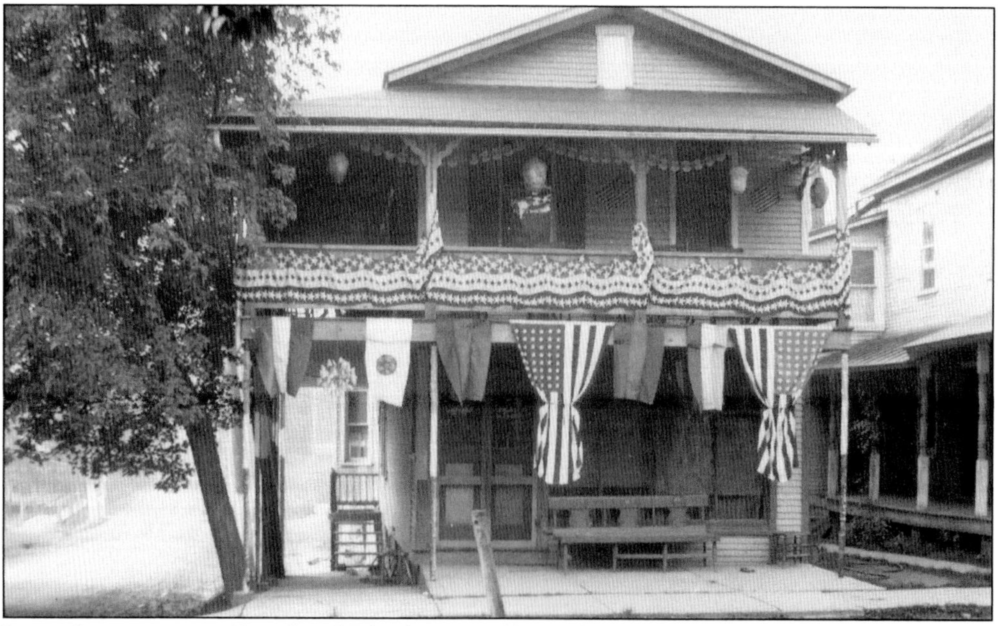

In its glory at current Broad and Third Streets (formerly Old Route 15), Byerly's Meat Market (and grocery) was a celebrated landmark for 90 years. John A. Byerly bought the lot in 1910 for the business where sons William B., Charles, and John Jr. worked, as well as grandson George N. Byerly. Now located on new Route 15 and Colonel John Kelly Road, Byerly Meats is operated by Donald and Richard Byerly. (UCHS 1990.6.3)

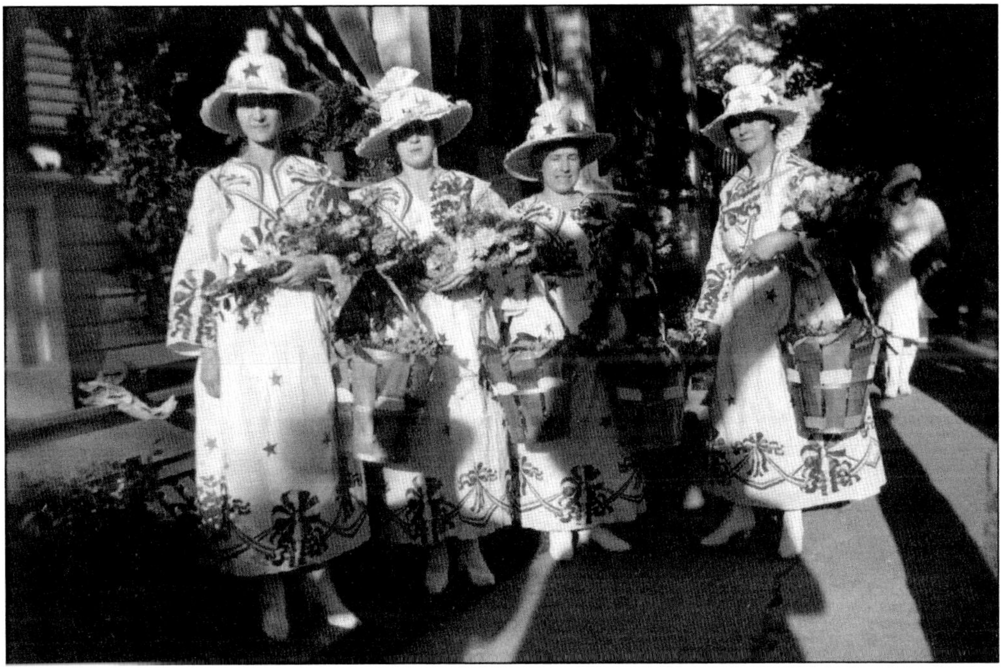

Pictured above and below, participants dress in celebratory regalia for a West Milton parade. The event must have been in the fall, as the ladies pictured above carry sprays of mums and peck baskets of flowers. (Both, UCHS 2007.14.2-.3)

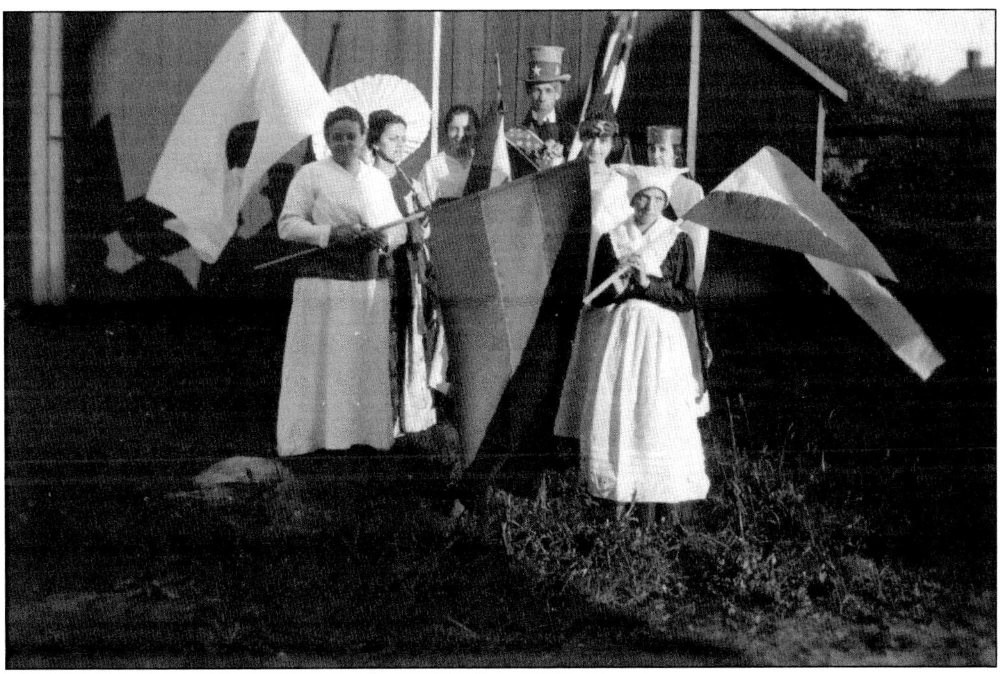

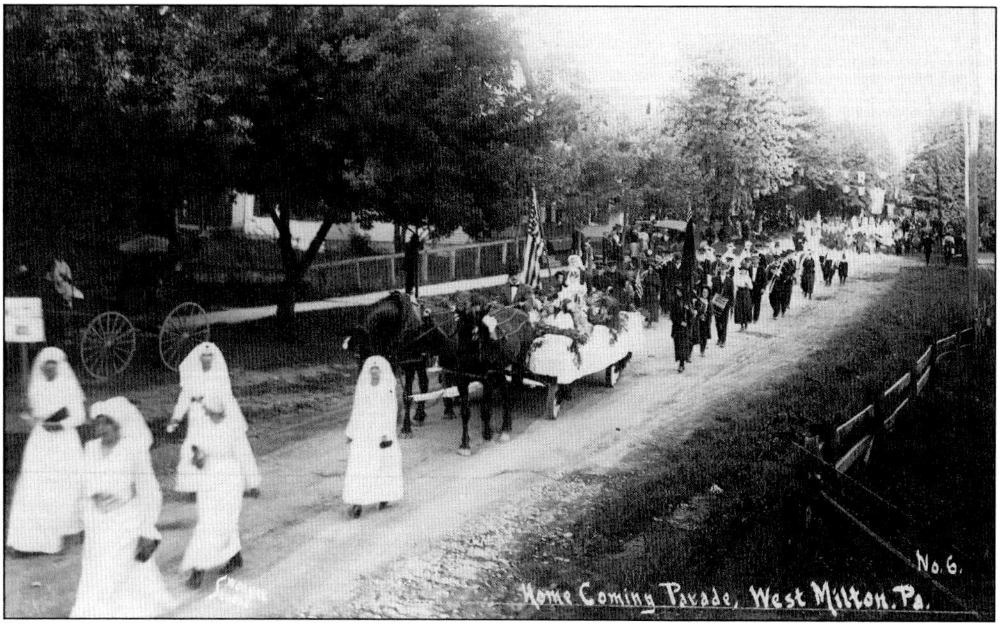

The 1919 Homecoming Parade in West Milton for World War I soldiers and nurses heads west on a then-unpaved Broad Street. The horse-drawn farm wagon float is followed by a band, then a keystone sign, and what appears to be a person dressed as the Statue of Liberty. This is the sixth in a series of real-photo postcards of the parade by Milton's Swanger Studio. (UCHS 97.1.13.)

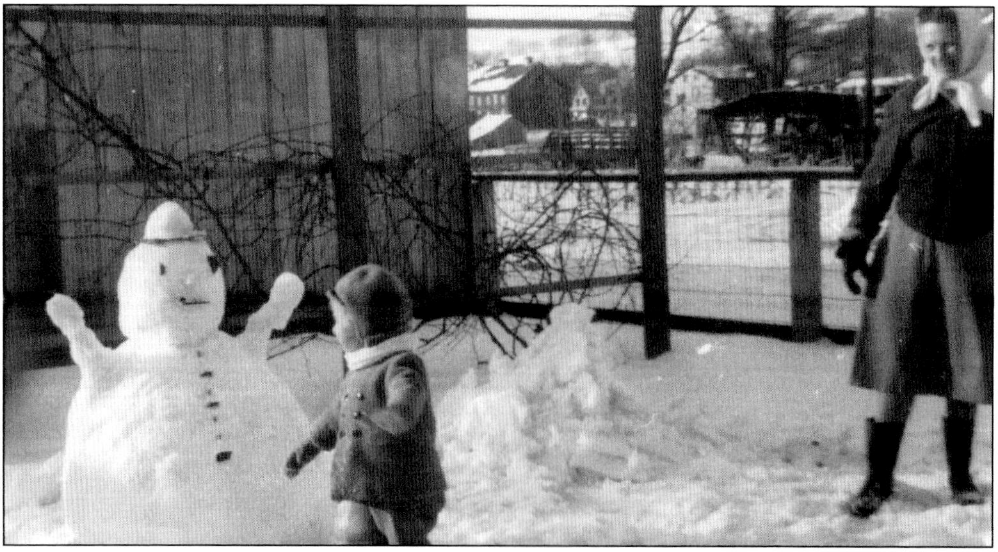

Sarah Meyers Ohl and daughter Nancy Susan Ohl celebrate the season by making a snowman in their backyard at 101 South Third Street (later Route 15) in a candid photograph from 1950. In the upper middle background is the Kling dairy barn. It no longer stands, having been razed for the ramp from West Milton to Route 15 going south. (Susan Ohl Wirth.)

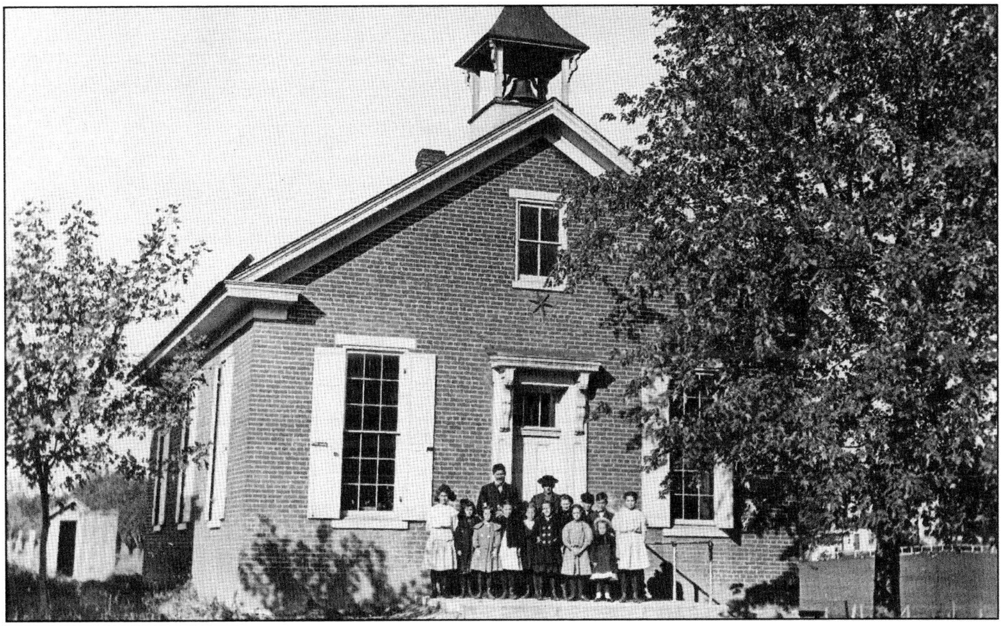

In 1892, a brick, one-room schoolhouse for grades one through eight, seen in this real-photo postcard, was constructed on a parcel from B.F. Keiser's farm. An addition in 1917 provided for another room and teacher: the north side was for grades one through four, and the south side was for grades five through eight. Below, the grammar school "A Class" has Reverend Hollenbach as a substitute teacher. Students include John Arner, first male at right in the first row, and Bright Byerly, the third male from the right in the first row. On the far left in the second row is Benjamin Bieber Schmick II. The school closed in 1957. Until 2007, the former school was owned by the Washington Camp Patriotic Sons of America No. 749. In 2008, George Zeyn Jr. (a Keiser descendant) purchased the building, which presently houses West Milton Schoolhouse Antiques. (Above, UCHS 89.59.5; below, Susan Ohl Wirth.)

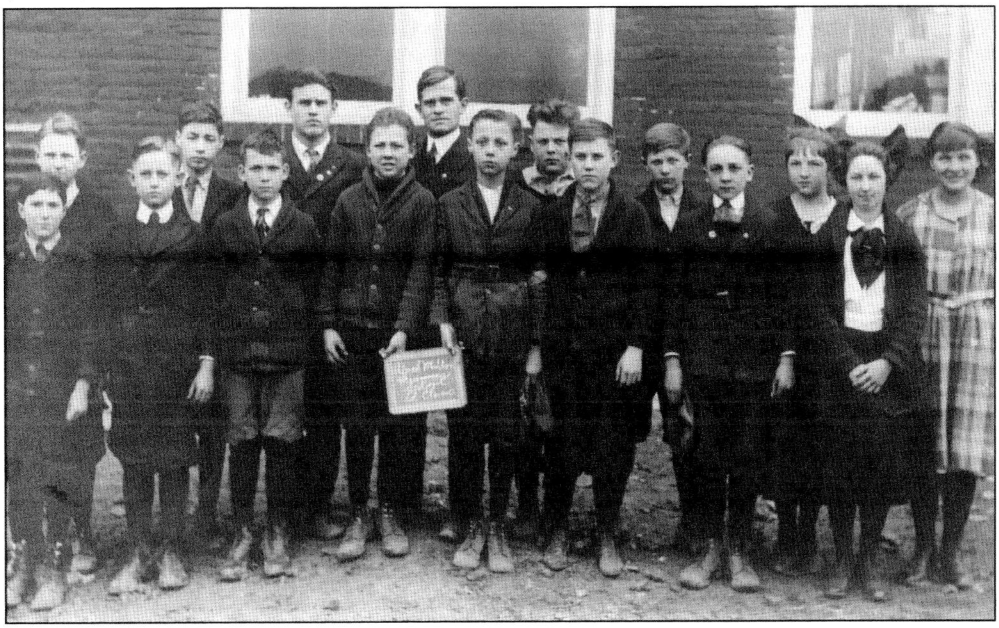

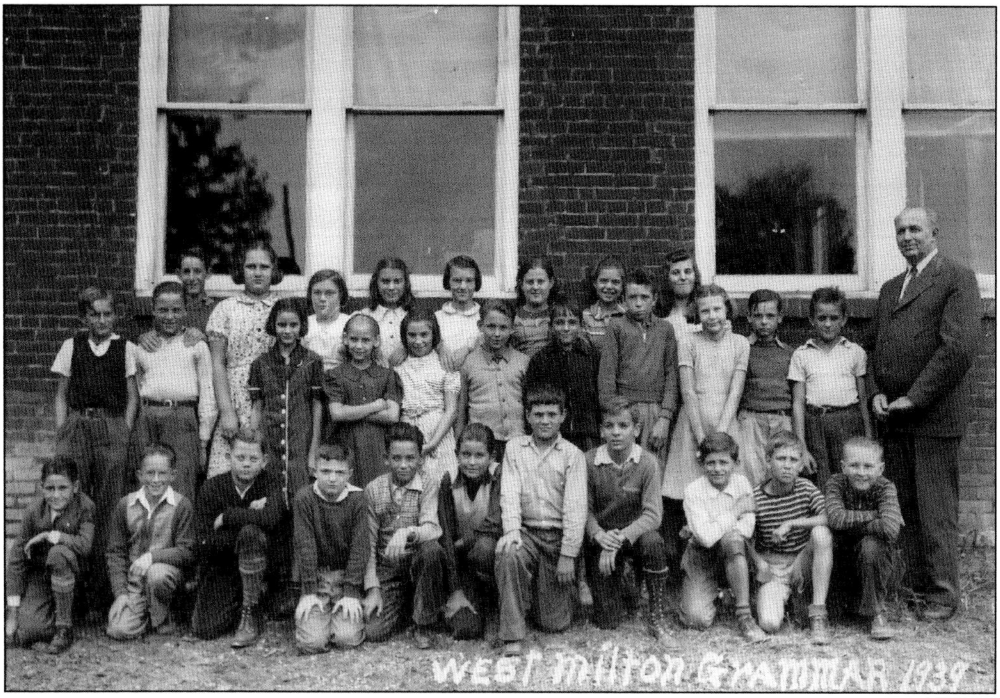

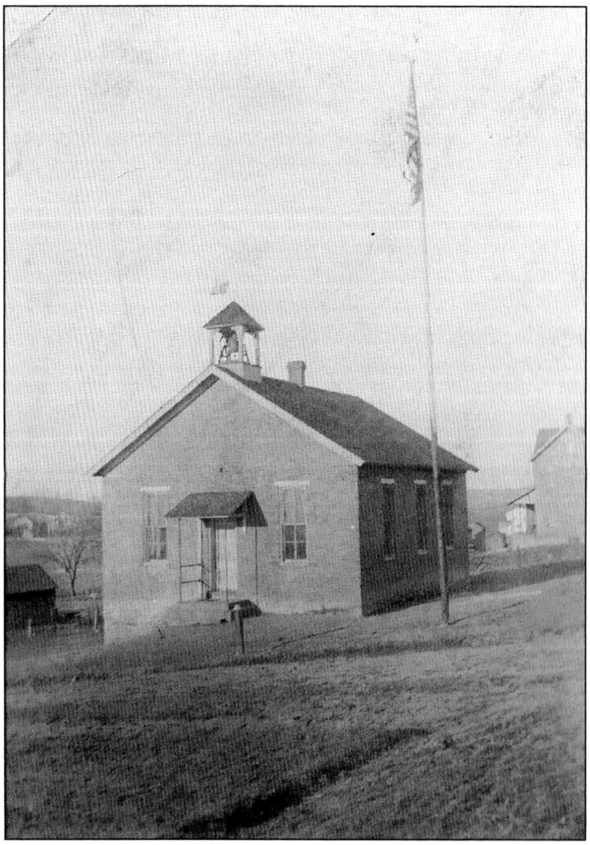

Above, teacher LeRoy Keifer poses with students. From left to right are (first row) Nicholas Mitidieri, Albert Snyder, Bert Freas, Paul Zeyn, George Byerly, Kenneth Bigger, Warren Diefenderfer, Norman Hanes, Richard Wagner, LeRoy Byers, and Dudley Vincent; (second row) Barton Wagner, Melvin Noll, Frances Campbell, Helen Poeth, Ida M. Smith, Bright Shreck, Eugene Baker, Nevin Zimmerman, Corinne Noll, Howard Bird, and Mahon Coup; (third row) John Campbell, Beatrice Edinger, Phyllis Stahl, Louise Machamer, Jean Young, Lena Shanner, Betty Tillinghast, and Gladys Gensel. Increased growth in West Milton necessitated the building of the Washington School on High Street in 1903, the last brick, one-room school approved by the White Deer Township School District. It is pictured at left in a candid real-photo postcard. (Both, UCHS 92.9.50 and 2010.1.13.)

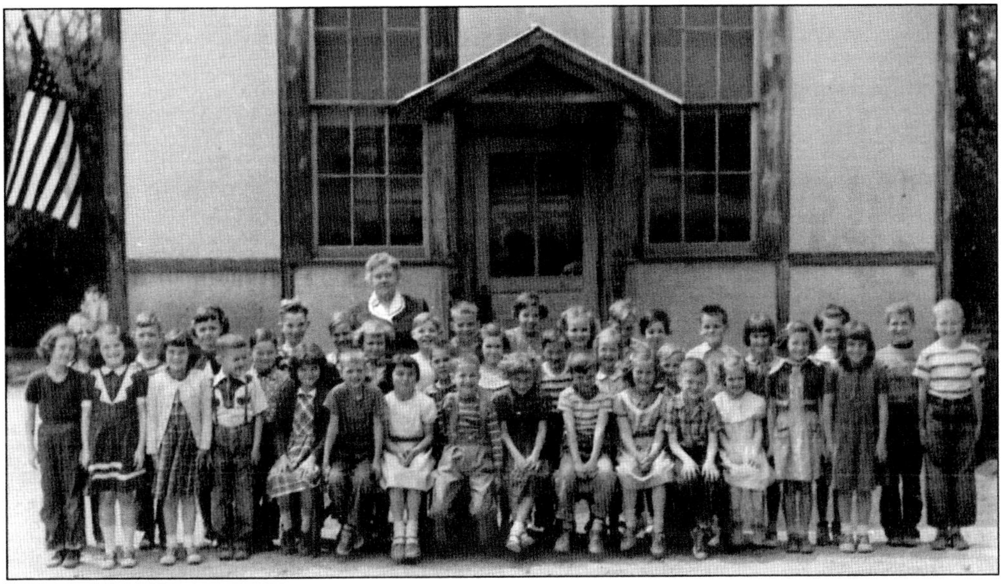

By 1926, the West Milton area student population again required more space. A prefabricated frame building named Washington Primary School was constructed to accommodate grades one through four, while the brick school from 1903 was renamed the Washington Grammar School. Consolidation took place in 1955, with students attending Kelly Elementary School in Lewisburg or the White Deer Elementary School in New Columbia. The prefabricated building was then razed. A late-1920s Washington School photograph features students of the Baker, Baylor, Bergenstock, Bowman, Confer, Coris, Criswell, Deiffenderfer, Dieffenbach, Engleman, Grove, Hartman, Hornbeck, Huntington, Mausteller, Maxfield, Musser, Rovert, Smith, Stump, Wagner, Walter, and Wright families. The school building has since been converted into a home. (Both, Susan Ohl Wirth.)

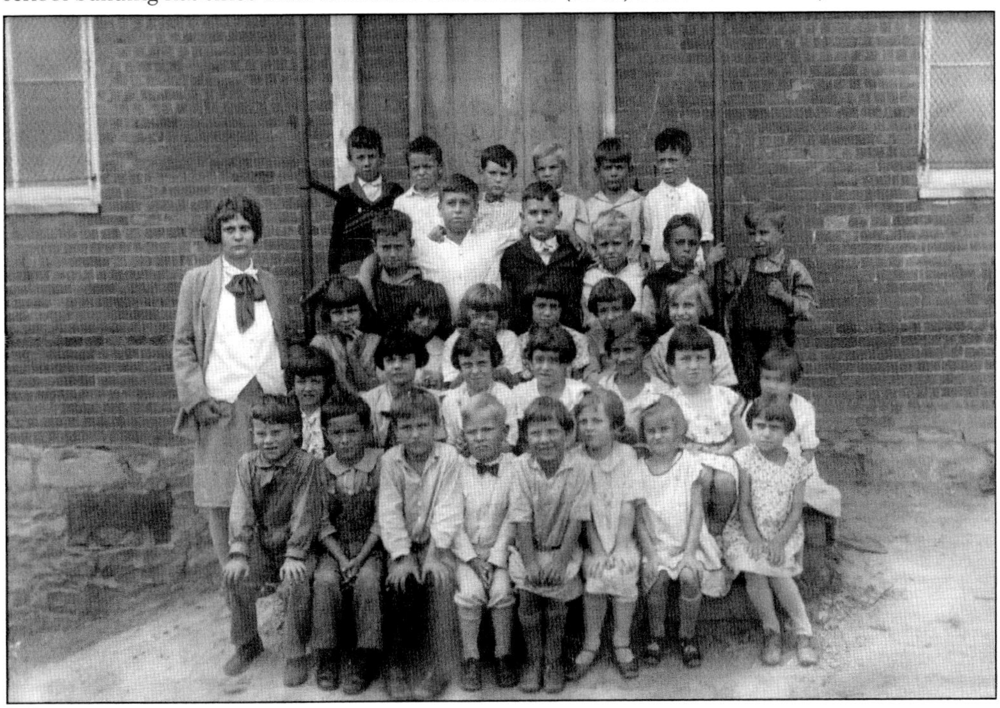

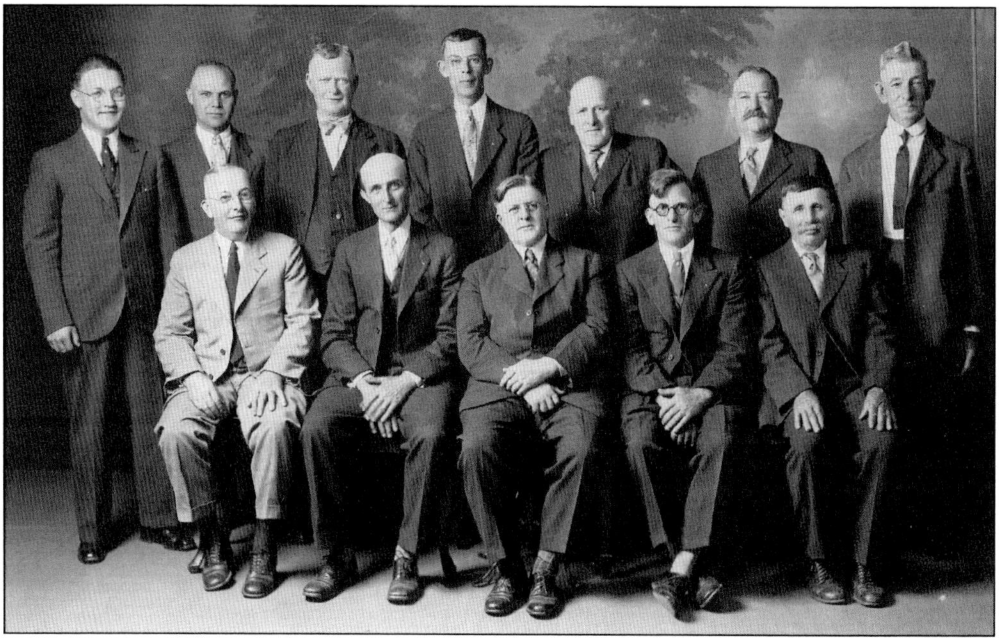

West Milton Bank's board and staff were photographed around 1931. Pictured in the first row, from left to right, are Daniel Meckley, Ray Keiser, vice president Lee R. Rank, president Owen Bergenstock, and Oscar Keefer. Some of the men in the second row are identified as clerk William Weaver, cashiers Bickel Huntington and Benjamin Specht, Clarence Grove, John Byerly, and Daniel R. Harbeson. In the 1970s, the bank built anew on High Street. In 2010, it celebrated its 90th anniversary. (UCHS 91.32.17a.)

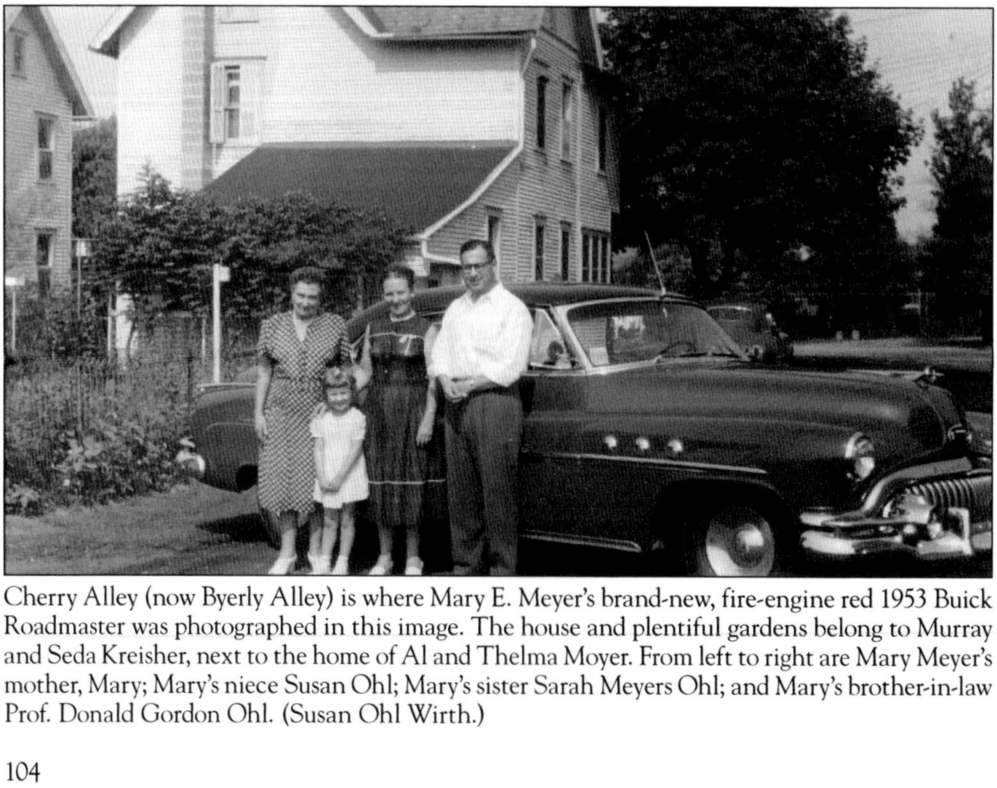

Cherry Alley (now Byerly Alley) is where Mary E. Meyer's brand-new, fire-engine red 1953 Buick Roadmaster was photographed in this image. The house and plentiful gardens belong to Murray and Seda Kreisher, next to the home of Al and Thelma Moyer. From left to right are Mary Meyer's mother, Mary; Mary's niece Susan Ohl; Mary's sister Sarah Meyers Ohl; and Mary's brother-in-law Prof. Donald Gordon Ohl. (Susan Ohl Wirth.)

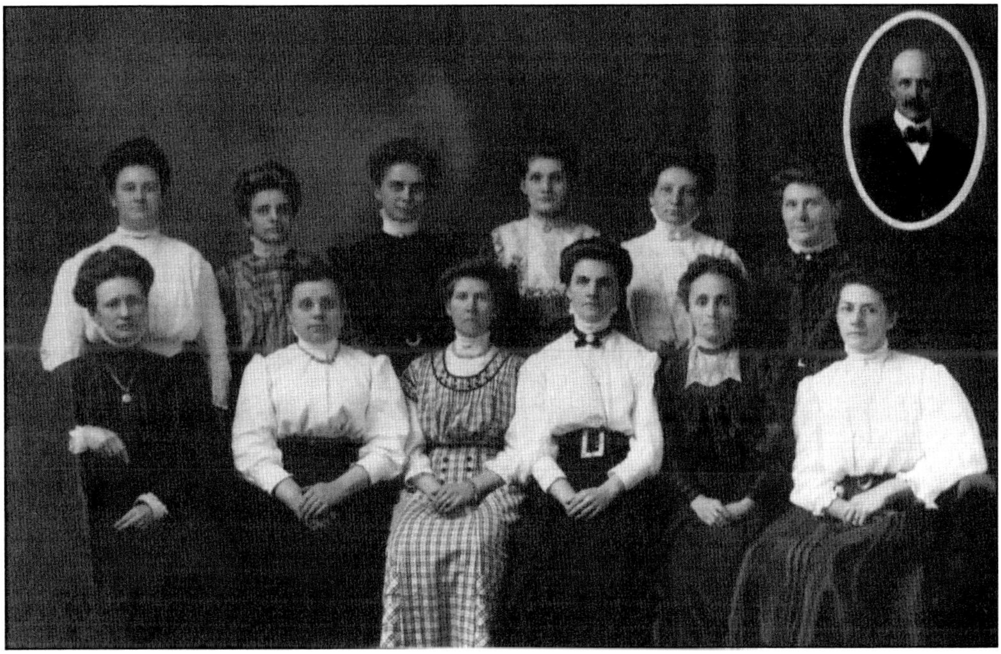

The Reformed Sunday School Ladies Aid Society, West Milton, is pictured. Members are, from left to right, (first row) ? McClellan, ? Dunkelberger, ? Pardoe, ? Gearhart, ? Shrek, and ? Leopold; (second row) Hester and Margaretta Huntington, Cora Bickel, Blanche Dennis, Margaret Grove, and Annie Hollenbach. (UCHS 2010.28.2.)

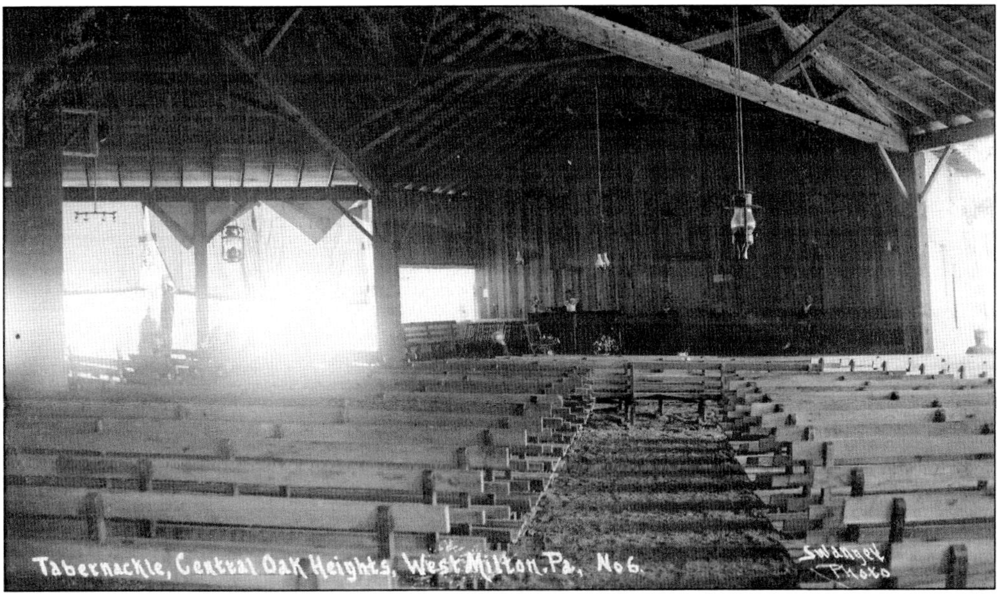

Since the United Evangelical Church's (UEC) founding of Central Oak Heights (COH)—a seasonal campgrounds and worship center—in 1909, the wood-framed tabernacle was the focal point on this oak-covered promontory near West Milton. This real-photo postcard captures auditorium-style interior seating and lighting details and the tabernacle's openness to the outdoors beyond its canvas shades. Initially, nearly 1,000 could be accommodated; now, 585 can be seated for concerts, lectures, and services. (Ronald Nornhold.)

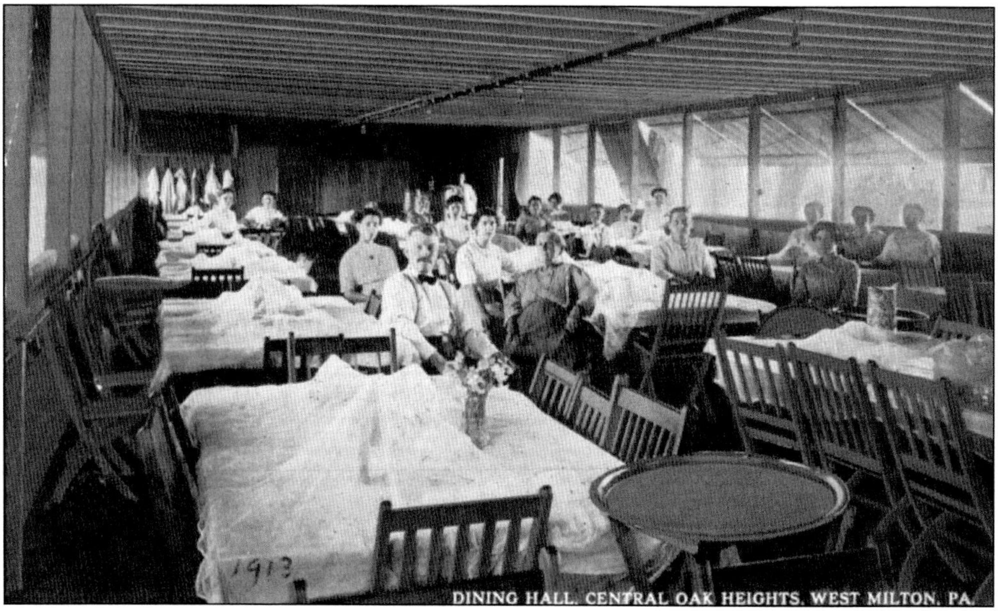

A dining facility was built on the original 40-acre purchase of Central Oak Heights. Its interior with gauze netting covering the table settings was among the first postcards issued of the site. Sixteen adjoining acres were purchased in 1966 with money for the land that was taken in the widening of Route 15. Pictured below, the Hornberger-Woodlawn Cottage was the grandest of 62 frame homes built at Central Oak Heights (COH). Houses owned by individuals on leased land was a long-standing tradition. Built by Edward Martin of Milton, this home was purchased in 1919 by Jerome Hornberger. In the 1990s, the whole site was acquired by the nonprofit Central Oak Heights Association, which rents several residences and other facilities from April 15 to October 15. The 2010 schedule included evening vesper services at the Sylvan Chapel, weekend performances, Sunday worship services in the tabernacle, a public archeological dig, and music camps. (Above, UCHS 94.5.16; below, Ronald Nornhold.)

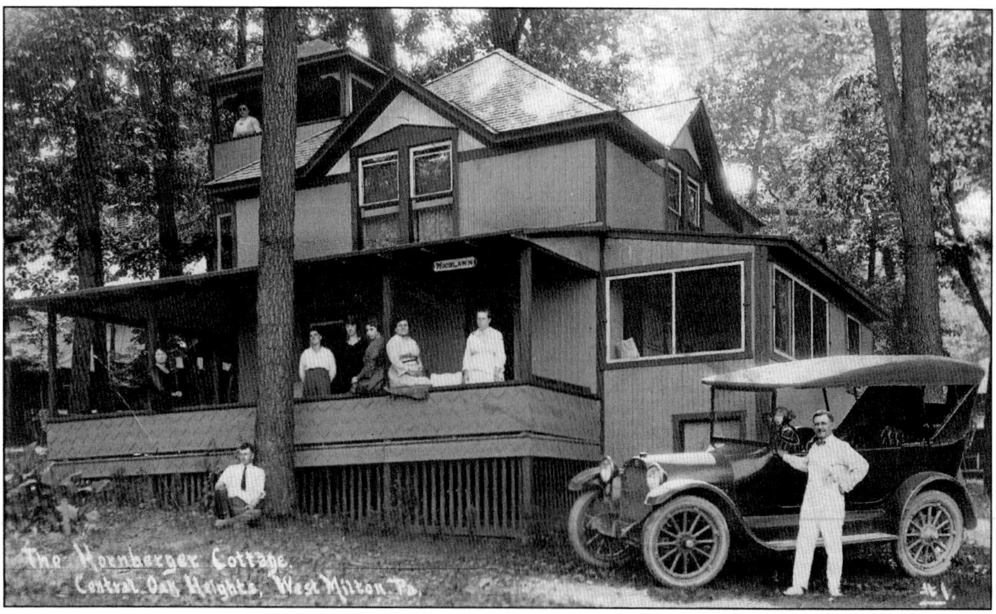

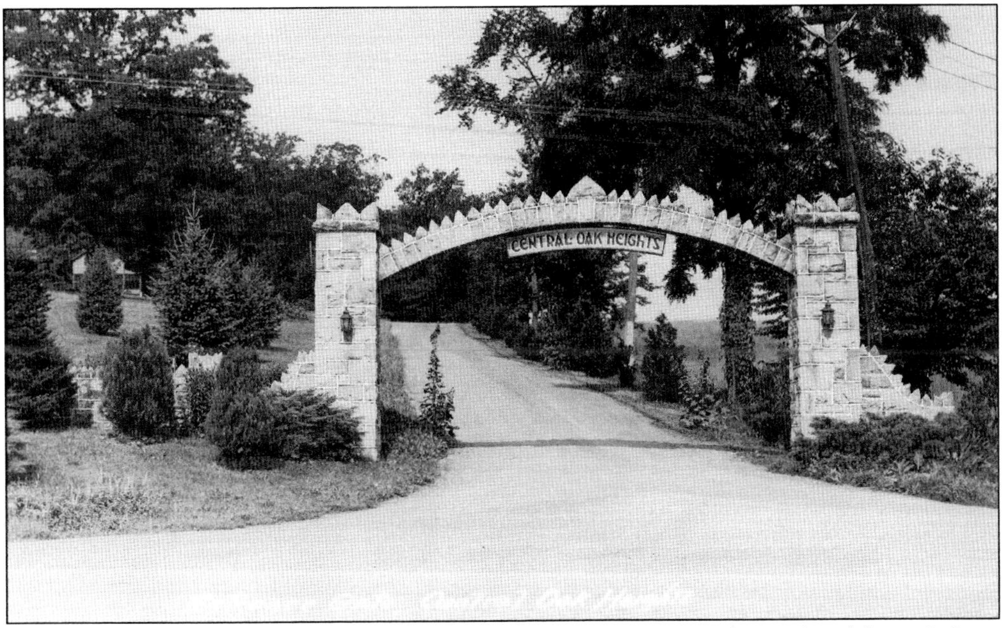

The entrance to COH is seen as it welcomes summer visitors in 1946. The sender of the real-photo postcard above remarks that more than 200 young people were there. In the postcard below, the monument (far right) erected on August 6, 1932, by the Pennsylvania Historical Commission, the Union County Historical Society, and the United Evangelical Church Historical Society at Chief Shikellamy's lookout can be seen near the administration building. The monument's plaque reads, "On the Plain stretching south east from this ridge was situated the Indian village of Shikellamy's Old Town which was visited by Conrad Weiser in 1737. . . Shikellamy was appointed Vice Regent of the Iroqouis Confederacy in 1745 and made Shamokin [Sunbury] his headquarters." (Above, UCHS 89.15.6; below, Ronald Nornhold.)

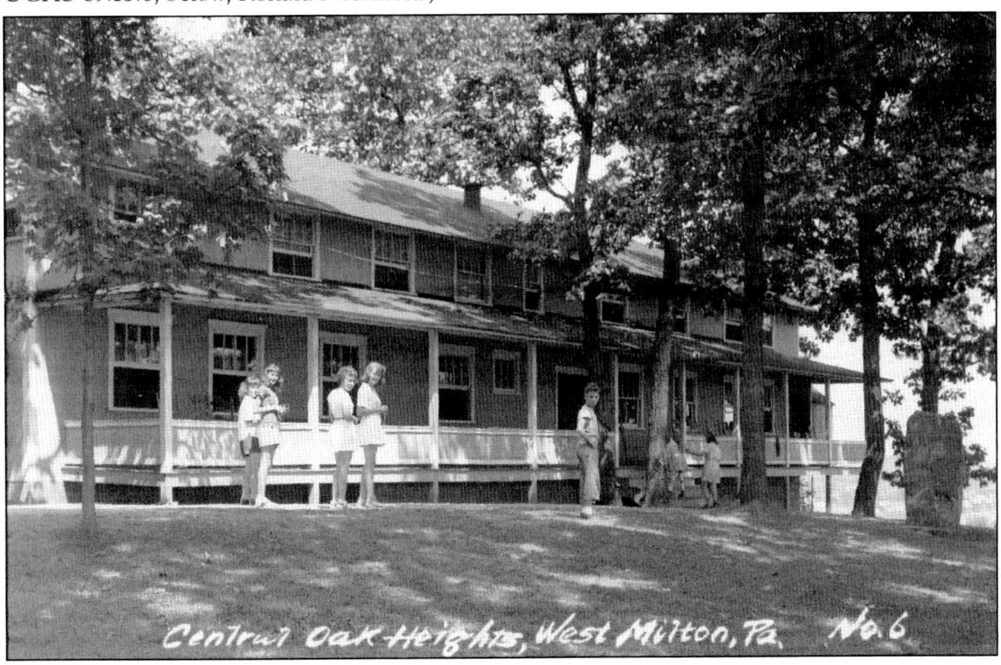

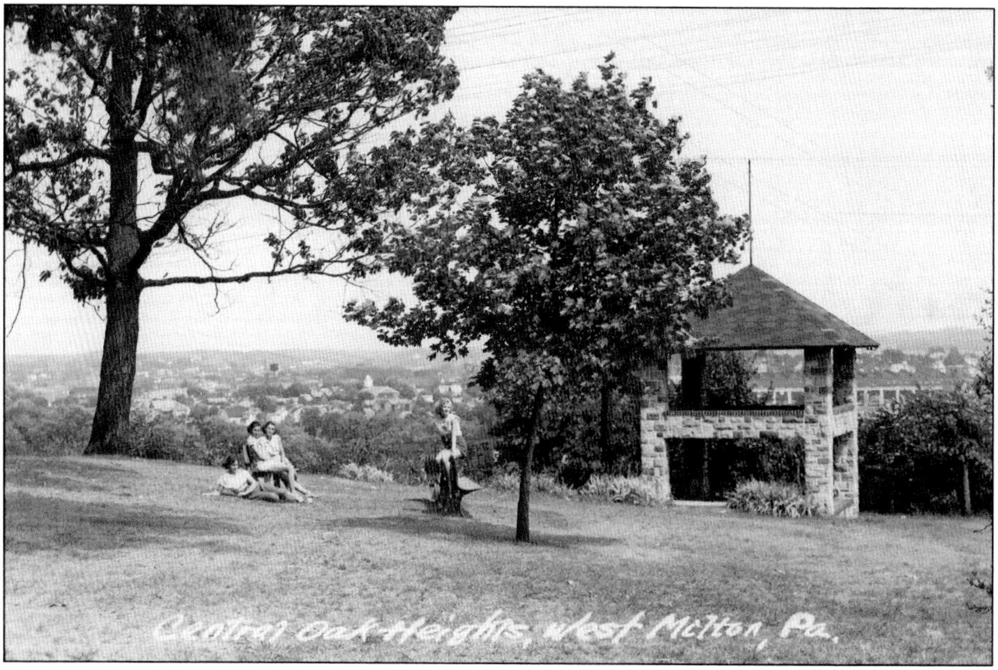

A series of real-photo postcards with postmarks as late as 1962 illustrates different vantage points on the 55-acre site of Central Oak Heights. Many views included the Susquehanna, the West Milton–Milton Bridge, and Milton in the far distance. On the reverse of one postcard is written, "Becky, Brad and I are here at camp. It cost me one week's pay but I can't think of a better way to spend it. It is rather cool here but hot in the sun." The camps were very popular in the 1950s to 1980s, after which they stopped being held. During that period, the Sylvan Chapel, a large dining hall, and an improved swimming pool were built. (Both, UCHS 90.21.12 and 94.9.15.)

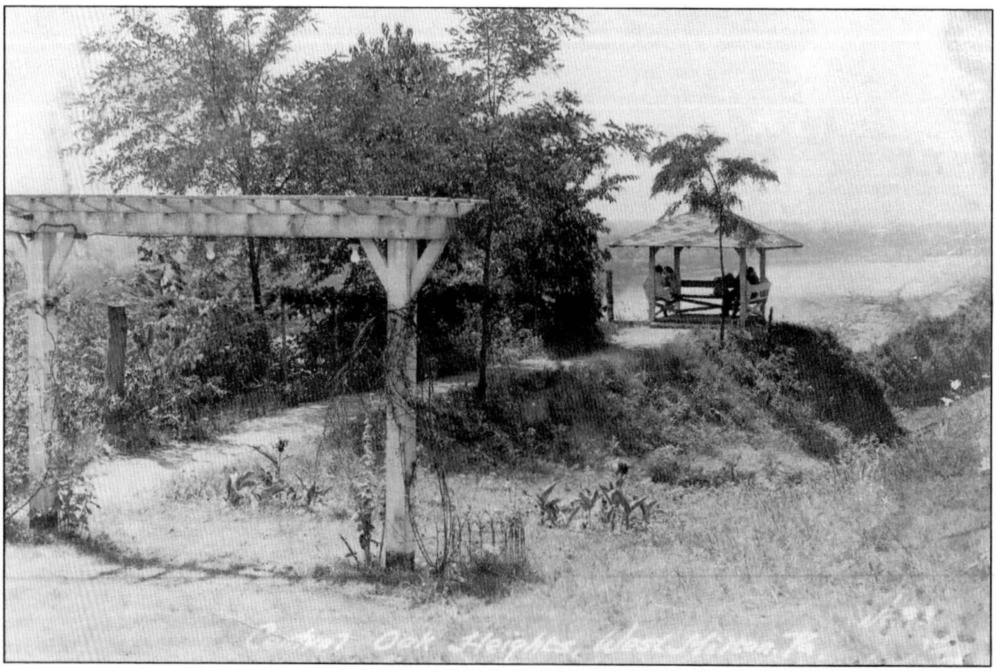

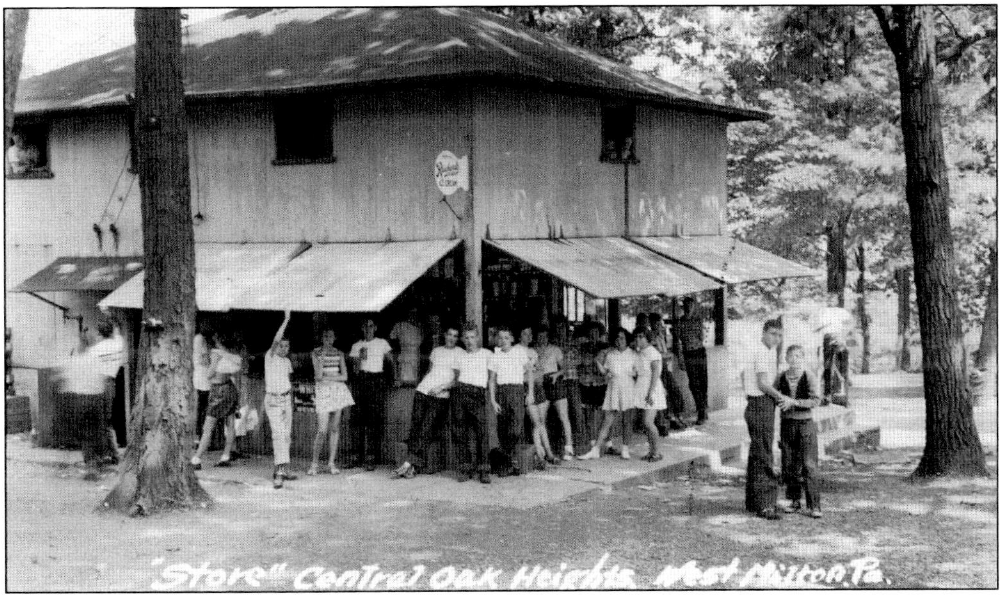

Outside "the Store," the 1950s real-photo postcard above shows youth in a more modern dress than seen in the 1909 views of the Store. Boys still wear trousers in the image on the postcard, which is postmarked 1962. Below is an interior photograph of the Store, also taken in the 1950s. Central Oak Heights was conveniently located roughly in the center of the Central Pennsylvania Conference of the United Evangelical Church (UEC) and drew many young people to its camps. The UEC then became united with the United Brethren Church in 1946 to become the Evangelical United Brethren Church (EUB). In 1968, the EUB and the Methodist church became the United Methodist Church. Since 1990, the site has been owned and administered by the nonprofit COH Association. The requirement is that a cottage owner be active in some denomination of a Christian church. (Above, Ronald Nornhold; below, UCHS 2006.65.1.)

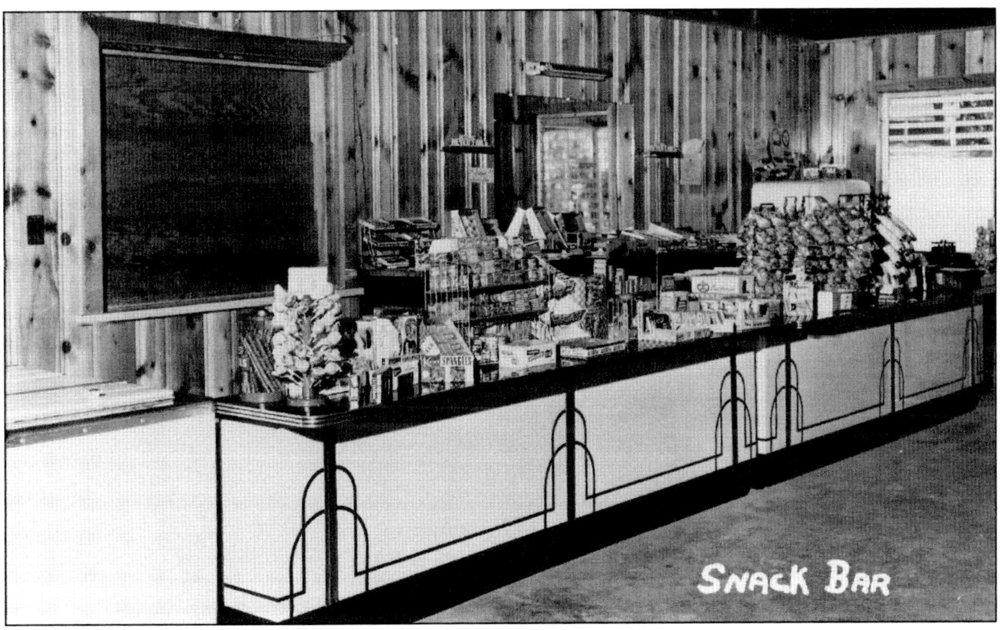

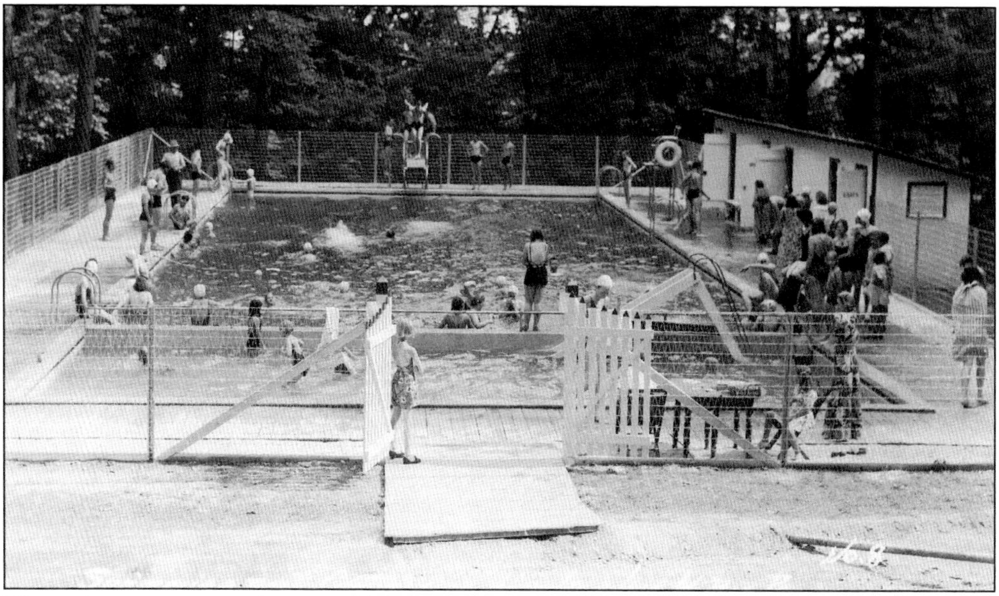

The earliest summer residents would swim in the Susquehanna River, but the first swimming pool was a welcome addition at Central Oak Heights when it was built in 1939. In 1962, a modern pool with a circulation and filtration system was constructed. Now, Scout, athletic camps, and wedding receptions are held at COH, in addition to performances given by groups like the Williamsport Youth Symphony. Events are open to all, and a schedule of annual events and available rentals is posted at the COH website. (Both, UCHS 92.9.89.51 and 2007.6.9.)

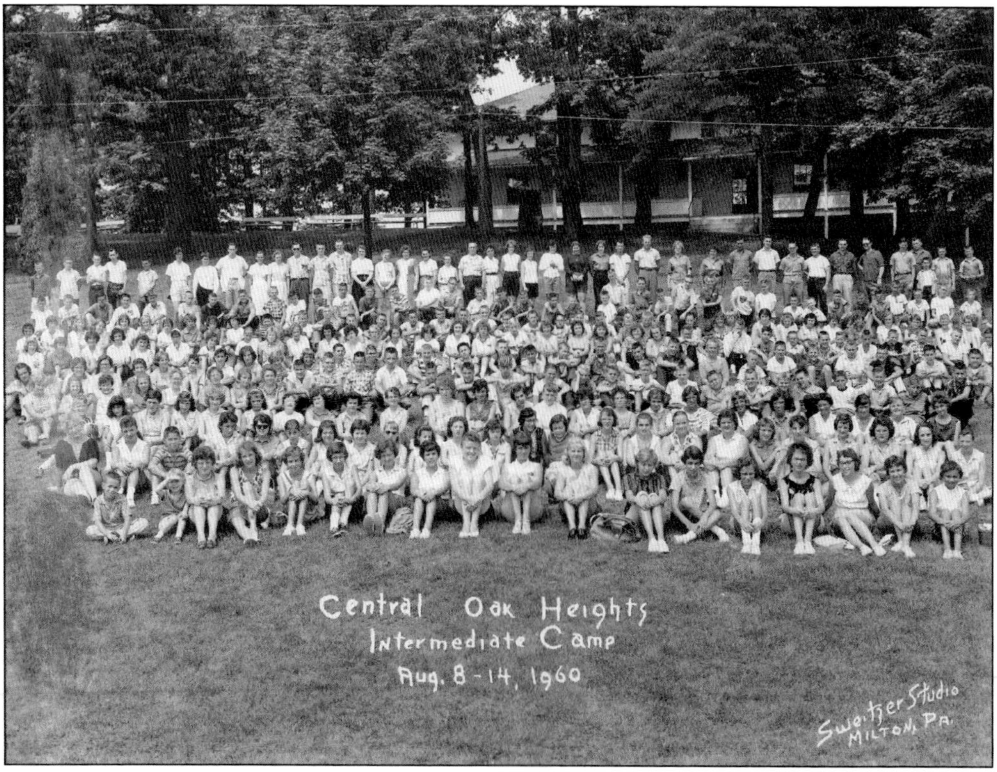

Five

WINFIELD

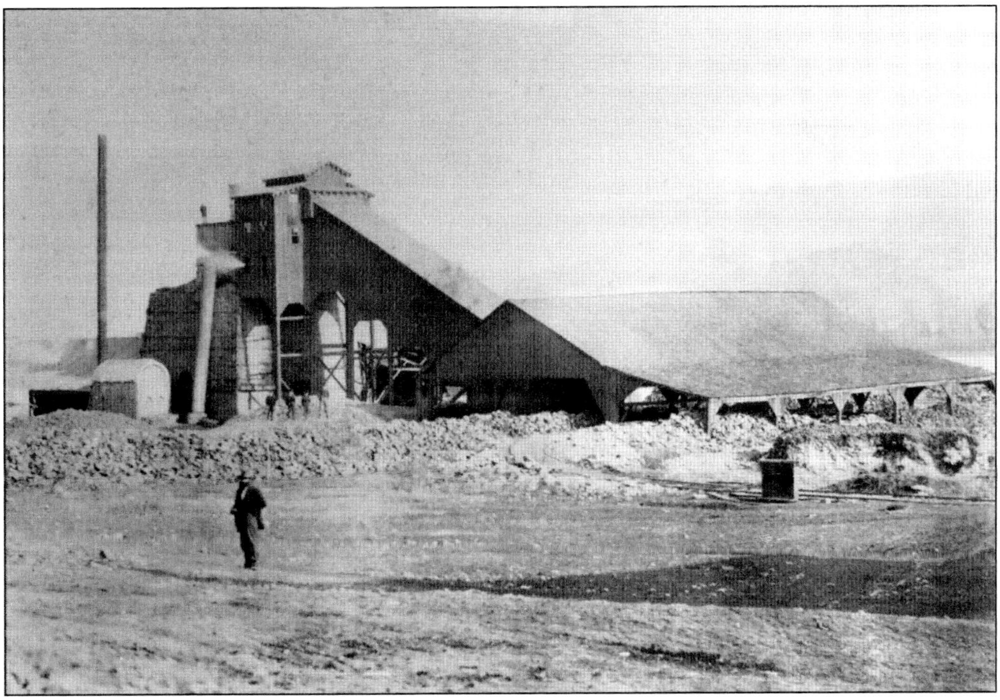

Winfield residents utilized the town's natural resources of iron ore, limestone, and timber in quarrying and iron-casting industries. Later, water access provided recreation opportunities. Pictured is the only overview photograph of the Beaver, Geddes, Marsh, and Company ironworks taken prior to its closing in 1891. One can appreciate the specialized mid-19th-century industrial operation that took hold in Winfield, White Deer, and Glen Iron in Union County. (Hagley Museum and Library.)

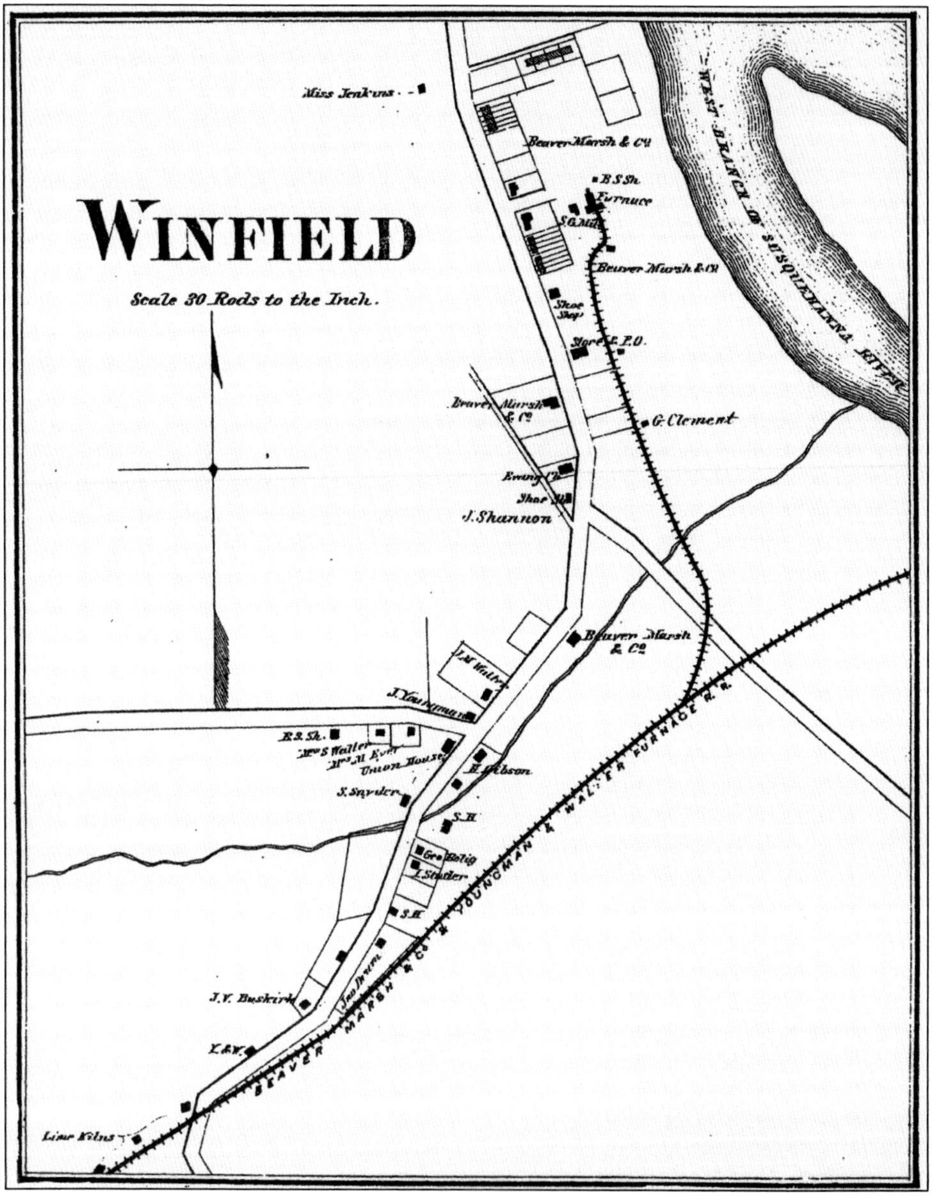

In 1841, iron ore was dug from the length of New Berlin Mountain, which extended west from the Susquehanna. From Miner's Hollow and Yankee Springs near Winfield, ore was hauled in wagons on what became Furnace Road, then it was transported by ferry across the Susquehanna to canal boats and, ultimately, to furnaces in Danville. Once the Union Furnace was built in Winfield in 1853–1854, ore could be smelted closer to its source. Winfield, as shown in the 1868 *Pomeroy's Atlas of Union and Snyder Counties,* had a narrow gauge track that went from the lime kiln site (lower left), to the furnace/blacksmith shop (upper right), and to a landing on the Susquehanna (middle right). Other sites on the atlas map and referenced in area photographs or postcards are the Van Buskirk and Drumm residences; the "S.H." or Winfield school; the Union House, later called Hyman Hotel, which was built on the 60-acre tract known as "Hospitality" and held by one family for nearly 200 years (lower half); the Evangelical Church, and the Union Furnace company store and post office (upper half). (UCHS.)

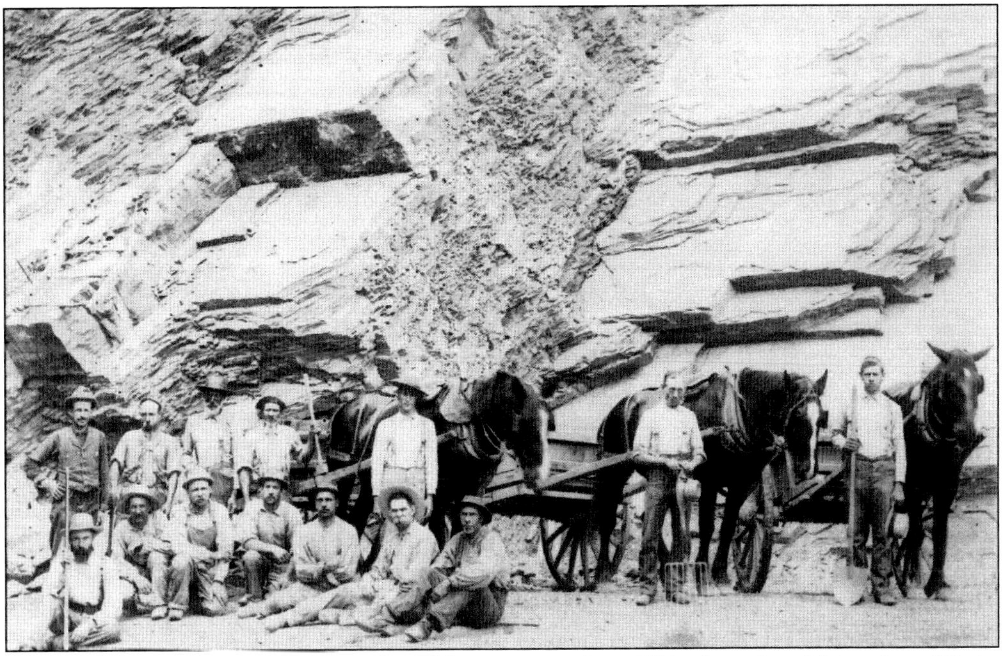

Winfield's limestone quarry was presumably operational in 1854 when then Union Iron Works commenced operations. This photograph was taken when work was still being done manually and the transportation method was horse-drawn carts. Pictured from left to right are, (first row) William Bennett, Newt Long, Sam Long, Frank Renn, Daniel Crabb, Albert Stetler, and ? Fetter; (second row) Charles Rooke, Theo Long, Jim Dunlap, John Renn, Harry Shannon, Henry Blyler, and Edward Rokland. The Union Iron Works employed 25 to 30 people, many living in company-owned housing and shopping at the company store, ledgers of which are in the Union County Historical Society collection. In those ledgers are entries for some of the workers above. Below, the entrance to a cave at the quarry made a mysterious nighttime scene complete with a fancifully created full moon by Winfield shopkeeper and resident Mildred Drumm around 1908. (Above, Fred Blyler; below, Ronald Nornhold.)

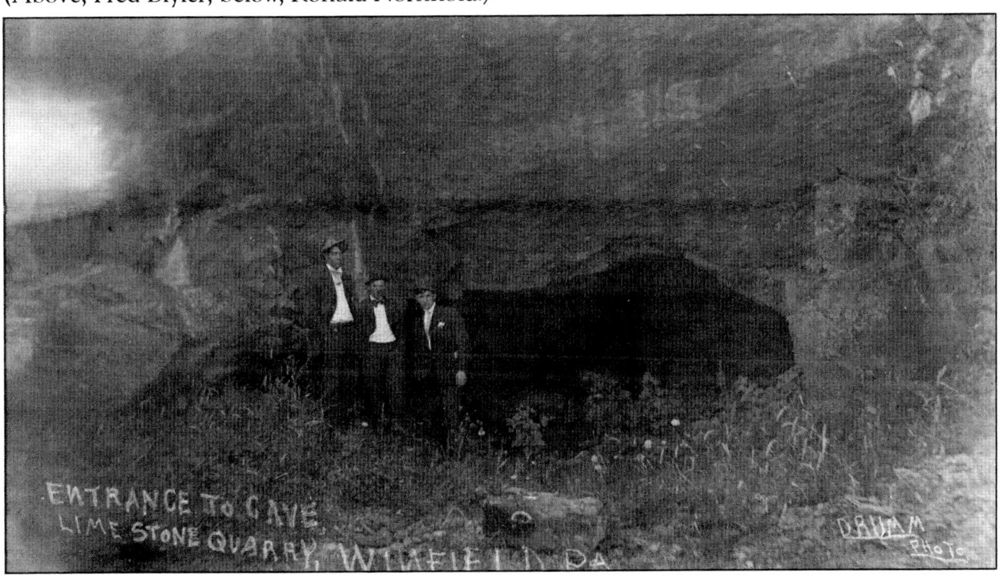

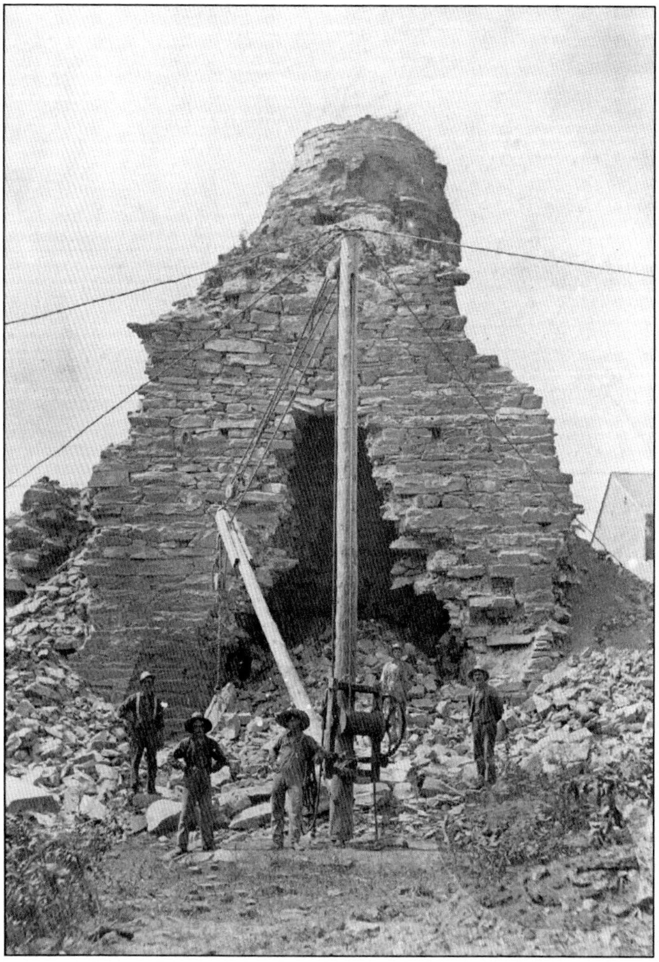

In the mid-1850s, foundry owners and operators Samuel Geddes, James Marsh, Elisha Marsh, and Joseph Shriner built the cast iron furnace complex below Turtle Creek. Thomas and Peter Beaver, Charles Morris, and Levi Rooke brought additional financial and technical assistance to the endeavor. Rooke eventually became superintendent. The Union Iron Works' smelting stack was said to rise more than 100 feet high. Alternate layers of charcoal, iron ore, and limestone were smelted and cast into pig iron ingots. The operation closed in 1891 and was photographed various times during the demolition of its furnace stack, seen at left in a *carte de visite* around 1912. In the 1907 real-photo postcard below, glimpses of several Union Iron Works buildings can be seen on the right side of the tracks, including the furnace in the right foreground. (Both, UCHS 2010.1.26 and 97.37.2.)

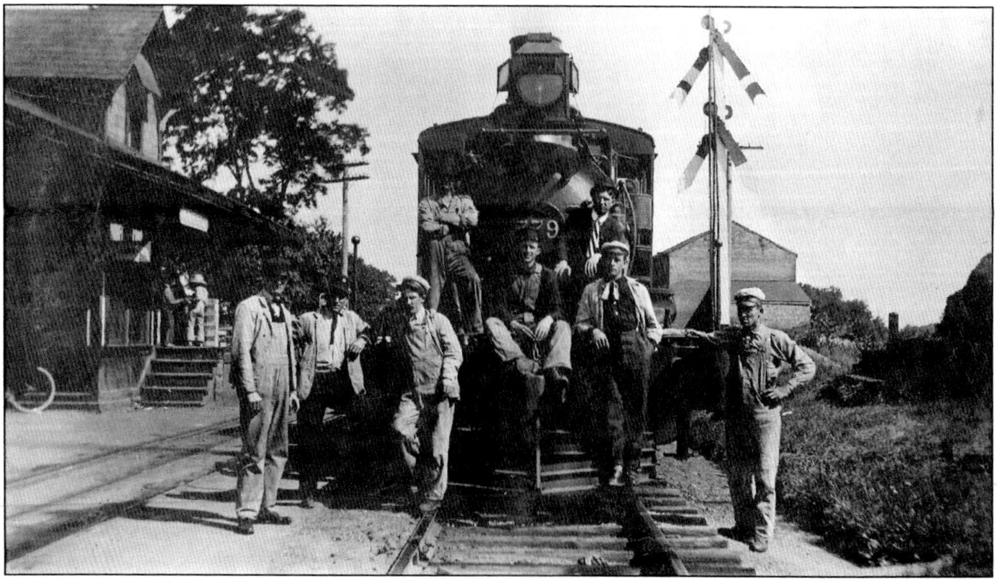

The Baptist Church of Winfield (right), built around 1875 on land given by Beaver, Marsh, and Company, was photographed by Stephen Horton of West Milton in 1911. Horton usually confined his photography to streetscapes that often included the stores where he sold Uneeda Biscuits, but in Winfield he photographed other subjects. Another real-photo postcard (below) features the United Evangelical Church. It was built in 1856 under the pastorate of A.L. Reeser, then it was rebuilt and dedicated on January 20, 1906, when Rev. Samuel Edward Koontz was minister. Below, two negatives were developed together in a composite card that commemorated the church's 50th anniversary in 1906. (Both, UCHS 92.9.92.27 and 2004.16.1.)

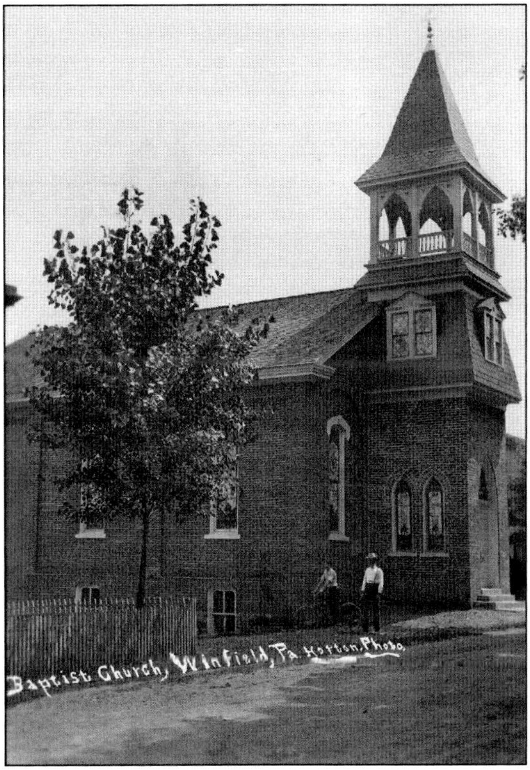

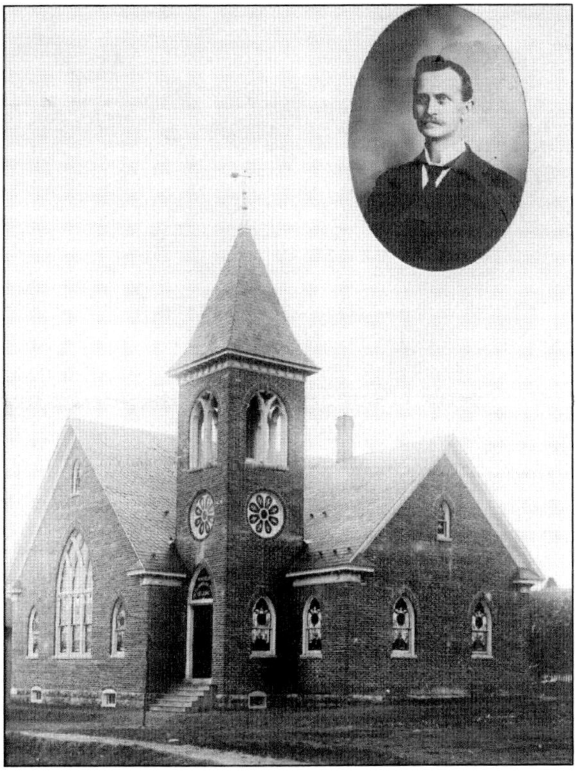

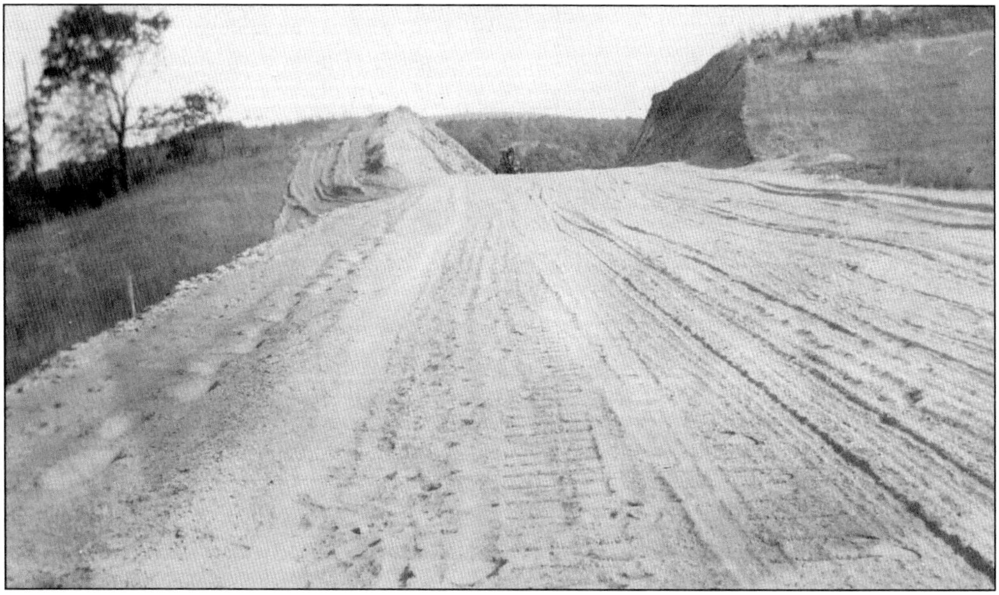

The Lewisburg-Winfield Road, later called Route 15, was graded and then paved around 1930. It passed 0.1 miles east of the junction of Route 304 and Quarry Road. There, Hotel Hyman was poised for visitors as seen in the photograph below from 1905. Charles and Bertha Hyman, owners of Hotel Hyman, stand in the foreground with their daughters, Anna (left) and Grace. Son, Grover, is on the bicycle. The hotel became a boardinghouse in the 1930s and was converted by the Hymans into apartments in the 1950s. (Above, UCHS 2000.2.1; below, Drew Hyman.)

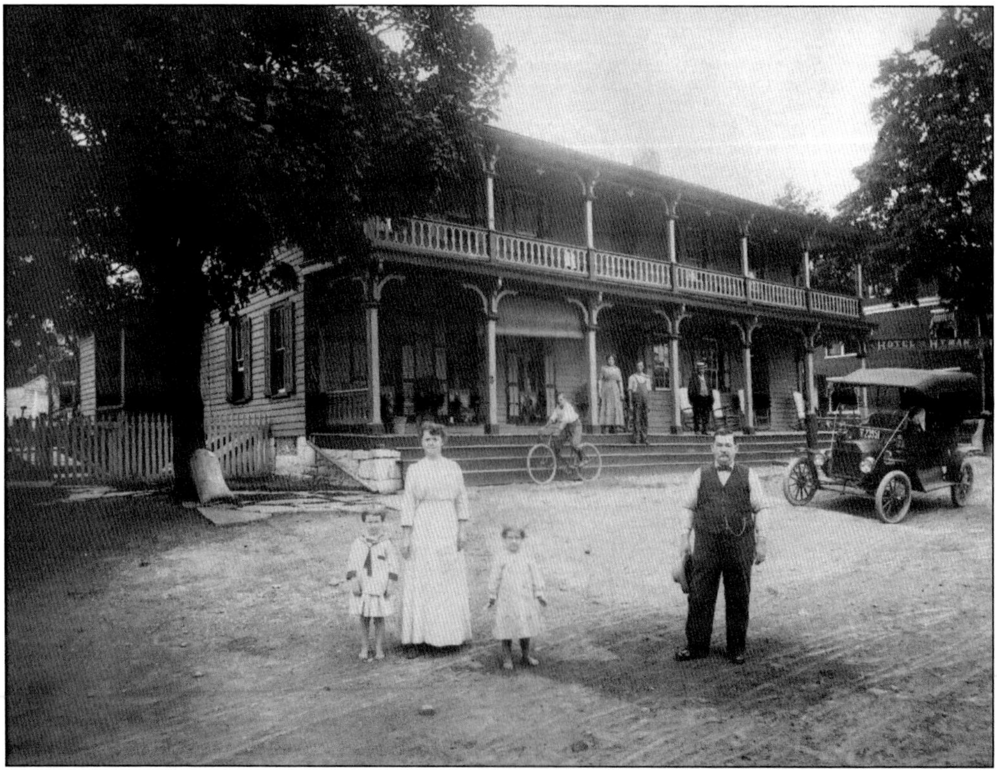

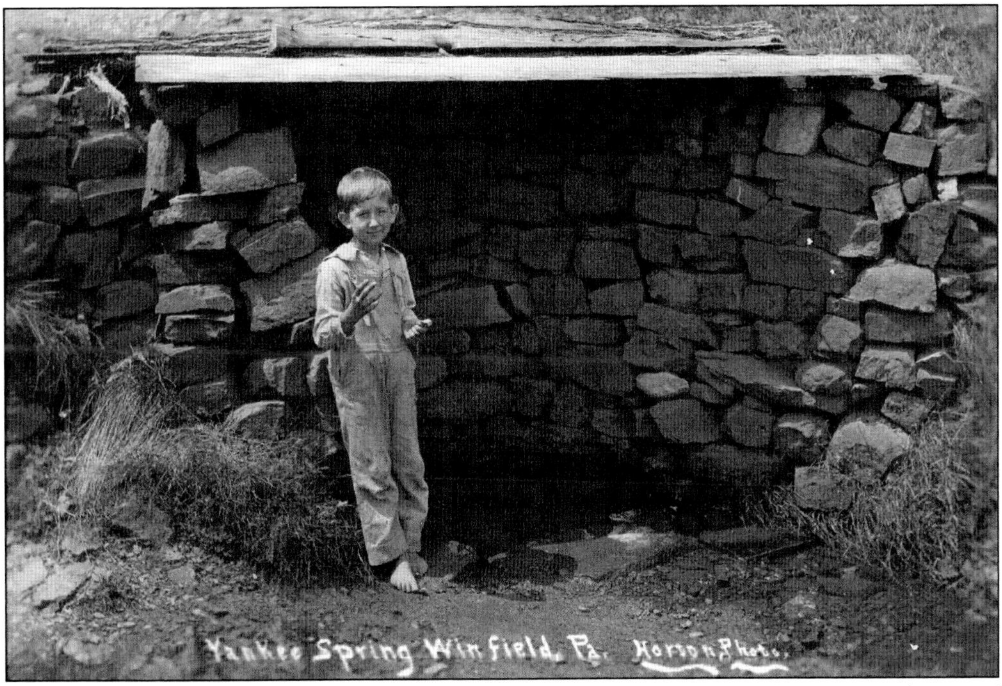

Two Winfield landmarks that were demolished and paved over in the subsequent widening of Route 15 around 1960 were Yankee Spring, a natural water source, and the Eyer Barn. The long stone barn (upper right of the composite card below) was built in 1805 on Abraham Eyer's farm in Winfield. It was the site of an important Evangelical church conference in 1816, which the postcard commemorates along with the drawing of the first Evangelical church in New Berlin built in 1817 and the East Prospect, Pennsylvania, conference anniversary site of 1917. (Above, Alan Richard; below, UCHS 2004.17.2.)

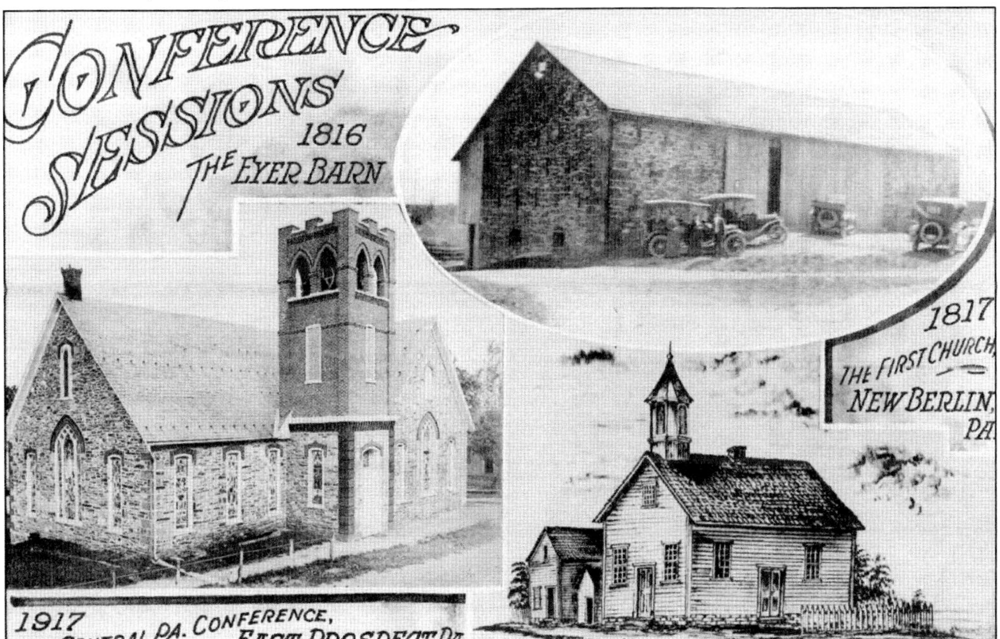

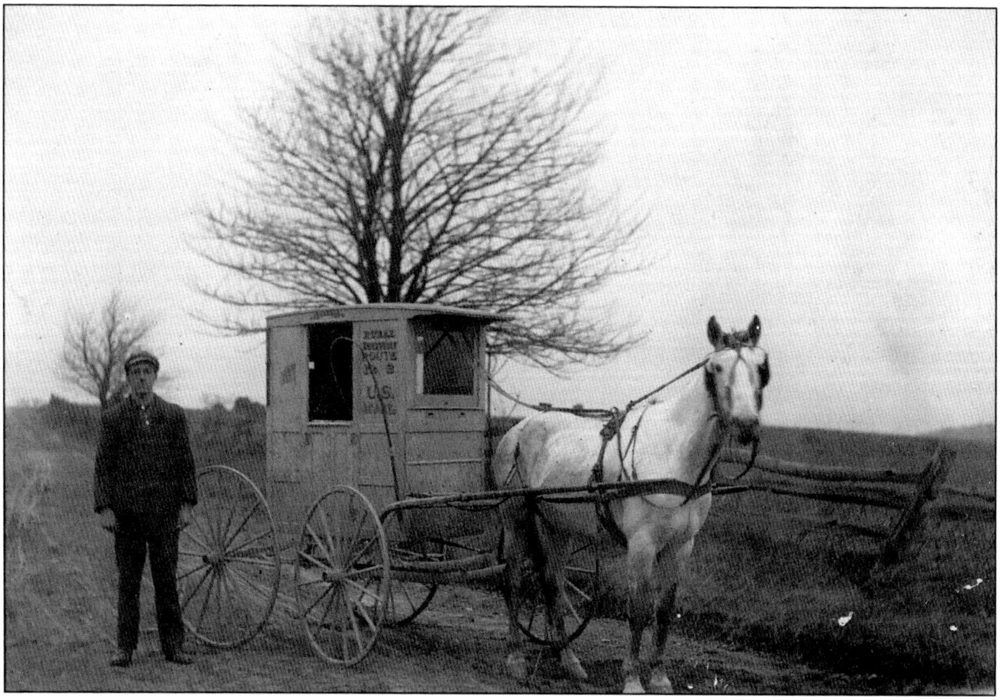

Pictured above and below, John Van Buskirk (1888–1971) sent the real-photo postcard above as a Christmas greeting to rural route customer Mrs. Boyer and family in 1912. Still a mail carrier for the Winfield Post Office in the 1930s, Van Buskirk is shown below prior to loading his vehicle. In 1851, a post office was built and named Winfield in the area previously called Dry Valley. Today, Dry Valley is a small crossroads community 3.2 miles west on Route 304 to New Berlin. (Above, Ronald Nornhold; below, UCHS 2000.2.2.)

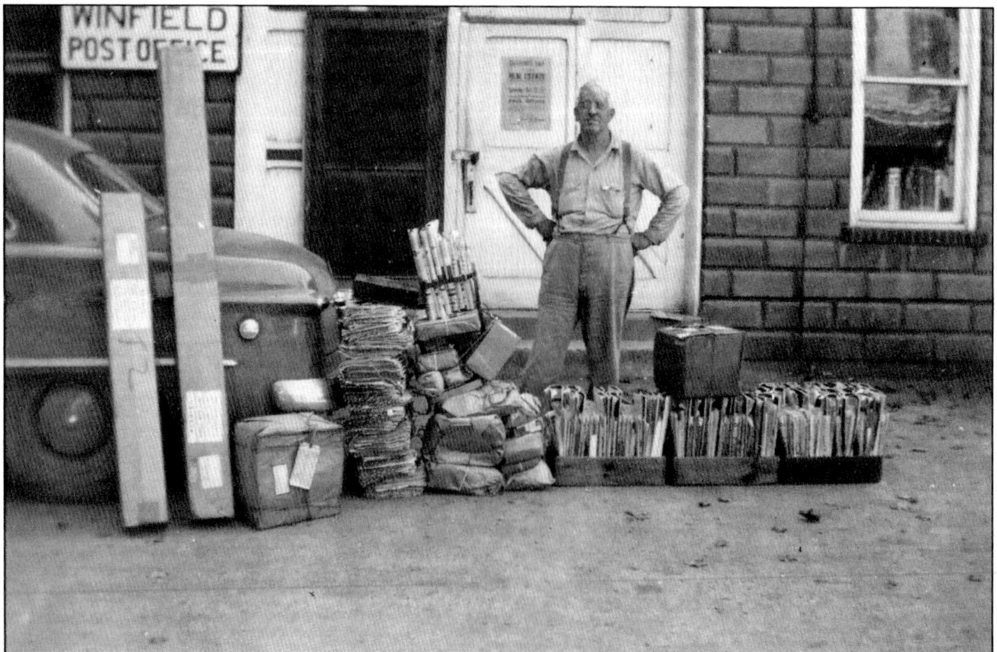

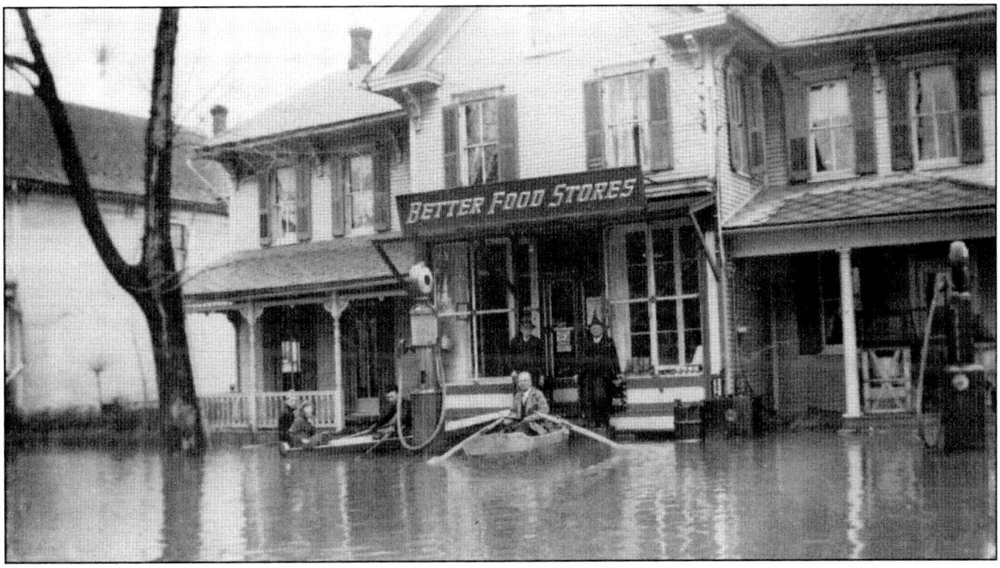

The Dyer Store property (above) on Winfield Road was given to Hannah Elizabeth (Dreese) Dyer by her parents. It was owned and operated by Mahlon Dyer (1868–1940), then Hannah, followed by their son Willard I. Dyer and his wife, Nina. William and Nina's son Willard Jr., who died in 2003, was the last Dyer family member to own it. It is pictured during the flood of 1936 with Charles Reagan in a rowboat. Another flood image (below) looks west past the 18th-century John Lee house (left), which is in front of the Lee stone springhouse and the Baptist church. They were all hard hit during the spring flood of 1936. Not until the Susquehanna River flooded in 1972 did the river rise higher. (Both, UCHS 2000.2.5 and 2000.2.3.)

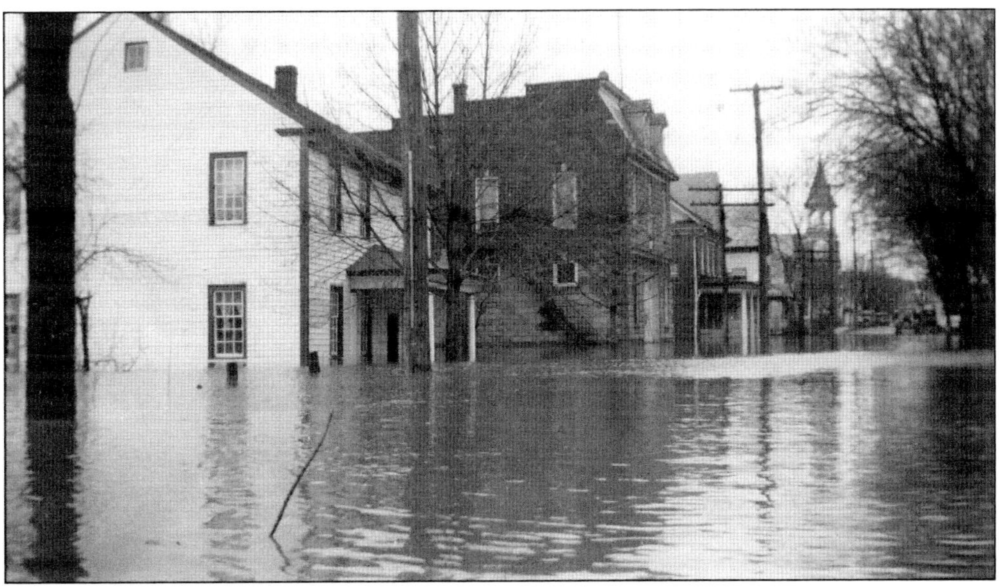

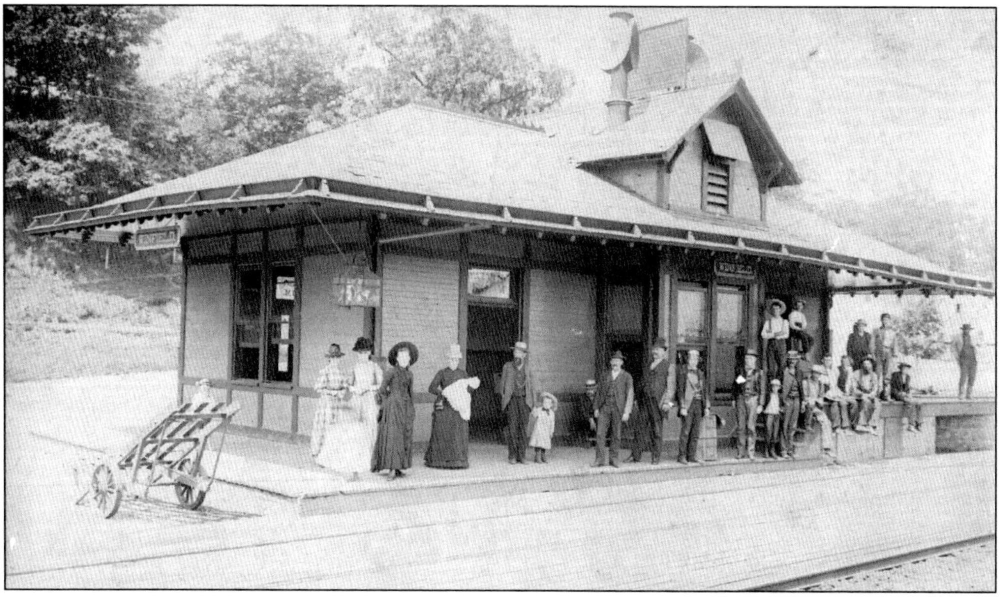

A few dozen passengers waiting at the Winfield Train Station are captured in a cabinet photograph. The Shamokin-Sunbury-Winfield-Lewisburg-West Milton line went farther north to New Columbia, White Deer, and Allenwood, and on to Williamsport. A short-lived narrow gauge line (1905–1916) connected Winfield with New Berlin, Union County's former county seat. The nine-mile passenger and freight line was underwritten by the Burd family of Shamokin and New Berlin. The freight line never made a profit. (UCHS 81.1.12.3.)

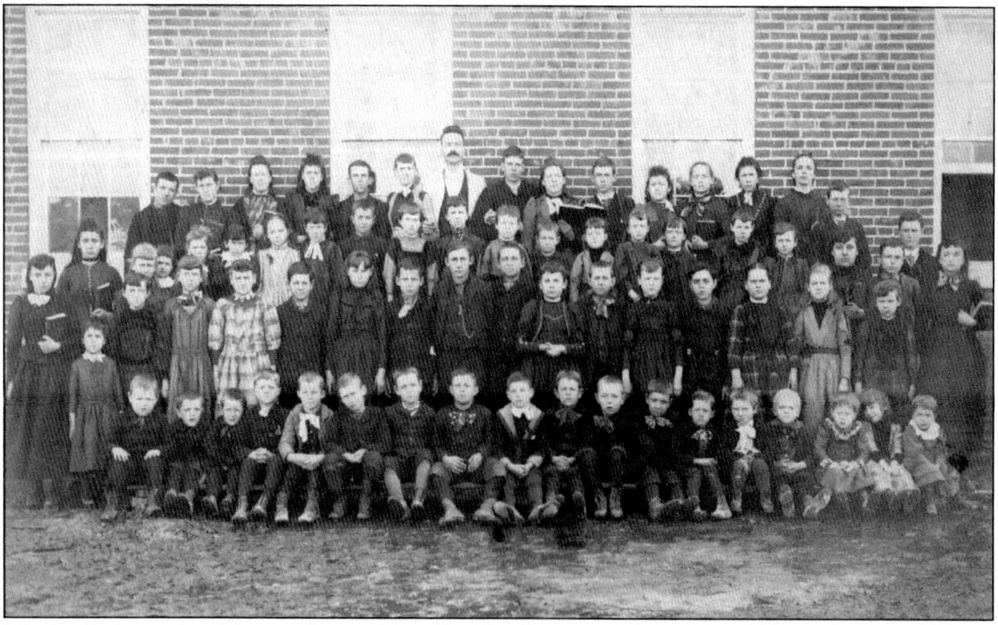

Winfield's first school was a private school built of logs in 1815 called Old College. After Union Township adopted the Free School Act (1834), a frame building was erected in 1842, followed by this brick one in 1874. For a time, primary and grammar school pupils used the frame and brick schools simultaneously. Students in 1890–1891 were captured on film by Lewisburg studio photographer James S. Brown for this cabinet photograph. (UCHS 81.1.12.2.)

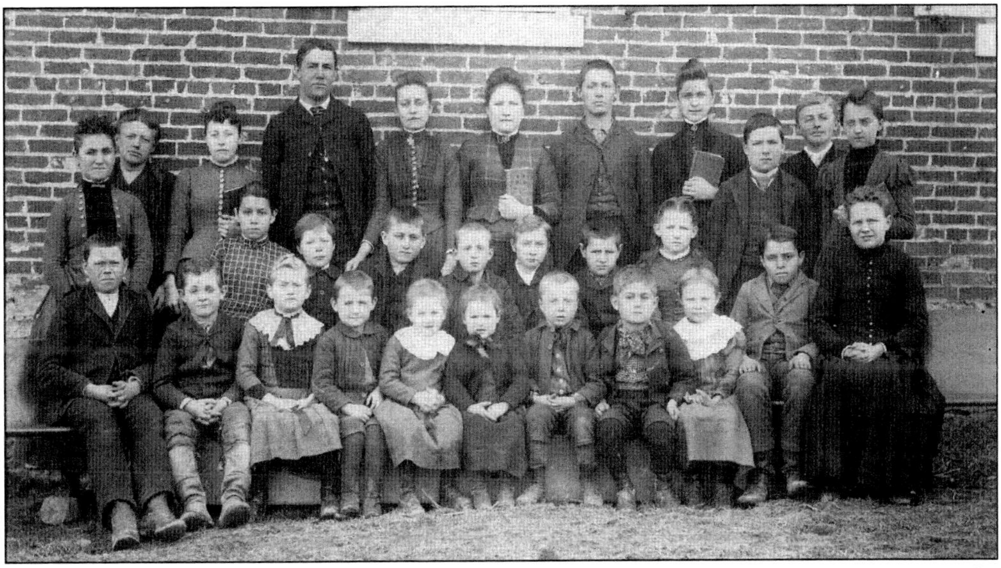

The intersection of Steven Kitchens and Mulls Hollow Roads, south of Winfield, was a site for the Merrill, Bettilyon, and Hollow or Sandels School (which was built of brick in 1878). In 1888, James S. Brown photographed schoolmates (above) of the Baker, Bennett, Brown, Chappell Dunkelberger, Eagle, Hummel, Kunkle, Sandel, Shadel, Troxell, Snyder, and Wiand families with teacher Fannie Kerstetter on the far left of the second row. In the photograph below from the 1929–1930 school year are, from left to right, (first row) Marlin Felmey, Elmer Muff, Boyd Roush, Marlin Fertig, and William Willow; (second row) Mary Alice Roush, Wilma Reitz, Ethel Felmey, Ruth Berge, Mildred Sandel, Ruth Sandel, Evelyn Hess, Doris Roush, and Betty Hunt; (third row) Geneva Hess, Martha Felmy, Eva Berge, Randel Bennett, John Berge, Simon Felmey, and teacher Alice Rabuck. The last school year at Sandels School was 1951–1952, when Union and Buffalo Township schools consolidated. (Both, UCHS 91.15.7 and 95.24.3.)

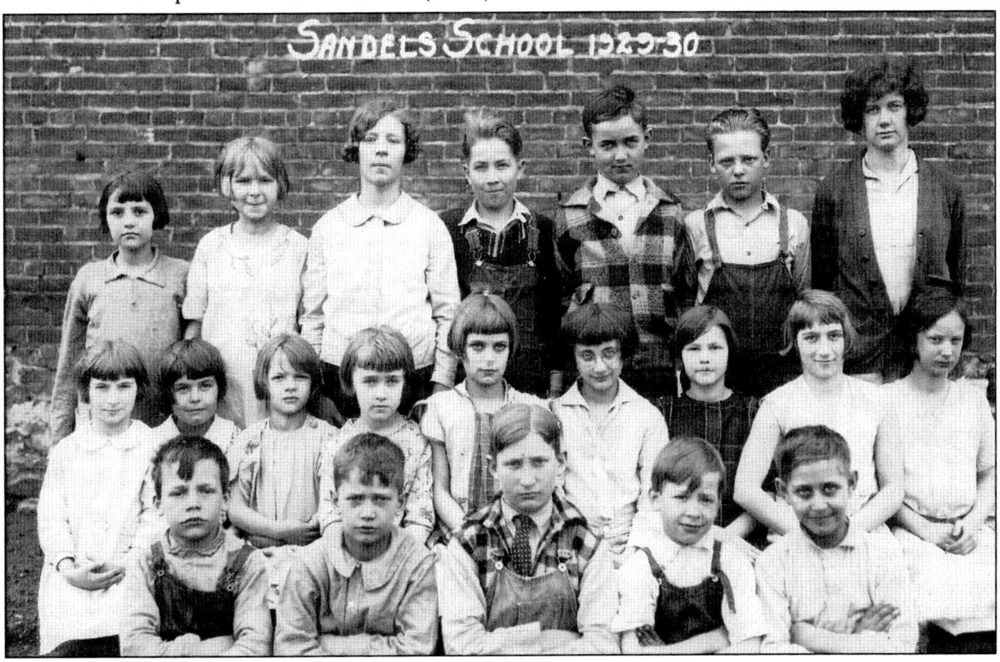

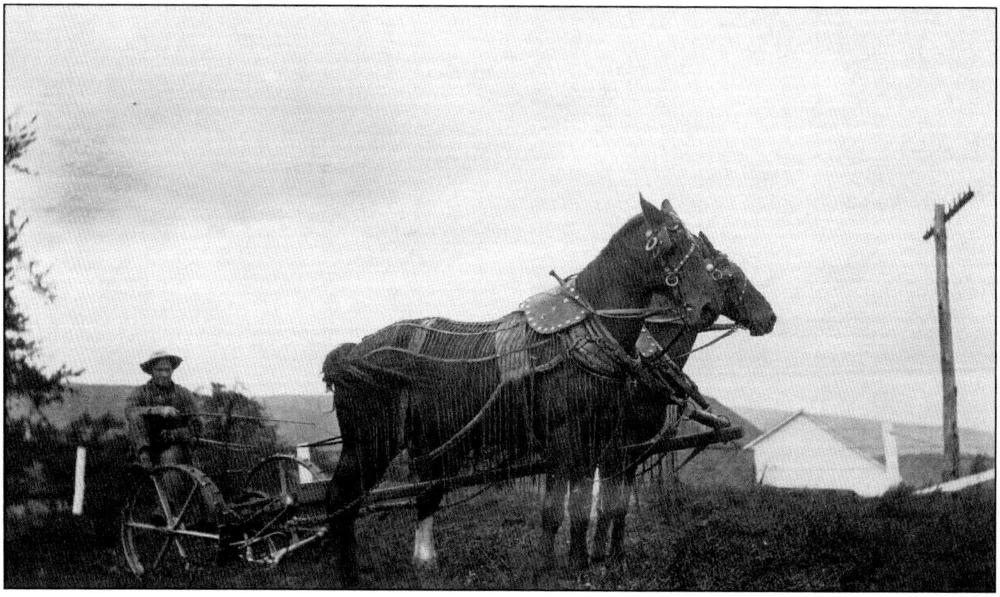

Both work and recreation play major roles in Winfield—historically as well as today. Above, Winfield farmer Charlie Ruhl was photographed, by the Youtz Brothers of McKeesport around 1907, with his horses Doc and Prince and his new Deering mower. A note written on the postcard's back says that Doc was bought from Sam Youtz and Prince was purchased from John Bingaman. On the real-photo postcard below labeled "Camp Moxie," Frank wrote to Gertrud Burns of Winfield in 1909, "Come Down to see the camp this evening and bring three lady friends along." (Above, UCHS 2009.15.5; below, Ronald Nornhold.)

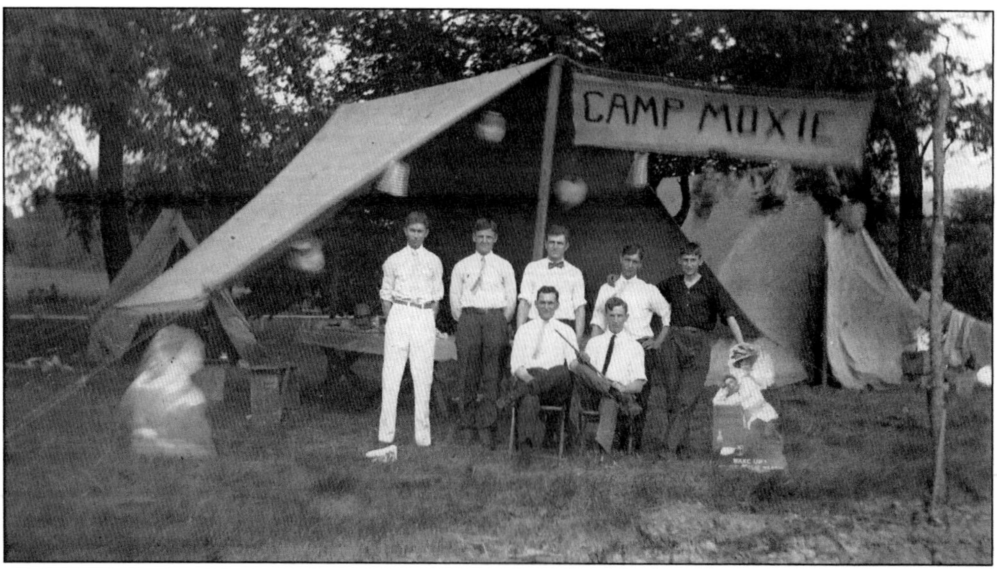

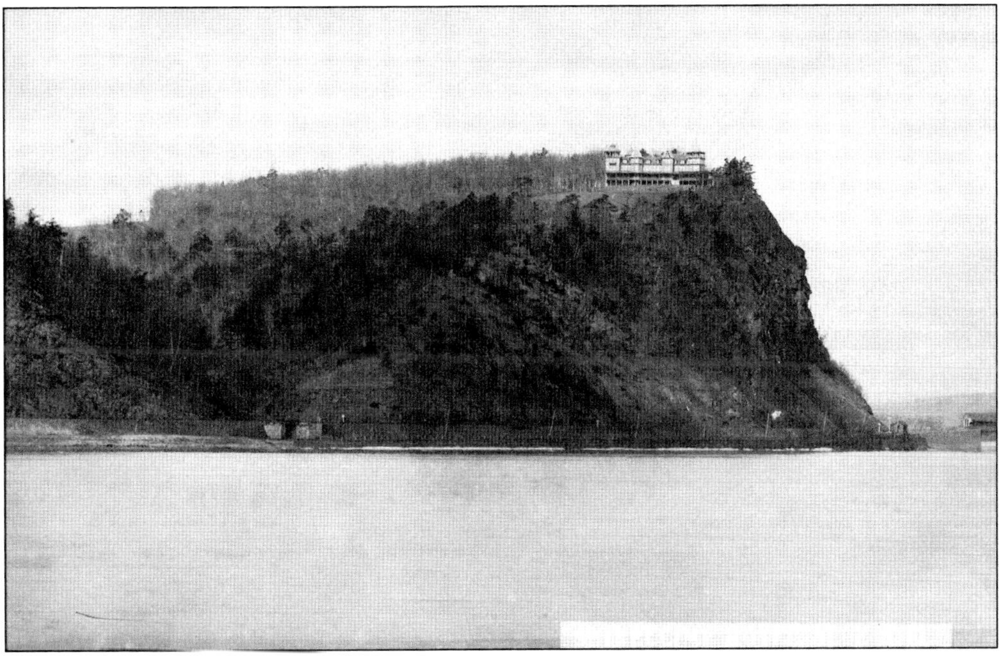

Located at the most southern edge of Union County and below Winfield, Hotel Shikellamy was conceived of and built by the Drumheller Brothers, who ran the City Hotel in Sunbury. Hotel Shikellamy was a 125-foot-by-145-foot, multi-gabled wooden structure designed to accommodate many guests. It also had ball and billiard rooms, smoking and writing rooms, a bowling alley, and a ladies reception room. Atop the crest of Blue Hill on the Union County side of the Union-Snyder county line, and 500 feet above the Susquehanna, the hotel was destroyed by fire on May 4, 1898, as it was being prepared for a new summer season. Hotel Shikellamy had cost about $50,000 to build but was insured for only $19,000. It was not rebuilt, but these postcards, issued several years after the fire, reminded all of its splendor and dramatic setting. (Both, Carl R. Catherman.)

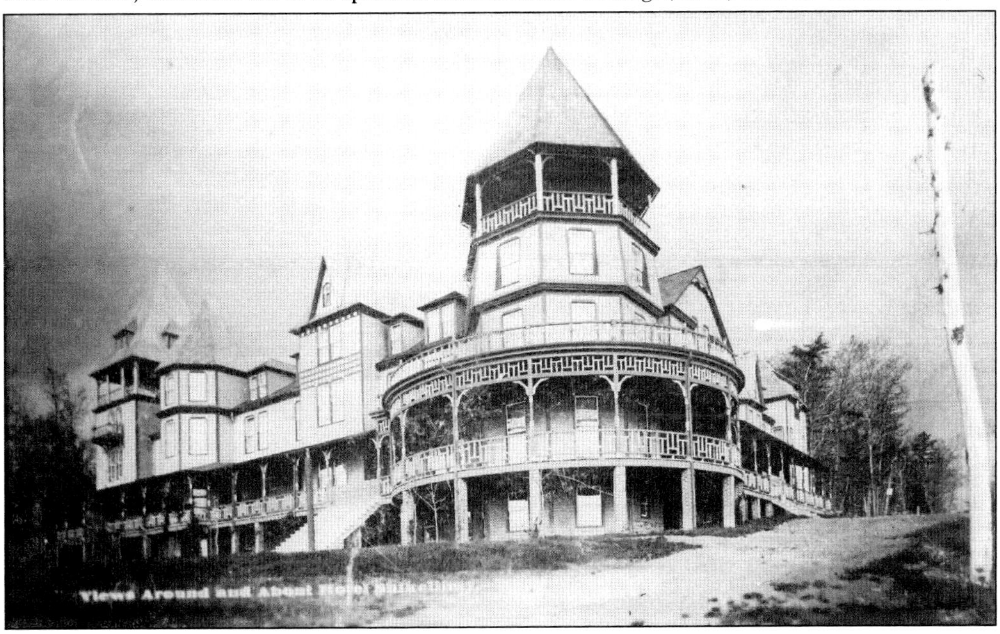

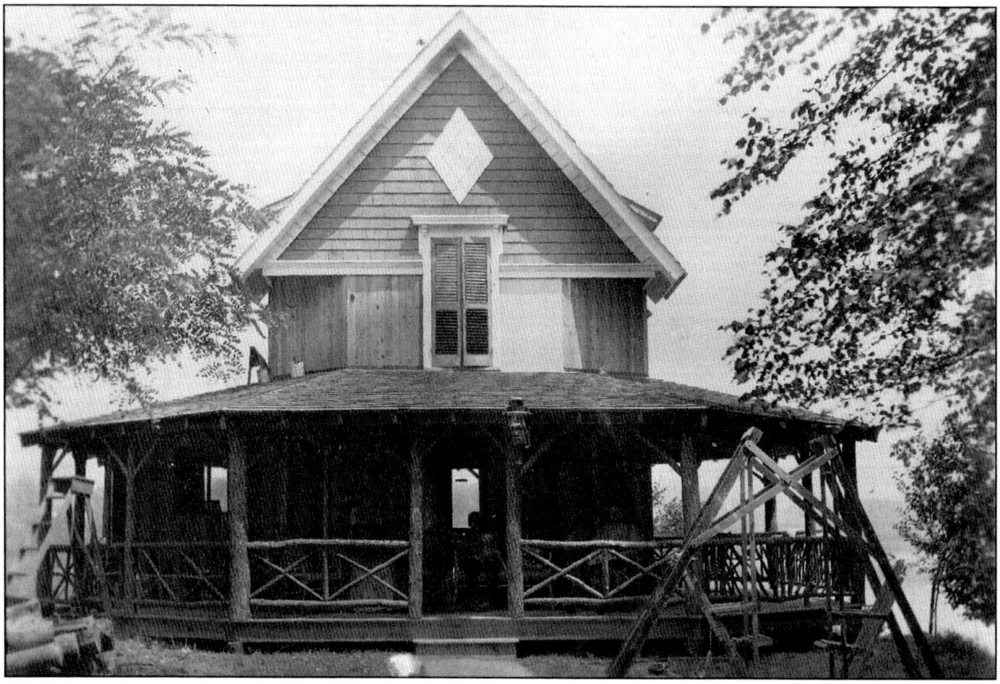

The rustic camp Sunnyside (above), situated alongside the Susquehanna at Winfield, was photographed by Matilda Drumm. The camp appears newly built or to be having some work done with the ladder on the left and a paint can on the roof. Sunnyside contrasts to the later mode of riverside living—the RV and trailer encampment. A Kodachrome postcard (below) issued by Garrison Color Corp. in New Jersey advertised George and Jeanette Vought's River Edge Camp Grounds in Winfield, "located in the beautiful Susquehanna Valley near the point where the north and west Branches of the Susquehanna River meet." There were hot showers, modern facilities, fishing, boating, swimming near the world's largest Fabridam, square dances, and hayrides in the 1970s. (Above, Ronald Nornhold; below, UCHS 2009.17.16.)

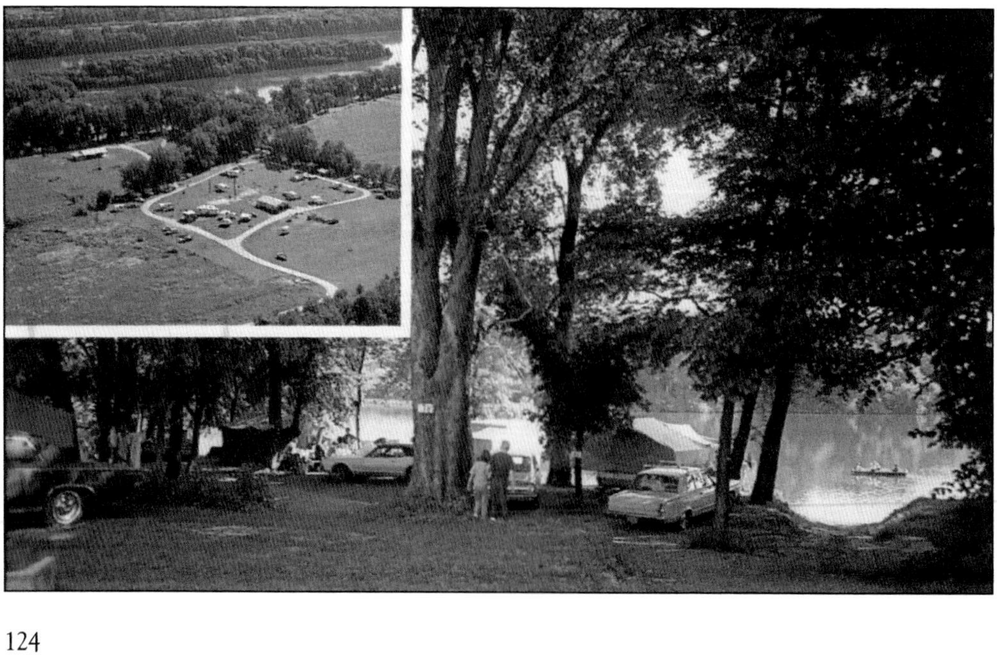

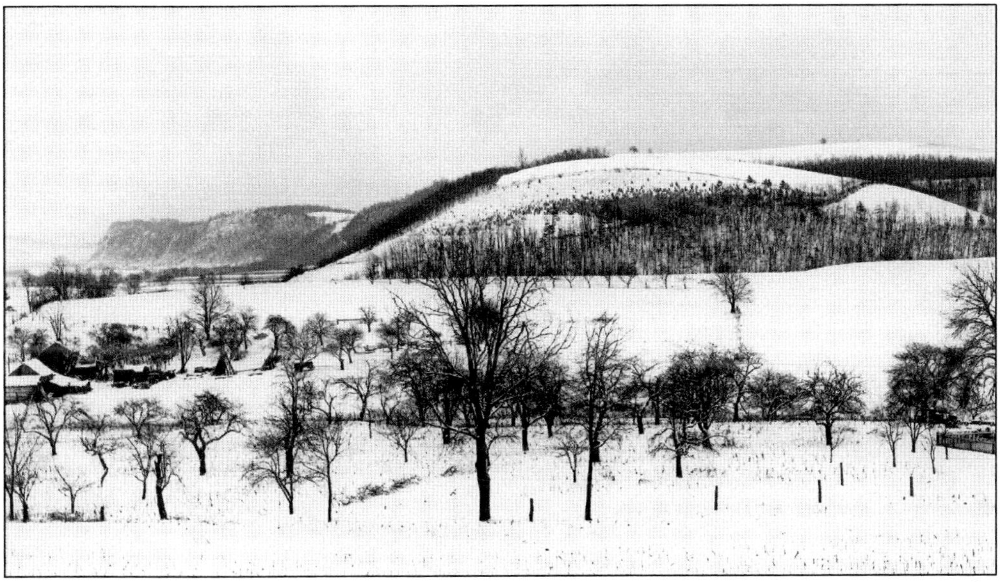

As currently planned, a Route 15 bypass and interchange will redirect ever-increasing traffic across the Susquehanna River near Winfield. A new bridge to Interstate 180 would pass below where the Sandel Farm, photographed above in February 1922 by George Grant of the National Park Service, was located. The new bridge will angle across the Susquehanna and cross over the northern tip of the southernmost island near Winfield. Early male enclaves along the Susquehanna at that spot included Camp Skidoo on Cat Bird Island, seen below complete with tents, tables, and a chef wearing a toque. Men could come for the day and pay by the meal. (Above, UCHS 91.14.1; below, Ronald Nornhold.)

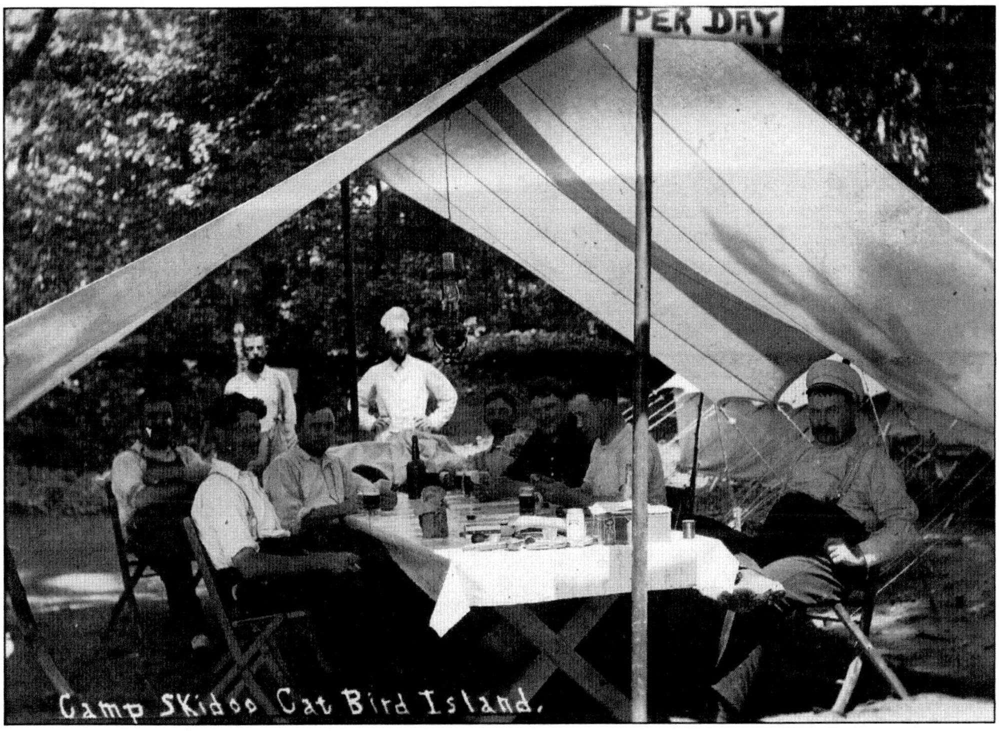

Tomorrow's River Towns

The impact of Union County's river towns of Allenwood, White Deer, New Columbia, West Milton, and Winfield will be different in the 21st century, diminished to a certain degree because of their small populations, which presently range from 1,427 to 4,687 by their respective townships. Yet, there are distinct advantages to their locations at or very near the juncture of Interstate 80 and US Route 15 that, if fully realized, will contribute greatly to the region's growth and importance.

In Allenwood, the completion of the Great Stream Commons mixed-use business park—on lands formerly slated for a toxic waste incinerator that was soundly defeated by citizens—is designed to create employment opportunities at a hub for regional commerce, an expansion of Allenwood's residential neighborhoods (which started in 2005), and more than a mile of riverfront park. The Allenwood Federal Prison Complex, located nearby, currently provides 800 to 900 stable jobs and perhaps more, should it grow.

The county's largest block of land planned for future industry and manufacturing, which is more than 1,000 acres, stretches from White Deer to New Columbia. Blue collar employment has been declining, but there is potential for a slight resurgence due to interest from businesses serving the Marcellus gas development to the north.

Near Winfield, the construction of the stalled US Route 15 bypass and interchange will redirect traffic across the Susquehanna River to Interstate 180, relieving congestion throughout the highway corridor while providing shorter travel times to points south for area residents.

Allenwood and White Deer remain gateways to the White Deer Hole and White Deer Creek Valleys, including thousands of state-owned acres in State Gamelands 317 and the Bald Eagle and Tiadaghton State Forests. Other outlying areas near Union County's small river towns will retain farming traditions and agricultural vistas, some conserved forever.

Last but not least, the Susquehanna Greenway and river trail have been designed to, when fully implemented, bring area residents and their visitors near and sometimes through these river towns so that people explore the same water route and its shores that Native Americans did centuries ago.

—Shawn McLaughlin, Director of Union County Planning

BIBLIOGRAPHY

Beers, D. G. *Atlas of Union & Snyder Counties Pennsylvania*. Philadelphia: Pomeroy & Beers, 1868.

Blake, Jody and Jeannette Lasansky. *Rural Delivery: Real-photo Postcards from Central Pennsylvania 1905–1935*. Lewisburg, PA: Oral Traditions Project of the Union County Historical Society, 1985.

Dershem, Arna. *The History of White Deer Township from Colonial Days to the Present*. New Columbia, PA: White Deer Twp, Bicentennial Commission, 1976.

Ellis, Franklin and A.N. Hungerford, eds. *History of the Susquehanna and Juniata Valleys embraced in the counties of Mifflin, Juniata, Perry, Union and Snyder in the Commonwealth of Pennsylvania*. Vols. 1 and 2. Philadelphia: Everts, Peck & Richards, 1886.

Huddy, Stephen and Paul Metzger. *Alvira and the Ordnance: An American Dream Denied*. Montgomery, PA: Montgomery Area Historical Society, 2009.

Lincoln, Richard Van Boskirk. *History of Union County, including the townships of Kelly, White Deer, Gregg, East Buffalo, and Union* (originally published in the *Mifflinburg Telegraph*, 1899–1900) reprinted as Union County *Heritage*. Lewisburg, PA: Union County Historical Society, 1998.

Linn, John Blair. *The Annals of Buffalo Valley, Pennsylvania, 1755–1855*. Harrisburg, PA: Lane S. Hart, 1877.

Lontz, Mary Belle. *History of the Schools of Union County*. Milton, PA: 1984.

New Columbia Sesquicentennial 1818–1968. New Columbia, PA: New Columbia Sesquicentennial Association, 1968.

Snyder, Charles M. *Union County Pennsylvania: A Celebration of History*. Lewisburg, PA: Union County Historical Society, 2000.

Swope, Robert Jr. *Watsontown, McEwensville, and Delaware Township: A Real-photo Postcard History*. New Hope, VA: Heritage Trails, 2006.

Tabor III, Thomas T. Notebook and photographs of Union County narrow gauge railroad lines, 2006.

Tax assessments and land deeds. Union County Courthouse, Lewisburg, PA.

Thomas, Marlin A. *Lewey and Mary Ellen: Moving On*. Airleaf Press, 2005.

Looking Through Lewey's Lens 100 Years Ago. Sandy, UT: Aardvark Global Publishing Company, 2010.